Anonymous

Studia Biblica et Ecclesiastica

Essays chiefly in Bibliocal and patristic criticism. Vol. 1

Anonymous

Studia Biblica et Ecclesiastica
Essays chiefly in Bibliocal and patristic criticism. Vol. 1

ISBN/EAN: 9783337424695

Printed in Europe, USA, Canada, Australia, Japan

Cover: Foto ©Lupo / pixelio.de

More available books at **www.hansebooks.com**

STUDIA BIBLICA

ESSAYS

IN BIBLICAL ARCHÆOLOGY AND CRITICISM

AND KINDRED SUBJECTS

BY

MEMBERS OF THE UNIVERSITY
OF OXFORD

Oxford
AT THE CLARENDON PRESS
M DCCC LXXXV

[*All rights reserved*]

PREFACE.

In the autumn of the year 1883, finding ourselves recently appointed to the three chairs which represent the interpretation of Holy Scripture in the University, we took counsel together to find some means of assisting students in our department outside the formal way of instruction by lectures. Since then we have met on four Monday evenings in every Term for the purpose of reading and discussing papers on Biblical Archæology and Criticism, including also some other kindred subjects which it seemed very desirable to embrace in our programme. The Essays contained in this volume have all been read at these meetings, but they have since been recast and in some cases substantially modified by the writers, each of whom is responsible for his own paper or papers, and for none of the rest. We cannot doubt that the meetings have been of use both to those who read papers and to those who heard them. We believe that they have done something to stimulate an independent study of the Holy Bible and of the history of the periods during which its books were written. They have also, we hope, deepened the sense of fellowship in work, which it is one great privilege of University life to foster, and drawn together younger and older men who are labourers in the same important field. These Essays are now published by the kindness of the Delegates of the Clarendon Press in the hope that they may reach a larger circle than can be gathered in a single room.

The papers are arranged (with the exception of the last) in a kind of historical order, beginning with those that relate to the Old Testament and coming down, through the New Testament, to the second century A.D. The volume has been some little time in preparation, but we cannot wholly regret the delay in its appearance, as it has enabled us to add the last two papers in the volume, which were read more recently than the rest.

Should this volume be favourably received we shall hope to continue the series as material is gathered together in our hands.

S. R. DRIVER.
WILLIAM SANDAY.
JOHN WORDSWORTH.

May 7th, 1885.

CONTENTS.

                                                                                           PAGE

I. Recent Theories on the Origin and Nature of the Tetragrammaton 1
      S. R. DRIVER, D.D., Christ Church, Regius Professor of Hebrew, Dec. 3, 1883.

II. The Light thrown by the Septuagint Version on the Books of Samuel 21
      F. H. WOODS, B.D., Tutor of St. John's College, May 5, 1884.

III. On the Dialects spoken in Palestine in the time of Christ 39
      AD. NEUBAUER, M.A., Exeter College, Reader in Rabbinical Hebrew and Sub-Librarian of the Bodleian Library, Feb. 18 and May 12, 1884.

IV. On a new Theory of the Origin and Composition of the Synoptic Gospels proposed by G. Wetzel . 75
      A. EDERSHEIM, M.A., Christ Church, Nov. 19, 1883.

V. A Commentary on the Gospels attributed to Theophilus of Antioch . . . 89
      W. SANDAY, M.A., Exeter College, Ireland Professor of Exegesis, Oct. 29, 1883.

VI. The Text of the Codex Rossanensis (Σ) . 103
      W. SANDAY, Feb. 4, 1884.

VII. The Corbey St. James (ff), and its relation to other Latin versions, and to the original language of the Epistle 113
      JOHN WORDSWORTH, M.A., B.N.C., Oriel Professor of Interpretation. Feb. 11, 1884.

CONTENTS.

	PAGE
VIII. A Syriac Biblical Manuscript of the Fifth Century with special reference to its bearing on the text of the Syriac version of the Gospels . .	151
G. H. GWILLIAM, M.A., Fellow of Hertford College, May 26, 1884.	
IX. The date of S. Polycarp's Martyrdom . . .	175
T. RANDELL, M.A., St. John's College, Feb. 25, 1884.	
X. On some newly-discovered Temanite and Nabataean Inscriptions	209
AD. NEUBAUER, Nov. 17, 1884.	
XI. Some further Remarks on the Corbey St. James (ff).	233
W. SANDAY, Feb. 9, 1885.	

I.

RECENT THEORIES ON THE ORIGIN AND NATURE OF THE TETRAGRAMMATON.

[S. R. Driver.]

In the Khorsabad inscription of Sargon[1], that monarch names, among those who had attempted insurrection against him, one *Ia-u-bi-'i-di*, king of Hamath; the word is accompanied by an indication that part of the compound is the name of a deity: and the supposition that this name is *Yahu* is confirmed by the remarkable fact that in a parallel inscription the same king bears the name *Ilubid*. A Hamathite king, it appears, could be called indifferently *Yahubid* or *Ilubid*, much in the same way that the king of Judah who before he came to the throne bore the name of Eliakim, was known afterwards as Jehoiakim. The discovery that the name *Yahu* was thus not confined to the Israelites led Schrader, in 1872, to the conjecture that it may have come to both Hebrews and Hamathites alike from Assyria; and the conjecture was adopted, and supported with positive arguments, by Friedrich Delitzsch, son of the well-known commentator, in his book *What was the Site of Paradise?* published in 1881.

I will begin by stating briefly Professor Delitzsch's theory, and the grounds upon which he defends it.

---

[1] Schrader, *Die Keilinschriften und das A. T.*, 1872, p. 3 f.; 1883, p. 23 : *Records of the Past*, ix. p. 6.

Origin and Nature

The view generally held hitherto by scholars has been that *Yahweh* is the original form of the sacred name, of which *Yahu* (found only in proper names) and *Yah* are abbreviations. Professor Delitzsch adopts an opposite opinion, arguing as follows:—

1. Yahweh was never the name of the God of Israel in the mouth of the people; the popular name was always יהו or יה, as is shown by the fact that the former constitutes part of no proper name, while large numbers are compounded with the latter.

2. The abbreviations themselves show that the significant part of the word was felt to lie in the *ya*, which was always retained, although upon the usual theory this would be merely a prefix.

3. It is improbable that a name handed down from remote times would have included the abstract idea of *being*: such a signification bears the impress of a later period of theological reflexion.

4. Yahu was a name of God among other Canaanite nations besides Hebrews. In addition to Yahubid just cited, there are besides, the Damascene *Ya'-lu-'* found in an inscription of Esarhaddon[1]; the Phœnician *Abdai*[2], *Yoel*[3], *Bithias*[4], the Philistine *Mitinti*, *Sidká*, *Padi*, names of kings of Ashdod, Ashkelon, and Ekron respectively, mentioned by Sennacherib[5], and formed precisely like the Hebrew Mattithiah, Zedekiah, and Pedaiah, the Hamathite *Yoram* (2 Sam. viii. 10), the Hittite *Uriah*, and the Ammonite *Tobiah*[6], all of which show traces of the same name. If Yahu was thus a general Canaanite name, it cannot well be derived from הוה: for this root,

---

[1] KAT., p. 24, *note*; p. 207, 24.
[2] A Tyrian Suffete, named in Menander Schröder, *Phœn. Gramm.*, p. 152.
[3] יאל, on the fifth Maltese inscription (Wright, in the ZDMG. xxviii. 143 f.; Nestle, *Israelitische Eigennamen*, 1876, p. 86).
[4] Verg. Aen. i. 738; Schröd., p. 114.
[5] KAT., pp. 289-290 (on the Taylor-cylinder).
[6] The name of the Hebronite *Hoham* (Josh. x. 3) is too uncertain to be added (Baudissin, *Studien zur Semitischen Religionsgeschichte*, 1876, i. p. 224).

though known to Aramaic and Hebrew, is not Phœnician[1]. Its source, therefore, must be sought not in Palestine, but in Babylonia, the common home of nearly the entire Canaanitish Pantheon; and remarkably enough, a sign denoting God (*ilu*), which hitherto had been read ideographically, has been discovered to have a phonetic value, and to be pronounced *i*, or with the ending of the Assyrian nominative *ya-u*. In other words, among the old Accadian population of Babylonia, from whom the Semitic immigrants derived their cuneiform writing, the supreme God bore the name *I*, which, in the mouths of the Semitic Babylonians, would readily become *Ya-u*.

Delitzsch accordingly propounds the following theory. The forms *Yahu*, *Yah*, current among the people, are of foreign origin. The form *Yahweh*, on the other hand, is distinctively Hebrew: it is a modification of *Yahu*, so formed as to be connected with הוה *to be*, and designed to express a deep theological truth: this prevailed among the prophets and priests, but not among the people generally. A distinction, it will be observed, is drawn between *Yahu* and *Yahweh*, and the theory is guarded thereby against the objection to which it might otherwise be exposed from a theological point of view. Delitzsch does not divest *Yahweh*, the usual form met with in the Old Testament, of the associations attached to it on the ground of Exod. iii and vi: he argues, on the contrary, that *Yahu* is the foreign word which was transformed into *Yahweh* just for the sake of giving expression to the truths taught in those passages. In fact, *Yahu* has no real connexion with *Yahweh*, and is merely the material framework upon which it is modelled.

The theory, however, though not open to objection upon theological grounds, is not free from difficulties in other directions, and exception was taken to it in most of the notices

---

[1] In Phœnician, as in Arabic and Ethiopic (הי *fieri* by the side of ⴱⴼⴲ *esse*), the substantive verb is כון (e.g. יכן לכהנם in the remarkable inscription, relating to sacrifices, found at Marseilles).

of Professor Delitzsch's book. C. P. Tiele, in the *Theologisch Tijdschrift* for March 1882, declared himself unconvinced, and recently it has been examined at greater length by F. A. Philippi[1] in the second part of the *Zeitschrift für Völkerpsychologie* for 1883[2], whose arguments against it I proceed now to state.

1. It is an exaggerated and untenable view to treat *Yah* as the popular form. In all colloquial expressions, in the language of every-day life, we uniformly in the Old Testament find *Yahweh*: it is used even in formulae of swearing and other common phrases, where a shorter form, if in use, might have been naturally expected to occur: of the shorter forms, *yahu* is confined entirely to proper names (where the longer one would have been cumbrous; imagine such a word as מלכיהוה!), and *yah* to proper names and poetry,—and even in poetry chiefly in later liturgical forms (e.g. Halleluyah, twenty-four times out of forty-seven[3]). Against the suggestion that possibly editors or scribes substituted at a later date the longer form, the testimony of Mesha is decisive; on his stone (line 18) he writes *Yahweh*[4]: the longer form must accordingly have been in popular use in the ninth century B.C. And in proper names abbreviations in accordance with the normal methods of the language (as יהו and יה would be) would not be against analogy.

2. The contractions do not cause difficulty. The transition from *Yahweh* to -*i* (י ָ) would not be made at once, but gradually. The last syllable being apocopated, after the

---

[1] Author of several important contributions to the comparative study of the Semitic languages, in particular, *Wesen und Ursprung des Status constructus* (1871), an article on the Root of the Semitic verb in *Morgenländische Forschungen* (Leipzig, 1875), on the numeral *two* in Semitic, in the Z.D.M.G., 1878, p. 21 ff., etc.

[2] P. 175 ff.

[3] According to B. Davidson's *Concordance* (London, 1876). [Is. xxxviii. 11 *bis*.]

[4] The reading admits of no doubt: Nöldeke and Dr. Wright do not question it; and the suggestion made since this paper was read to vocalize *Yahu'a* and to treat this as the name of a man (E. King, *Hebrew Words and Synonyms*, i. p. 35) is devoid of probability. The sense of יהוה is determined naturally by the context, which is here strongly in favour of יהוה being the name of a God.

analogy of verbs ל״י and ל״ו, there arose first *yahw*; next, the final *w* being first vocalized and then dropped, came *yahu* and *yah* (with the aspirate sounded — יַה)[1]: after a while the aspirate ceased to be sounded, though it continued always to be written: and thus, though it is true that at last, in proper names, only the sound *ya* remained, its continuity with the earlier stages was unbroken, so that its real origin would always be felt. The forms, moreover, in which ‎ ‎‎וֹ‎ or ‎‎יִ‎ alone appears (as מַתְּנַי, עַבְדִּי) are at best of uncertain derivation: it is possible that they are not connected with *yah* at all [2].

3. The objection drawn from the abstract nature of the idea shall be considered presently; the name, it is probable, was understood to express a moral, not a metaphysical, conception of being.

4. The Philistine names are too uncertain in their formation for an argument to be based upon them; and the others [3] are too isolated to prove a general worship of a deity

---

[1] The apocopation causes no difficulty: it is in strict accord with other analogies presented by the language. The habit of apocopating the imperfect tense of verbs ה״ל was so familiar to the Hebrews that a word of similar formation, especially when forming the second part of a compound name, must have lent itself to it quite naturally. The phenomenon is isolated because other names of the same form from verbs ה״ל do not occur (the form is itself a rare one): יהוה is shortened as naturally to יהו in יְשַׁעְיָה as יִשְׁתַּחֲוֶה to יִשְׁתַּחוּ after the *waw* conversive in וַיִּשְׁתַּחוּ (in pause וַיִּשְׁתָּחוּ).

[2] Renan, in an article *Des Noms Théophores apocopés* in the *Revue des Études juives*, v. (1882), p. 161 ff., regards the termination in these cases as disguised forms of the suffix of the 3rd pers. sing., referring to God. Others treat at least the *-ai* as adjectival (see Ewald, § 273 *e*; Olshausen, § 217 *a*, *b*). In an appendix to this essay will be found a representation and description (which I owe to the kindness of R. S. Poole, Esq., Keeper of Coins and Medals at the British Museum) of a remarkable coin found in the neighbourhood of Gaza, and bearing the letters יהו.

[3] As regards *Yo'el* (יואל), Dr. Wright, in the *Transactions of the Bibl. Archaeol. Soc.*, 1874, p. 397, had already remarked that the vocalization is conjectural. Whether, however, Nestle (*l. c.*) is right in connecting it with יאל, *voluit* (הואיל), and interpreting *strong-willed*, must remain uncertain: it is at any rate precarious to seek support for this meaning in the וילו and ראלו of the Sinaitic Inscriptions (Levy in the Z D M G. xiv. pp. 408, 410): for the proper names in those inscriptions appear mostly to have Arabic affinities (Blau, *ib.*, xvi. p. 377; Nöldeke, xvii. p. 703 f.). See also the *Corpus Inscr. Sem.*, p. 163.

Yahu—individual cases of borrowing from Israel are no improbability.

5. Admitting a Babylonian *yau*, it is difficult to understand how a Hebrew *yahu* can have arisen from it: the form which the regular phonetic laws would lead us to expect is *yô*; and if *yau* became in Hebrew indiscriminately יְהוֹ, or יְהוּ, how is it that the latter appears never at the end of a compound proper name, the former never at the beginning? This difference can be accounted for upon the ordinary view, but not by Delitzsch's theory. 'The יְהוֹ abbreviated from יַהְוֶה, when standing at the beginning of compound names became *y'hau*, *y'hô*, after the analogy of דְּבַר from *דָּבָר, because *yăhû*, in such a position, as part of a compound word with an accent of its own, would have drawn the tone unduly back, whereas יָהוּ for יָהְוְ, in the second part of the compound, was excellently adapted to receive the tone.'

The question of a Babylonian *yau* is an intricate one, and cannot be satisfactorily discussed except by those who have made the cuneiform inscriptions their particular study. But the discussion may fortunately be dispensed with. Not only do both Tiele and Philippi raise objections to Delitzsch's reasoning, contending, for example, that the Assyrian *I* itself is not satisfactorily established as the name of a deity, but Professor Sayce, whose authority is not less than that of Professor Delitzsch, has declared[1] that his attempt to derive *Yahweh* from an Accadian origin is unsuccessful. Our knowledge of Babylonian mythology, he remarks, is tolerably complete: and no such name as *Yahweh* is contained in it. A derivation from the Accadian, which Professor Sayce abandons, need surely not occupy our attention further[2].

The rejection of a Babylonian origin for the Tetra-

---

[1] *The Modern Review*, 1882, p. 853.

[2] Mr. King, *u. s.*, pp. 15, 24, is of opinion that the ultimate source of יהוה is the Accadian *An* or *Ana*; but such a position as may readily be imagined, is defensible only by aid of a series of assumptions, philological and critical, of the most questionable kind. An examination in detail is, I venture to think, needless.

grammaton does not, however, preclude the possibility of its having some other foreign, non-Hebraic, origin. Older scholars had indeed already suggested this, on the strength of certain notices in Greek writers[1]; and as the view has been recently revived, I may be allowed, for the sake of completeness, to consider it briefly here, referring for further particulars to the full examination of it by Count Baudissin in the first volume of his *Studien zur Semitischen Religionsgeschichte* (1876), p. 181 ff. Several ancient authorities (e.g. Diodorus Siculus[2], Origen, Theodoret, Jerome) speak of the God of the Jews under the name Ἰαώ: and the same name appears in some of the Gnostic systems[3]. Here it is evidently derived from the Old Testament, being found by the side of other names plainly of Hebraic origin. This is the case not only in the lists given by Irenaeus and other ancients, but also on the Gnostic rings and amulets, representations of which have been given by Macarius[4], Montfaucon[5], Kopp[6], C. W. King[7], and others. Abrasax, for example, we learn from Irenaeus, was the name given to the First Cause in the Basilidean system[8]. If therefore we find the name ΙΑѡ coupled with CΑΒΑѠΘ or ΑΔѠΝΑΙ under the strange composite figure which denoted Abrasax—the head of a hawk, or

---

[1] See the article Jehovah, by Mr. W. A. Wright, in Smith's *Dict. of the Bible*, i. p. 953 f.

[2] i. 94 Παρὰ δὲ τοῖς Ἰουδαίοις Μωυσῆν [sc. προσποιήσασθαι τοὺς νόμους αὐτῷ διδόναι] τὸν Ἰαὼ ἐπικαλούμενον θεόν.

[3] The names of the spirits which, according to the Ophites, presided over the seven planets, are thus given by Irenaeus (i. 30, 5):—'Eum enim qui a matre primus sit Jaldabaoth vocari; eum autem qui sit ab eo, Iao; et qui ab eo Sabaoth; quartum autem Adoneum et quintum Elaeum et sextum Orcum, septimum autem et novissimum omnium Astaphaeum.' Origen (*c. Cels.*, vi. 32) rightly perceived that the third, fourth, and fifth of these were derived from the Hebrew Scriptures.

[4] *Abraxas seu Apistopistus* (Antwerp, 1657).

[5] *L'Antiquité expliquée et représentée en figures*, Paris, 1722 (vol. ii. p. 353 ff.: *Supplém.*, 1724, p. 209 ff.).

[6] *Palaeographia Critica* (Mannheim, 1817-1829), vols. 3 and 4.

[7] *The Gnostics and their Remains* (London, 1864). Specimens of the inscriptions (without, however, the figures) are given in abundance by Baudissin.

[8] Iren. i. 24, 7. Abrasax (the letters of which, estimated numerically, equal 365) was the *princeps* or ἄρχων of the 365 heavens.

sometimes of a jackal, the arms of a man, one arm often bearing a whip, with two serpents diverging below as legs—

Reverse: ΙΑω ϹΑΒΑω[1].

it will not surprise us; some mystic meaning or magical power may well have been supposed to reside both in the figure and in the name. If it was known (as it certainly must have been[2]) that the Jews hesitated to pronounce the name, its value as a magical token would be the greater. But what are we to say when we read the name ΙΑΩ, as we often can, associated with the image of the youthful Horus, resting on a lotus leaf—Horus, the Egyptian god of the awakening life of spring?

From 'The Gnostics and their Remains,' pl. iii. 8[3].

[1] King, pp. 35, 234.
[2] Allusions are frequent, e.g. Philo, *Vita Mosis*, iii. 25 and 26 (ii. p. 166, Mangey). See Lev. xxiv. 16 in the Versions.
[3] Elsewhere the Abrasax and Horus figures are combined (also with the name Ἰάω), as in pl. vii. 4.

Here 'Ιάω stands alone, unaccompanied by any Jewish or Christian symbol. From this evidence, taken in conjunction with some notices (especially the reputed oracle of the Clarian Apollo[1]) which appeared to connect 'Ιάω with the Phœnician Ἄδωνις[2], Lenormant, in 1872[3], considered it clear that the populations of Phœnicia and Syria recognized a god 'Ιάω, and threw out the suggestion that the name was an old one, denoting properly *the existent*, which, as being the least closely attached to a definite mythological personage, might have been the model upon which the Mosaic *Yahweh* was constructed. Not, however, that Lenormant supposed *Yahweh* to be *derived* from 'Ιάω: from the beginning, he adds, the Israelitish name was used in an altogether different sense from the Phœnician; the resemblance was purely external: though the similarity of name, he thought, might help to explain the readiness with which the Israelites afterwards exchanged the worship of *Yahweh* for a Canaanitish cult. But the grounds for such a theory are precarious: the Hamathite and Phœnician names are not numerous enough to bridge over the chasm which separates the late classical times (at which 'Ιάω is first attested) from the age of Moses. Baudissin, after a careful examination of the facts, concludes, with great probability,

---

[1] Macrobius (fifth cent. A.D.), *Saturnalia*, i. 18:—

Ὄργια μὲν δεδαῶτας ἐχρῆν νεοπενθέα κεύθειν
Ἐν δ' ἀπάτῃ παύρῃ σύνεσις καὶ νοῦς ἀλαπαδνός.
Φράζεο τὸν πάντων ὕπατον θεὸν ἔμμεν' Ἰάω,
Χείματι μέν τ' Ἀίδην, Δία τ' εἴαρος ἀρχομένοιο,
Ἠέλιον δὲ θέρευς, μετοπώρου δ' ἁβρὸν Ἰάω.

The verses are cited for the purpose of establishing the identity of Helios and Dionysus.

[2] The grounds for the identification may be seen in Lenormant, *Lettres Assyriologiques*, First Series, tom. ii. pp. 193 f., 209-212, or more fully in Movers, *Die Phönizier* (1841), i. 542-547. They consist chiefly in the similarity (πάντων ὕπατος) or identity (ἁβρός) of the epithets applied in the oracle to 'Ιάω, and in other ancient writers to Adonis (e.g. Theocr. xv. 128 ἁβρὸν Ἄδωνιν); partly also in a connexion supposed by some of the ancients to subsist between Dionysus and Adonis on the one hand (Plutarch, *Symp.* iv. 5, 3), and the God of the Jews on the other (on account, probably, of observances connected with the Feast of Tabernacles: *ib.* iv. 6, 2; Tacit. *Hist.* v. 5, who, however, himself rejects the identification).

[3] *L.c.* pp. 196-201.

that 'Ιάω with the Horus figure is simply derived, as in the previous cases, from the Old Testament, and its occurrence in that connexion is merely a piece of religious syncretism, such as meets us often elsewhere in Gnosticism, especially when its home is in Egypt (pp. 205-207). Baudissin discusses at the same time the identification of this 'Ιάω with Dionysus or Adonis, and the oracle of Apollo: his conclusion with regard to the latter is that even if it be admitted to be the work of a Greek in pre-Christian times [1], it would not follow that the 'Ιάω named in it was other than the God of the Jews himself: and that consequently that name could not be alleged as the source whence the Jewish *Yahweh* was derived. The Greek 'Ιάω, it may be concluded, is everywhere dependent on the Hebrew יהוה [2].

Professor Sayce, lastly, though, as we saw, not admitting its Accadian origin, still attaches weight to Delitzsch's arguments for *Yahu* being the original and popular form; and expresses himself inclined to assign to it a Hittite origin. How important the great Hittite empire of Kadesh on the Orontes was in the ancient world we know now from many sources. Hamath, Professor Sayce remarks, appears to have been a sort of Hittite dependency: Abraham had dealings with Hittites: David had not only a Hittite warrior, Uriah, but was on friendly terms with a king of Hamath: the kings of the Hittites are spoken of, long after David's time, as ready to give help to a king of Israel (2 Kings vii. 6): and the inscriptions mention no names compounded with *yahu*, except in Israel and Hamath. *Yahweh*, he concludes,

---

[1] This oracle has been usually regarded as spurious, but the authority of Lobeck has led it to be viewed in some quarters with greater favour; and it is defended accordingly by Land (see the next note) and Lenormant (*l. c.*). Kuenen, *Religion of Israel*, i. 399 ff., argues strongly on the other side.

[2] The theory of a Canaanitish origin of the name יהוה had been proposed in a somewhat different form by J. P. N. Land in the *Theol. Tijdschrift*, 1868, p. 156 ff. It was criticized by Kuenen in 1869 *Religion of Israel*, i. 400, who pointed to the song of Deborah, as in his judgment conclusive against it. Land's reply may be read in the *Tijdschrift* for 1869, p. 347 ff. Tiele, *Histoire Comparée des Anciennes Religions* 1882), p. 349 f., agrees with Kuenen.

was as much the supreme God of Hamath as of Israel[1]. Should this conjecture be discarded, he is disposed to fall back on the view of Professor Robertson Smith (see below), that the word denoted originally the sender of lightning or rain.

The general conclusion at which we arrive is, that while there are no substantial grounds for abandoning the ordinary view that *yahu* and *yah* are abbreviated forms of *Yahweh*, the *possibility* of a foreign origin for the latter cannot, in face of the Phoenician and other non-Israelitish names in which it seems to appear, be altogether denied. This, indeed, is the opinion of the most competent scholars of the present time. Thus Hermann Schultz, writing in 1878[2]: 'The opinion that the word may once have been current in a wider circle of peoples than Israel alone, cannot be said to be exactly refuted.' While concluding himself that it is *most probably* of Hebrew origin, he concedes that a different view is still tenable and that the name 'may have only acquired a definite religious significance in Israel.' Dillmann[3] and Delitzsch[4] express themselves similarly: the latter remarking that more ought perhaps, under the circumstances, to be granted than the conclusion of Baudissin (p. 223) that the God of the Jews was adopted by some of the neighbouring peoples into their Pantheon. But, like Schultz, both these scholars are careful to add, that, even if that be so, the name received in Moses' hands an entirely new import[5].

---

[1] Stade (*Gesch. Israel's*, i. p. 130 f.) following Tiele (*l. c.*, p. 350 f.) conjectures that it may have been borrowed by Moses from the Kenites. The Egyptian *anuk-pu-anuk*, which was compared (after Brugsch) by Ebers, in *Durch Gosen zum Sinai*, 1872, p. 528 (the note is omitted in the 2nd edition of 1882), is declared by Le Page Renouf (*Hibbert Lectures*, 1879, p. 244 f.; *Academy*, xvii. (1880), p. 475) to mean *I, even I*, and not to be capable of the rendering *ich bin, der ich bin.*

[2] *Alttestamentliche Theologie*, p. 488 f.

[3] *Exodus und Leviticus* (1880), pp. 33 *bottom*, 34.

[4] Herzog's *Real-encyclopädie*, vi. (1880), article JEHOVAH, p. 507.

[5] Kuenen expresses himself most emphatically against such theories as have been here discussed, *Hibbert Lectures* (1882), pp. 58-61, 310 f. And Dillmann, notwithstanding his concessions to logical possibility, views them evidently with disfavour. The history of the name (on Israelitish ground) prior to Exod. iii. 14 is uncertain. As is well known, the two main sources of the Pentateuch,

Assuming then *Yahweh* to be a derivative of הוה *to be*, we may proceed now to consider the signification attaching to it. In form, *Yahweh* belongs to a class of words hardly found in Hebrew beyond a few proper names[1], but used somewhat more widely in Arabic and Syriac[2], which are considered to denote an object or person from some active or prominent attribute. Jacob, the supplanter, Isaac, the laugher, Jephthah, the opener, Jair, the illuminator, are familiar examples of the same formation. Hebrew scholars will, however, at once perceive that the vocalization *Yahweh* (which we may here assume to be the correct one, or at least the most probable by far that has been proposed[3]) may belong to two conjugations or voices, may have a neuter or a causative force, may express grammatically either *he that is*, or *he that causes to be*. Formerly the name was supposed almost

P (the Priests' Code) and J, differ in their representation of the antiquity of the name: in J it is used from the beginning (cf. Gen. iv. 26), P consistently eschews it till Ex. vi. 3. (The passage Ex. iii. 9-14 is assigned by critics to E.) But though promulgated anew, and with a fresh sanction, by Moses, it can hardly have been *unknown* before, though its use may have been more limited. It is an old and not improbable conjecture of Ewald's *Hist.*, ii. p. 156 f., based partly on the name of Moses' mother *Yochebed*, partly on the early occurrence of the abbreviated form *Yah* (in the Song, Ex. xv. 2), and confirmed by the singular expression in the same verse, 'God of my *father*' (cf. iii. 6, xviii. 4), that the name was current in the family of Moses (comp. Delitzsch, *Genesis*, p. 29 f.; Dillmann, pp. 28, 54); see also, now, König. *Die Hauptprobleme der altisraelitischen Religionsgesch.*, 1884, p. 27. The derivation of מריה is obscure: but philological reasons are decisive against the opinion that it means *shown of Yah*; for not only are proper names compounded with *participles* almost unknown in Hebrew, but a transition such as that from מראיה, which such a compound would have given (cf. קיישה, מהסה) to מיריה, is altogether without precedent: where does the disappearance of א *lengthen* a preceding vowel, or indeed take place at all after a quiescent *shwa*? (Comp. Delitzsch on Qoh., xii. 5.)

[1] See Olshausen, *Lehrbuch*, § 277 g; Stade, *Lehrbuch* (1879), § 259.
[2] Dietrich, *Abhandlungen zur Hebr. Grammatik* (1846), pp. 136-151.
[3] See the correspondence between Dietrich and Delitzsch (bearing in particular on the vocalization of the second syllable), published recently in Stade's *Ztsch. für Alttestamentliche Wissenschaft*, 1883, pp. 280-290; 1884, pp. 21-28.
On the origin of the form יהוה, which appears on the margin, and sometimes also in the text, of Greek MSS. of the Old Testament (cf. Field, *Hexapla*, on Ps. xxv. 1), and which passed thence into Syriac MSS., see, in addition to Jerome, *Ep.* 136 ad *Marcellam*, the Scholion of Jacob of Edessa (A.D. 675), published with explanations by Nestle, in the ZDMG. xxxii. (1878), pp. 465-508 also p. 735 f. and xxxiii. 297 ff.).

universally to convey the sense *he that is*, but latterly there has been a growing consensus in favour of *he that causes to be*. Not, indeed, that this interpretation is a new one; it is as old as Le Clerc, who, in his Commentary on Exod. vi. 3 (1696), both gives the pronunciation *Yahweh*, and explains the name as = γενεσιουργόν. In more modern times the same view has been favoured (in some instances independently) by authorities of considerable weight: it was thrown out as a suggestion by Gesenius[1] in 1839 (*creator* or *life-giver*), and is adopted by Land[2], Lagarde[3], Kuenen[4], Schrader[5], Baudissin[6], Nestle[7], H. Schultz[8], Tiele[9]. Not by all, however, quite in the same sense. Kuenen, for instance, interprets the name as denoting the giver of existence: Schrader and Schultz as the giver of life and deliverance: Lagarde and Nestle, following Le Clerc[10], as *he who bringeth to pass*, i.e. the performer of his promises. Lagarde finds similarly in Exod. vi, in the contrast between *El Shaddai* and *Yahweh*, the transition from the idea of God's might to that of his covenant faithfulness. The thought is a suggestive one; but even in this, the most favourable form of the causative view, there are difficulties which are a serious obstacle to our accepting it.

It is true that היה is used of the fulfilment of a promise or prediction (1 Kings xiii. 32 כִּי הָיֹה יִהְיֶה הַדָּבָר), but hardly

---

[1] *Thesaurus*, p. 577 *note*. [2] *L.c.*, 1868, p. 158 (de levengever, Schepper).
[3] ZDMG. xxii. (1868), p. 331; Symmicta, i. 104: supported with further arguments in the *Psalterium juxta Hebraeos Hieronymi* (1874), p. 153 ff. (originally *creator*) and *Orientalia*, ii. (1886), pp. 27–30. [*Gött. Gel. Anz.*, 1885, p. 91: '*He who calls into existence the events of history*, whence the idea of *performer of promises* must have necessarily developed.']
[4] *Religion of Israel*, i. 279, 398 ('probably').
[5] In Schenkel, *Bibel-Lexicon*, s.v.   [6] *L.c.* (1876), p. 229.
[7] *Isr. Eigennamen*, p. 88 f.   [8] *L.c.* (1878), p. 487 ff.
[9] *Histoire Comparée*, etc., p. 345 (*Celui qui fait être:* the explanation *Je suis celui qui suis* is an adaptation, not the primitive sense of the word).
[10] 'Uno verbo Graece non ineleganter dixeris γενεσιουργόν *existentiae effectorem*, qua voce Clemens Alexandrinus aliique Patres usi sunt, ut significetur ὡς τὴν γένεσιν πάντων ἐργάζεται.' The Patriarchs, he continues, had known God as El Shaddai, but had not seen the fulfilment of his promises which 'jam (יִהְיֶה) *ut esset facturus erat*. Hinc Deus hic orationem ordihur his erbis יהוה אֶ׃, hoc est, is sum *qui re praestiturus sum* quod olim promisi.'

in the abstract, without the object of the promise being indicated in the context: and the fact that scarcely any Semitic language uses the causative form of היה, whether in the sense of creating or bringing to pass, appears to make it additionally improbable[1]. The same lexical consideration tells further against the view that the name had in its origin, before it was spiritualized as in Exodus, some other causative force, such as, e.g. *he who causes to fall* (sc. rain, or lightning[2]). It is true, as Arabic shows, that *to fall* was almost certainly the primitive meaning of the root; it even occurs once with this sense in Hebrew[3]: but it is questionable whether the causal form used absolutely would have conveyed such a special meaning as this, without the object being distinctly expressed. Rather, as Professor W. H. Green observes[4], it would signify *the destroyer*—أَهْوَى is used in the Qor'an (53, 54) of God's *ruining* or *throwing down* the cities of the Plain.

[1] The exception is in the case of Syriac: but even there, to judge by Payne Smith's *Thesaurus*, the use is rare, the few examples given being of late date, and apparently artificial formations such as Syriac lends itself to readily, so that they justify no inference as to what may have been the usage some 2000 years previously. The question has been recently a subject of controversy in Germany. Delitzsch, in the *Zeitschr. für Luth. Theologie*, 1877, p. 593 ff., criticizing the explanation of יהוה as a *hifil*, had observed that whenever, in post-Biblical times, a causative of היה was required (in philosophical terminology) the *piel* was the form employed; and quotes an explanation of יהוה by Aaron ben Elijah, of Nicomedia, the Karaite (in his עץ החיים, written in 1346, and published by Delitzsch in 1841 in the *Anekdota zur Gesch. der mittdalterlichen Scholastik*, p. 93) as the יהיה כל היה, מהוה מצב, the source of all being. Nestle, in the *Jahrbücher für Deutsche Theologie*, 1878, p. 126 ff., answers that this explanation of יהוה by the *piel* may have been determined by the *shwa'* under the י, and appeals in support of its having been a *hifil* to the examples in Syriac. He appears, however, to make more of these latter than they deserve. Lagarde's most recent discussion of the subject is in his *Orientalia*, ii. (1880), p. 28 f., which is in fact a reply to Delitzsch, though that scholar is not named. It remains a possibility that יהוה may have had a causal idea, but the arguments advanced by Lagarde do not appear to me to have made it probable. Even Schultz, though inclined to regard the causal sense with favour, nevertheless expresses himself with reserve, when he says (p. 487), 'It cannot be denied that the view has great probability: but in no case can it be regarded as certain.'

[2] W. Robertson Smith, *Old Test. in the Jewish Church*, p. 423.

[3] Job xxxvii. 6. See Fleischer in Delitzsch's Commentary (Engl. Tr.); or Dr. Wright's luminous note in the *Trans. Bibl. Arch. Soc.*, iii. (1874), p. 104 ff.

[4] *Moses and the Prophets* (New York, 1883), p. 42.

It appears then that *Yahweh* cannot be safely regarded except as a neuter (*qal*); and we must take as our guide in its interpretation the parallel passage in Exod. iii, which, indeed, is clearly meant as an exposition of what it implies.

In an instructive essay on this question, in the *British and Foreign Evangelical Review* for 1876, Professor Robertson Smith observes that the modern disposition to look on *Yahweh* as a causal form is in large measure a protest against the abstract character of the exegesis of Exod. iii. 14. A double exegetical tradition, he proceeds to remark, is connected with that verse, the Palestinian, deriving from it the idea of God's eternity and immutability, and the Hellenistic or Alexandrian, deriving from it the idea of his absolute nature (already in LXX. ὁ ὤν). Either of these views, but especially the latter, assigns to the revelation an improbably abstract, metaphysical character, and moreover does not do justice to the word or the tense employed. היה is γίγνομαι, not εἰμί; and אהיה suggests the meaning *come to be*, or *will be*, rather than *am*. The phrase denotes thus not γέγονα ὃ γέγονα, but either γίγνομαι ὃ γίγνομαι or ἔσομαι ὃ ἔσομαι. This was seen by Franz Delitzsch[1] and Oehler[2], who, adopting the former of these alternatives, observe that the name does not express fixity, but change,—not, however, a change regulated by caprice, but by design and conscious choice— '*I am*,'—not that which fate or caprice may determine, but— '*that I am*,' what my own character determines. It implies that God's nature cannot be expressed in terms of any other substance, but can be measured only by itself (cf. the phrases iv. 13; xxxiii. 19; 2 Kings viii. 1). But further, since היה is not mere existence, but emerging into reality (*werden*, γίγνομαι, come to pass), it implies a living and active personality, not a God of the past only, but of the future, one whose name cannot be defined, but whose nature it is ever to express itself anew, ever to manifest itself under a fresh aspect

---

[1] *Commentar über die Genesis* (1872), pp. 26, 60 (der Begriff des V. היה, oder היה, nicht sowol der des ruhenden, als des bewegten Seins, oder der Selbstbethätigung ist, *u. s. w.*).

[2] *Theology of the Old Testament*, § 39.

(ein immer im Werden sich kundgebendes), whose relation to the world is one of ever progressive manifestation (in stetem lebendigem Werden begriffen ist). It denotes him, in a word, not as a transcendental abstraction, but as one who enters into an historical relation with humanity.

If we interpret אהיה as a future, we get a somewhat different meaning. This rendering is found in Rashi (eleventh century), who paraphrases '*I will be* with them in this affliction *what I will be* with them in the subjection of their future captivities[1].' So Ewald, in his last work[2] (regarding Exod. iii. as an effort to import new meaning into a word the sense of which had become obscure and forgotten), explains '*I will be* it,' viz. the performer of his promises; ver. 12, God says, 'I will be with thee:' ver. 14 explains how: '*I will be* it! I (viz.) *who will be* it,' will be, viz. what I have promised and said. This is the view adopted also by Professor Smith, though he construes more simply, 'I will be what I will be.' From the use of *I will be* just afterwards by itself, he argues that אשר אהיה is epexegetical and not part of the name itself. He next points out how this *I will be* rings throughout the Bible,—'I will be *with thee, with them, their God*,' etc., and finds in this often-repeated phrase the key to the name here. '*I will be*'—something which lies implicitly in the mind of him who uses the name: in the mouth of the worshipper, '*He will be* it,' an assertion of confidence in Jehovah as a God who will not fail or disappoint his servants: in one word, *He will approve himself*. At the same time *what* he will be is left

---

[1] The paraphrase is suggested evidently by *Berachoth*, 9 b (quoted in the commentaries *ad loc.*):— אהיה אשר אהיה א"ל הק"בה למשה לך אמיר להם לישראל אני הייתי עמכם בשעניד וה ואני אהיה עמכם בשעבור מלכיות אמר לפניו רבינו של עולם דיה לצרה בשעתה אמר ליה הק"בה לך אמיר להם אהיה שלחני אליכם. Similarly, Jehudah ha-Levi (twelfth century), who, commenting on אהיה, *Cusari*, iv. 3 (p. 262, ed. Buxtorf: p. 304, ed. Cassel), writes:— ורצה בו למנוע מהשיב באמתות העצם אשר ידיעתי נמנעת וכאשר שאלי יאמר ואמרו לי מה שמו מנהו לאמר מה לוהם לבקש מה שלא יוכלו להשיגי דומה למה שאמר המלאך למה זה תשאל לשמי והוא פלאי אך אמיר להם אהיה ופירושו אשר אהיה והעצם הנמצא אשר אמצא להם בעת שיבקשוני אל יבקשי ראיה גדולה מהמצאי עמהם ויקבלוני בו.

[2] *Die Lehre der Bibel von Gott* (1873), ii. p. 337 f.

undefined, or defined only in terms of himself, for the very reason that his providential dealings with his people in their ever-varying needs are inexhaustible—are more than can be numbered or expressed. The vagueness is intentional, as when Moses says, 'Send now by the hand of him that thou sendest,' i. e. send me, then, if it must be so. So here, 'I will be that which I am to be' to you: what I have promised and you look for; I will approve myself—though *how* he will approve himself is an ἀνεκφώρητόν. And in Hos. i. 9 Professor Smith finds an allusion to the phrase, 'I will save Judah by (*or* as) Jehovah their God;' but to Ephraim he says, 'Ye are not my people, and *I will not be* for you.' The promise made to Moses is there withdrawn from Ephraim.

This view is, undoubtedly, an attractive one. Dillmann, indeed, objects that the principal fact, viz. what Jehovah will prove himself, is not expressed, but must be supplied in thought: but the substantive verb may well be understood in a pregnant sense, *give evidence of being*. It differs, however, but slightly from that of Oehler and Delitzsch. The essential point in both is that they see in יהוה not the idea of abstract existence (such as is denoted by the unfortunate rendering *the Eternal*), but of active being, manifestation in history. The principal difference is that on the one view this is conceived as realized in history at large: on the other, in the history of Israel in particular. On the whole, the meaning of יהוה and אהיה אשר אהיה may probably be best explained as follows: יהוה denotes *He that is—is*, viz. implying not one who barely exists, but one who asserts his being, and (unlike the false gods) enters into personal relations with his worshippers. He who in the mouths of men, however, can only be spoken of as *He is* becomes, when he is speaking in his own person, *I am*; and the purport of the phrase in iii. 14 is, firstly, to show that the divine nature is indefinable, it can be defined adequately only by itself; and secondly, to show that God, being not determined by anything external to himself, is consistent with himself, true to his promises, and unchangeable in his purposes. The latter aspect of the name became certainly prominent afterwards: and the prophets, by many allusions[1], show that they saw in it the expression of moral unchangeableness[2].

To sum up briefly the substance of what has been said. The theories of the *origin* of the name, or the meaning once attached to it, relate to the time *prior* to Exod. iii. 14: their truth would in no way invalidate or affect the revelation there given, so that they may be considered impartially upon their own merits. Upon their own merits they cannot be regarded as established. The theory of an Accadian origin unquestionably breaks down; the theory of some other non-Israelitish origin rests, at least at present, upon an insecure foundation, and is rejected by the most competent Old Testament scholars of every shade of theological opinion. The Ἰάω of the Greek writers is late; and nothing can be built upon it till it has been shown not to be derivable from the Old Testament tradition itself. The Hamathite and Phœnician names cannot be explained away: the *possibility* of a point of contact with non-Israelites remains; but we await further discoveries. So much for the name, as a name. Then as to the meaning. The possibility of a stage in which the name denoted the author of some physical phænomenon is undeniable. There is no positive evidence adducible in its favour; though some minds may be influenced by the weight of analogy. Similarly, though from the time when Exod. iii. was written, the name must have been understood by Jews in the neutral sense ὁ γιγνόμενος, the possibility of a prior stage when it was interpreted in the sense *He that causeth to be* (or *to come to pass*) must be conceded. More than this cannot be said: positive evidence is again not forthcoming. Indeed, the advocates of this opinion hardly contend for more: both Kuenen and Schultz, for instance, speak very cautiously. The considerations advanced in support of the theories which have been discussed are not, I

---

[1] E.g. Isa. xxvi. 4, 8, xli. 4; Hos. xii. 6; Mal. iii. 6.
[2] Comp. Philippi, *l.c.* p. 179 f.; Dillmann, p. 35, both of whom regard the word as having the sense of a Qal.

venture to think, sufficiently strong to render them plausible : no ground appears at present to exist for questioning either the purely Israelitish origin of the Tetragrammaton, or the explanation of its meaning which is given in Exod. iii. 14.

Coin found near Gaza, referred to on page 5.

The following is Mr. Poole's description :—

'*Obv.* Bearded male head, three-quarter face towards r., in crested Corinthian helmet.

'*Rev.* 4∆2l (יהו). Deity resembling the Greek Zeus, clad in mantle, seated r. in a car to the axle of which wings are attached, holds in r. eagle or hawk; in front, below head of Bes or of a Satyr l.; the whole in a dotted square. Silver. Weight 50·7 grains.

'Published by J. P. Six in the *Numismatic Chronicle*, 1877, p. 229, as struck probably at Gaza, but for this there is no authority. See also Combe, *Vet. pop. et regum nummi qui in Mus. Brit. adservantur* (1814), p. 242', and pl. xiii. 12; De Luynes, *La Numismatique des Satrapies et de la Phénicie* (1846), p. 29¹, and pl. iv. ("Sohar").

'The legends in Phœnician and Aramaic characters on coins give (*a*) names of kings *or* satraps : (*b*) names of towns *or* gods of towns, so specified,—besides dates; generally (*a*) and (*b*) are combined on the different sides of the same coin. I know of no instance of the name of a god occurring without the qualification of the name of the mint, as *Baal-Turz* on coins of Tarsus. I am, therefore, inclined to read יהו as a proper name. That the reading is correct I am not sure, as the form of the second letter is strange for ה.'

Respecting the origin and use of אל and its relation to אלהים, a discussion has recently arisen in Germany which is sufficiently cognate to the subject of the preceding essay to be mentioned here, and which deserves the attention of those interested in such questions. It is contained in the following articles : 1. Lagarde, *Orientalia*, ii. (1880), pp. 3–10 [connects אל not with אול but with אלי]; 2. Nöldeke in the *Monatsberichte der Kön.-Pr. Akad. der Wissenschaften zu Berlin* for 1880, pp. 760–776 [adduces evidence, chiefly from inscriptions, to show that the vowel in *El* was originally long]; 3. Lagarde in the *Göttingische Nachrichten*, 1882, pp. 173–192 (=*Mittheilungen*, 1884, pp. 94–106), [reply to No. 2]; 4. Nestle in the *Theol. Studien aus Württemberg*, 1882, Heft iv. pp. 243–258 [conjectures אלהים to be the plural of אל]; 5. Nöldeke in the *Sitzungsberichte* of the same Berlin Academy, 1882, pp. 1175–1192 [criticism of No. 4, and answer to No. 3]; 6. Lagarde in the *Mittheilungen*, pp. 107–111 and 222–224. The course taken by the discussion has been indicated in outline; but no abstract of the argument is here attempted: the field covered by it is so wide that in order to be properly appreciated it must be studied *in extenso*[1].

My friend, Mr. D. S. Margoliouth, of New College, while examining an Ethiopic MS. recently acquired by the Bodleian Library (MSS. Aeth. 9. 5), and containing the same *Preces magicae xii discipulorum* as No. 78 in Dillmann's Catalogue of the Ethiopic MSS. of the British Museum, has observed יהוה vocalized almost exactly as by Epiphanius and Theodoret (Ἰαωέ). The passage occurs (fol. 6ᵇ) in a list of magical names of Christ said to have been given by him to his disciples. As the context is curious, I transcribe a portion of it (vocalization unchanged):—

ወእምድኅሬሁ፡ ነገሮሙ፡ አስማቲሁ፡ ኢያሄ፡ ብሂል፡ ግሩም፡ ሱራሄ፡ ብሂል፡ ዓቢይ፡ ዶሞናኤል፡ ብሂል፡ ኃያል፡ ......ሞርጎነ፡ ብሂል፡ ዓቃቤ፡ ኵሉ፡ አኤ፡ ብሂል፡ ረዳኤ፡ አፍራነ፡ ብሂል፡ መድኃኔ፡ መናቴር፡ ብሂል፡ ኖላዊ፡ ኤል፡ ኤል፡ ብሂል፡ ከዳኔ፡ ኵሉ፡ አኪ፡ ብሂል፡ ተዓጋሢ፡ አሱሂ፡ ብሂል፡ ዐፃሬ፡ ኵሉ፡ ......ያዌ፡ ያዌ፡ ብሂል፡ አማኒ፡ ርቱዕ፡

'And after that he told them his names: *Iyáhé*, i.e. terrible; *Súráhé*, i.e. great; *Demná'él*, i.e. mighty; ...... *Mergoa*, i.e. all-watching; *Oe*, i.e. helper; *Apháráa*, i.e. saviour; *Manátér*, i.e. shepherd; *'Él*, *'Él*, i.e. protector of all; *Akhó*, i.e. patient; *Elóhé*, i.e. supporter of all; ...... *Yáwé*, *Yáwé*, i.e. faithful (and) just.'

---

[1] See also Professor Francis Brown's note in the *Presbyterian Review* (New York), 1882, pp. 404–407; and (still more recently) M. Halévy in the *Revue des Études juives*, 1884 (ix), pp. 175–180 (pp. 161–174 on יהוה, maintaining its Israelitish origin, and explaining nearly in the sense of Rashi).

II.

THE LIGHT
THROWN BY THE SEPTUAGINT VERSION
ON THE BOOKS OF SAMUEL.

[F. H. Woods.]

THE object of the following paper is to attempt to give a fair estimate of the value of the LXX as a critical authority with special reference to the Books of Samuel; and at the same time to point out the most important passages in which that version throws light upon the original text, or the manner of its composition. The limits required in a paper of this kind compelled me in most cases to select only a few examples by way of illustration, and made a more complete view of the subject impossible.

The critical value of the LXX rests mainly on the fact of its great antiquity. At the lowest computation it must be many centuries older than the oldest existing Hebrew MS., and some centuries older than any other translation of the Hebrew text. Again its extreme literalness, in these books especially, gives it often much of the value which an actual Hebrew MS. would possess. Hebrew phrases are represented with an exactness which is defiant of Greek idiom and not unfrequently of Greek grammar as well. Such phrases as ἐξ ἡμερῶν εἰς ἡμέρας, 1 Sam. i. 3; καὶ προσέθετο ἔτι ... ὀμόσαι, 1 Sam. xx. 17; καὶ ἀπηγγέλη τῷ βασιλεῖ Δαυίδ, λέγοντες, 2 Sam. vi. 12; and ὥσπερ αὐτοὺς καὶ ὥσπερ αὐτούς, 2 Sam. xxiv. 3, enable us easily to reproduce the Hebrew text from which they are translated, and examples of such a kind might be multiplied indefinitely. In much the same way even the imperfect knowledge of Hebrew which the translators frequently exhibit is often a real gain to the critical student. The translations of בִּי by ἐν ἐμοί in 1 Sam. i. 26 and תֹאבֶה by προστεθήσεσθε in 1 Sam. xii. 25 (cf. xxvii. 1) are just such mistakes as a Hebrew novice might make. But in all such cases it is easy enough to see what is the reading which the LXX represents, and at the same time the disregard of an intelligible sense, in their scrupulous desire to reproduce exactly the Hebrew original, shows that the translators would never have altered the text to improve the meaning. Whenever they appear to have done so, we must assume, either that the LXX text represents a different reading of the Hebrew, or that the MS. which they translated from was defective. In another way also the imperfect knowledge of the translators serves the Biblical critic a good turn. They frequently transliterated the Hebrew words which they were unable to translate, showing again their almost superstitious anxiety to give an exact equivalent to the Hebrew. Thus in 1 Sam. ii. 18 we find ἐφουδ βάδ, though curiously enough the words are rendered στολὴν ἔξαλλον in 2 Sam. vi. 14, pointing perhaps to the work of a different translator or a later reviser. The words Ἰερίμ in 1 Sam. xv. 3, 8, and Νάβαλ in 2 Sam. iii. 33, 34 are evidently regarded as proper names[1]. Sometimes transliterations were made because the Hebrew words, being of a technical character, or for other reasons, were too well known to require translation. Thus such a phrase as Ἀδωραὶ σαβαώθ in 1 Sam. i. 11 is to be accounted for, and perhaps also ῥέβελ in i. 24. A more remarkable feature is the occasional representation of a Hebrew by a Greek word, which happens to have a similar sound, though no philological connexion. Thus in 1 Sam.

---

[1] Other examples are Μεσσάβ in I. xiv. 1, 6, 11, 12; ἐργάβ, xx. 19; εἰς τὴν ἁματταρί (הַמַּטָּרָה) in xx. 20; ἀραφώθ and σαφώθ in II. xvii. 19, 29. Not unfrequently we find the Hebrew word side by side with the translation, either preceding or following it, one of the two being the insertion of a later reviser, as τὰ ἐμπρόσθια (ἀμαφέθ), I. v. 4; θίμα (ἐργάβ), vi. 11, 15; (Ἰάαλ) δρυμός, xiv. 25; θεοῦ πίστις (φελλανὶ μαεμωνί), xxi. 2; συνεχόμενος (νεεσαράν), xxi. 7; (Μέσσερα) στενήν, xxiv. 23.

v. 4 ῥάχις seems to have been suggested by רק, and νυκτικόραξ is the translation of קרא in xxvi. 20[1].

Unfortunately we have certain drawbacks to set against these advantages of the LXX. In the first place the Hebrew MS., or MSS., employed by the translators, appear to have been in several places illegible, or at least defective. To this is due in a large measure the constant misrepresentation of names of persons and places, the interpreters not being able, as with ordinary words, to guess the meaning by what they expected to find. In this way only can we account for such renderings as εἰς δουλείαν in 1 Sam. xiv. 40 and ἐπάνω διακοπῶν in 2 Sam. v. 20. Again, the translators' imperfect knowledge of the language they were translating, if it has some advantage, as already maintained, has also some disadvantages. They occasionally seem to have omitted words or passages which they were unable to translate. This is the most natural way of accounting for the omissions of 1 Sam. xiii. 1 and 2 Sam. i. 18. The first is interesting as showing that the absence in the Hebrew of the numbers describing Saul's age and length of reign must belong to a very ancient condition of the text.

The greatest hindrance, however, to the use of the LXX for critical purposes is that the Greek text is itself obviously in a very different state from that in which it left the translators' hands. And we hope to show satisfactorily that many of the peculiar readings of the LXX, as we now have it, are not the fault of the translators, but have been introduced into the Greek text at a later date. The two oldest and best complete MSS. of the LXX are the Alexandrian (A) and the Vatican (B)[2]. These differ in some cases very considerably from each other. It is, however, pretty clear, by a comparison of each with the Masoretic text, that A has been revised by reference to the Hebrew, and so represents a later recension of the Greek text

[1] We find similar examples in the translation of הין by τόκος in Ps. lv. 12, lxxii. 14; קרע by τρώφη, Ps. cxi. 5; and וז by τοπάζιον in Ps. cxix. 127.

[2] The Sinaitic (א) contains only a fragment of 1 Chron. and the greater part of the poetical and prophetical books.

than B, though in a few isolated cases (as in 1 Sam. x. 12; xiv. 20, 41; 2 Sam. xxi. 1) the reading of B is evidently a corruption of A. We are therefore justified in general in taking B rather than A as the basis for comparative criticism.

Now if we compare B with the Masoretic text, we shall find that it contains a large number of short passages not found in the latter. By far the majority of these are alternative renderings of some passage already otherwise translated, and have most probably been inserted into the text from marginal glosses. The Hexapla, and other similar editions of Origen, no doubt, did much to produce this result. In the Book of Judges many of the passages so inserted are known to be from the translation of Theodotion. These alternatives are in most cases easily detected, as, for example, in 1 Sam. ii. 24; 2 Sam. v. 15, 16. One of the alternatives, generally the first in order, usually agrees nearly with the Masoretic text. Sometimes, however, both alternatives differ from it considerably, as in 1 Sam. xxi. 13. Not unfrequently one of the alternatives is derived from a different reading of the Hebrew text, and differs considerably from the other, so that at first sight it appears to be an arbitrary insertion. Thus in 2 Sam. ii. 22, 23. καὶ ποῦ ἐστι ταῦτα; ἐπίστρεφε πρὸς Ἰωάβ is merely an alternative of καὶ πῶς... Ἰωάβ, the former being probably a translation of ואיך מנה אלה אל־יואב, the latter agreeing verbally with the Masoretic text; so also ἐν ἰσχύϊ in 2 Sam. vi. 5 is the alternative of ἐν ὀργάνοις ἡρμοσμένοις, as shown by verse 14, where the latter alone is the rendering of the Hebrew בכל עץ; Μολχόμ in 2 Sam. xii. 30, ἀδελφὸν αὐτοῦ in 2 Sam. xiv. 6, τοῦτο ἐγὼ ἄρξομαι in 2 Sam. xviii. 14, καὶ ἐπίγνωθι σεαυτῷ in 2 Sam. xix. 7, are alternatives of a similar kind[1]. In some cases an attempt has been made to combine the alternatives into one sentence, as in 2 Sam. xviii. 18, by the insertion of the words ἐν ᾗ between the alternatives ἔλαβε ... στήλην and

---

[1] See also 1 Sam. xiv. 47; 2 Sam. xv. 34; xix. 7, 18, 43; xx. 18. In the last καὶ ἐν Δὰν (ודנה) is evidently a corruption of ונה.

ἐλήφθη ... στήλην, and the alteration of ἕκαστοι (B) into ἕκαστον (A) in 1 Sam. v. 4.

Besides these alternative renderings we find several clauses which are evidently additions to the original text. These are very various in kind. Thus the clauses καὶ οἶνον καὶ μέθυσμα οὐ πίεται, καὶ πάσας τὰς δεκάτας τῆς γῆς αὐτοῦ, and καὶ ἄρτοις, in 1 Sam. i. 11, 21, 24, appear to be additions derived from the Levitical law, not unlike the references to fasting so frequently inserted in the MSS. of the New Testament. In other cases insertions have been made to give greater fulness to the narrative, where the concise form of the story much better accords with the spirit of the Hebrew language. Of this we have a remarkable example in the words of David to Goliath in 1 Sam. xvii. 43, in answer to Goliath's question ὡσεὶ κύων ἐγώ εἰμι, etc. Can we imagine that any Hebrew writer would have put in David's mouth such a tame reply as οὐχί, ἀλλ᾽ ἢ χείρων κυνός? The words καὶ πορεύεσθε ... ἐνώπιόν μου, in 1 Sam. xxix. 10, appear to be an insertion of a similar kind. The long insertion in 2 Sam. xi. 22, πάντα τὰ ῥήματα ... τὸ τεῖχος, is evidently an expansion of the narrative derived almost verbatim from verses 19–21[1]. Such insertions are obviously analogous to the later paraphrastic expansions of the Targums, and are probably due to the influence of the oral teaching of Jewish Scripture. In many cases the insertion has been made of historical notes referring to a later stage of Jewish history, as in 2 Sam. viii. 7, 8; xiv. 27; xxiv. 25. Insertions of this kind may be the work of a later reviser, whether of the Hebrew text from which the LXX was made, or of the LXX translation itself, it is impossible to determine with certainty. The interpolation, however, of ὅτι μείζων ... πρώτη in 2 Sam. xiii. 15, suggested probably by our Lord's words

---

[1] The insertions διδοὺς εὐχὴν τῷ εὐχομένῳ in I. ii. 9, οὐχὶ πορεύσομαι ... Ἰσραήλ and τίς ... ὅς in xvii. 36, καὶ γυναῖκα in xxx. 2, and ἀπὸ Δὰν ἕως Βηρσαβεὲ in II. vi. 19, ὁ ποιήσας τοῦτο in xii. 7, καὶ ἐξελέξατο ... πυρῶν in xxiv. 15, are probably expansions of a similar kind.

in Matt. xii. 45, seems to show that additions of this kind were sometimes made at a very late date. We may compare with this last the remarkable insertion, in Ps. xiv, of the quotations in Rom. iii. 13-18, and of Jer. ix. 23, 24 in 1 Sam. ii. 10. The last, differing as it does verbally from the LXX text of Jeremiah, must either be derived from a Hebrew source or from an independent translation of the Hebrew.

It seems hardly consistent with the evident aim of the translators to represent with such scrupulous accuracy the Hebrew original, to suppose that any of these interpolations were added at the time of the translation. But, whatever be their origin, they are in most cases easy to detect, and cannot be considered to detract very materially from the critical value of the LXX. We now come to others which have more the character of *variae lectiones*. First, we may notice the addition of some word, such as the name of the person or place referred to, or some other short phrase, to complete the sense, as ἐπὶ Ἰσραήλ in 1 Sam. xv. 23, ὁ βλέπων in 1 Sam. xvi. 4, Ἰεβοσθέ in 2 Sam. iv. 2. On the other hand, we frequently find expressions of the same kind in the Masoretic text, and not in the LXX; so that, if we apply in such cases the canon by which the shorter reading is to be preferred to the longer, we must often accept the reading of the LXX to the exclusion of that contained in the Masoretic text. There is little doubt, therefore, that we should omit such readings as לפי־חרב in 1 Sam. xxii. 19 b, נבל in xxv. 19, אל־הבילך in xxvi. 14, בחברון in 2 Sam. iv. 12 b. The omissions in 1 Sam. xxix. 9, xxx. 7 are more doubtful.

There are also many instances in which an apparent insertion of the LXX ends or begins with the same, or nearly the same, words as have lately occurred, and should therefore more probably be regarded as an omission in the Masoretic text from *homoeoteleuton*. This will be easily recognised as the true explanation of the omissions of εἰς ἄρχοντα ... ἔχρισέ σε Κύριος in 1 Sam. x. 1, καὶ προσάγουσι τὴν φυλὴν Ματταρί εἰς ἄνδρας in x. 21, καὶ ἀναβαίνουσιν ἐπὶ Ἰσραήλ and καὶ τὸ κατάλειμμα ... Γαλγάλων in xiii. 5, 15. It is extremely improbable that Samuel would have gone, as the Hebrew text of this last passage has it, to Gibeah, Saul's home, instead of his own home at Ramah; whereas Gibeah was the most natural place for the assembling of Saul's forces, as it is stated in the LXX, and the place where, according to the next verse, we actually find them. This is doubtless too the true explanation of the additional clauses, τί ὅτι ... τῷ λαῷ σου Ἰσραήλ in 1 Sam. xiv. 41, which not only make what in the Masoretic text is unintelligible quite clear, but throw a most interesting light on the use of the Urim and Thummim as a sort of sacred lots, δῆλοι being a frequent rendering of אורים in the LXX (e.g. xxviii. 6), and ὁσιότης being here obviously a representative of תמים. In this instance we must, with A, omit the words δὸς δή, a curious insertion from δὸς δήλους above. I must leave it to others to decide whether we should on similar grounds accept ὃν ἂν ... υἱοῦ αὐτοῦ in verse 42, or regard it as one of those paraphrastic expansions above noticed. We have also good examples of omission by *homœoteleuton* in the Masoretic text of 2 Sam. xiii. 21 and 34.

It frequently happens, however, that what at first sight look like omissions from this cause in the Hebrew prove, on closer examination, to be merely alternative renderings of the LXX, because, from the nature of the case, these alternatives generally begin or end with the same words as the clauses to which they correspond. Thus in 1 Sam. xv. 3, καὶ ἐξολοθρεύσεις ... ἀπ᾽ αὐτοῦ is clearly an alternative of καὶ πατάξεις ... ἐξ αὐτοῦ, and we have no reason therefore to depart from the Masoretic text. In 2 Sam. xv. 18, which will be noticed again lower down, and in xix. 18 we have striking examples of the same ambiguity. There are other cases in which the additions of the LXX are probably accidental insertions, because we can trace the sources from which they appear to be derived. Thus in 2 Sam. xiii. 27, the words καὶ ἐποίησεν Ἀβεσσαλὼμ πότον κατὰ τὸν πότον τοῦ βασιλέως may have been inserted from 1 Sam. xxv. 36, the only other shearing feast described in the Old Testament. Similarly in 2 Sam. xix. 10 the words καὶ τὸ ῥῆμα παντὸς Ἰσραὴλ ἦλθε πρὸς τὸν βασιλέα are clearly derived from the eleventh verse. In both these passages, however, the differences in the wording of the Greek show that the insertions must have already existed in the Hebrew MS. from which the Septuagint translation was made[1].

On the other hand, we find several passages in which the LXX itself omits clauses by *homoeoteleuton* which are found in the Masoretic text. We have more or less certain examples of this in 1 Sam. ii. 32, xxv. 13, xxvi. 5, xxxi. 6, 2 Sam. xvi. 16, xviii. 18. If we accept the genuineness of the Masoretic text in all such cases, we ought in fairness to accept the so-called additions of the LXX where their insertion cannot be adequately accounted for, and their omission may be traced to such a frequent source of textual corruption.

Some few of the additions in the LXX are, on the other hand, *insertions* from *homoeoteleuton*. Thus in 2 Sam. vii. 25, the words Κύριε παντοκράτωρ Θεὲ τοῦ Ἰσραήλ have been inserted from verse 27, where they rightly follow the words ἕως αἰῶνος. In 2 Sam. xi. 18 there is a similar insertion of the words λαλῆσαι πρὸς τὸν βασιλέα from verse 19. And we find an example of precisely the same sort of insertion in the Masoretic text in 2 Sam. vi. 3 and 4, where a comparison with the LXX shows that the words חדשה ... בגבעה have got into the text from the same cause. For, had the LXX reading been the result of an *omission* from *homoeoteleuton*, that version would have read the words τὴν καινήν after ἅμαξαν in verse 4.

There are some passages in which the LXX is more than a critical authority in determining the text, and throws important light on the way in which the Books of Samuel were composed. The omissions of B in chapters xvii. and xviii.

---

[1] On the other hand the additions of I. viii. 18, II. xxiv. 13, are probably intentional amplifications derived from the immediate context.

of 1 Samuel seem quite conclusive in proving that these chapters are composed of two separate accounts of the encounter of David and Goliath, one of which only was found in the Hebrew MS. or MSS. to which the Septuagint translators had access. If we read separately and continuously the parts of these chapters omitted by B, xvii. 12–31, 50, 55—xviii. 5, xviii. 9–11, 17–19, 29 b–30, and the remaining parts contained in B, we get two nearly consecutive narratives throughout: whereas the difficulties are almost insuperable if we regard the whole, as it stands in the Masoretic text and our English version, as one continuous history. It will be sufficient to mention one difficulty which is removed, or at least greatly lessened, if we regard these separate portions as fragments of two independent accounts of this portion of David's career. One of the greatest puzzles of commentators is the fact that in xvii. 55 Saul asks Abner whose son David is, and Abner replies that he cannot tell; whereas, according to xvi. 21, David was Saul's own armourbearer. Various unsatisfactory explanations have been given of the remarkable ignorance which Saul and Abner both showed, as e.g. that Saul in his fits of madness did not know David by sight, or that a considerable interval had elapsed since his appointment and subsequent return to his home. But the difficulty is at once removed, or at least changed in character, when we find that both question and answer belong to the account, omitted by the LXX, in which David is said to have been sent by his father from Bethlehem as a stranger to his brothers; whereas in the other account, which the LXX preserves, it is implied that he was present with the army when Goliath uttered his challenge. The difficulty of reconciling the two accounts still remains; but becomes a historical, rather than a critical one, and hardly greater than we find in other parts of the Bible, where different accounts of the same event are preserved, as in the Gospels. The independence of these two accounts becomes clearer still if we omit certain connecting sentences, which by their omission in B are proved to have been inserted when or after the two were blended into one narrative. The first part of xviii. 6 and the last part of xviii. 21 are obviously additions of this kind, the first being inserted to justify the compiler in going back again to the events of the previous chapter, the second to connect the accounts of the offer by Saul of each of his two daughters. It is highly probable that similar connecting links were introduced in the portions of the narrative not found in B; but as this narrative does not exist in an independent form, these must be, more or less, a matter of conjecture. It is not improbable that xvii. 15, and perhaps 16, are additions of this kind: the first being added to account for David not being with Saul, and the second referring the reader back to the description of the Philistine in verse 4, whereas the first part of verse 23, as it exists in the Hebrew text, most naturally describes Goliath's first appearance. If this view is correct, there must have been some alteration, perhaps by omission of Goliath's words, of the last part of verse 23.

There are other instances in which the LXX seems to point to a combination of more or less distinct narratives of the same event. At the end of chap. iii. and the beginning of chap. iv. of 1 Samuel, we have a very remarkable addition in the LXX. The last part καὶ ἐγενήθη . . . πόλεμον is a natural commencement of the description of the battle with the Philistines, and has been probably omitted by *homoeoteleuton* from the Hebrew text. The middle portion from καὶ Ἡλὶ . . . Κυρίου is like statements which we constantly find scattered throughout the Hebrew narrative, but usually at the commencement of the subject. It is not therefore out of place if we regard it as an introduction to chap. iv, showing how the disasters which followed were a punishment to Eli and his sons. Nor is it unsuitable in connexion with what goes before, contrasting as it does the position of Samuel and Eli. Keil seems therefore needlessly severe when he writes, 'At the close of verse 21, the LXX have appended a general remark concerning Eli and his sons, which, regarded as a deduction from the context, answers no doubt to the paraphrastic treatment of our book in that version, but in a critical aspect is utterly worthless.' (Translation, Clark's Series, p. 52.) The first part of this insertion, καὶ ἐπιστεύθη ... ἕως ἄκρων, is evidently an alternative of verse 20. But it differs from the alternatives we usually meet with, partly in its paraphrastic character—the alternatives generally differ but little in form of sentences and order of words, the chief differences being due to variations of reading—partly also in not immediately preceding or following the passage it represents[1]. Now it is remarkable that the intermediate words, καὶ προσέθετο ... Σαμουήλ, resemble in their general meaning verse 19, so much so, that, if we had only the LXX without the help of the Hebrew, we might very naturally suppose that the whole of verse 21 to ἕως ἄκρων was another form of verses 19 and 20. Is it not possible that this is the true explanation, and that we have here an instance in which part of an alternative form of the narrative has got into the Hebrew text? We have a somewhat parallel example in the next chapter. Before verse 16 καὶ εἶπεν ... πρὸς Ἡλὶ is evidently an alternative of verse 14. But it also differs from the ordinary type of alternative in the same two respects as the last. The differences are just such as we should expect in two forms of the same narrative, and the alternatives are separated by an intermediate sentence. Now this intermediate καὶ Ἡλὶ ... ἐπέβλεπε more naturally precedes verse 16 than follows verse 14, explaining as it does the reason why Eli had to ask the question, the reason, according to the custom of Hebrew writers, generally coming first. Besides this it is difficult to reconcile the statement of verse 13 that Eli was 'watching' (Hebrew מִצְפֶּה) with the mention of his blindness in this verse. On all these grounds there seems considerable reason

---

[1] 2 Sam. i. 19-23 and xviii. 17 are no real exceptions to this rule, the intermediate words in each case being only a single phrase may fairly be regarded as part of the alternative, and pointing therefore to a variation in the order of the words.

for regarding verses 15 and 16 to πρὸς Ἡλί as an alternative of verses 13 and 14. So that here again we probably find part of an alternative form in the Masoretic text.

In chap. v. the LXX again seems to show that the narrative has been compiled from two different accounts of the events narrated. The last half of verse 3, καὶ ἐβαρύνθη ... τὰ ὅρια αὐτῆς, is obviously an alternative of verse 6, and agrees almost exactly with the Masoretic form of that verse, while verse 6 as it stands in the LXX differs very considerably from it, containing two additional statements in the phrases καὶ μέσον ... μύες and καὶ ἐγένετο ... πόλει, while it omits את אשדוד ואת גבוליה, to say nothing of the reading ναῦς, which, however curious it may be, is evidently the analogue of ἕδρας in the other form. In the fourth verse the words ἕκαστοι ... πρόθυρον are an alternative of καὶ κεφαλὴ ... ἐμπρόσθια (the Hebrew word ἀμαφέθ being of course a second alternative of ἐμπρόσθια, and probably the earliest reading). Here the differences are less considerable and more analogous to the usual type of alternatives: yet the word ἕκαστοι cannot easily be explained as originating from our present Hebrew text. For though ἕκαστον (the reading of A) might at first sight appear to be a translation of איש, a corruption of ראש, we cannot thus explain the omission of καὶ before, and Δάγων, or some word corresponding to it, after, ἕκαστον. But the difficulty is removed if we regard this as a fragment from another form of the narrative. The sentence may have originally begun καὶ βραχίονες ἕκαστοι, or in some such way. The reading of ἕκαστον in A is most probably a correction to make the word agree with ἴχνος, and so connect this with the other alternative. Now if we assume the integrity of the Masoretic text of this chapter, we must suppose that the original Septuagint translation contained only one of these alternatives in both the fourth and sixth verses (probably the latter in each case, as being the most unlike the Masoretic text), that a later reviser, comparing that translation with some Hebrew MS. or some other Greek translation of a Hebrew

MS. nearly resembling, if not identical with, the Masoretic text, introduced the other alternatives καὶ κεφαλὴ ... τὰ ἔμπροσθια (or ἀμαφίθ) and καὶ ἐβαρύνθη ... ὅρια αὐτῆς as marginal glosses; and that, lastly, what was probably the original form of the sixth verse was transposed by a still later reviser to the second verse, while the two glosses naturally enough found their way into the text. The great objection to this view is the number of hypotheses it involves. Can we not find a simpler solution of the difficulty? Now let us suppose for an instant that we only possessed this account in the LXX. We should, I think, strongly suspect (considering how frequent such alternatives are) that the first part of verse 4 is also an alternative of the first part of verse 3, with which it almost verbally agrees. If this is the case, we must conclude, as was shown to be highly probable in the last two discussed examples, that the narrative, even in its Hebrew form, has been compiled from two distinct accounts of Dagon's fall (which must have happened only once), much in the same way as it has been shown that the two accounts of David and Goliath have been combined. The only serious difficulty is the phrase, found both in the Hebrew and the Greek, in verse 3: 'And they took Dagon, and set him in his place again;' but this can be explained as a connecting-link inserted when the two accounts were combined, like those in the XVIIIth chapter already noticed. This theory of the origin of our present chapter cannot be considered as definitively proved, but seems on the whole to afford the simplest explanation of the differences which exist between the Masoretic text and the LXX. I have purposely not mentioned the remarkable insertion in verse 5, ὅτι ὑπερβαίνοντες ὑπερβαίνουσι, because it may very probably be a later gloss, arising out of a traditional explanation of Zeph. i. 9, and, if so, has no direct bearing on the question. We have, I believe, another example of the existence of alternative forms in the Masoretic text in 2 Sam. iv. 6. Here, at first sight, it is very tempting, with Thenius, Kirkpatrick, and others, to accept the LXX reading; but there are several objections to our doing so. (1) It does not altogether remove the awkward repetitions of the Hebrew text, the clause καὶ Ἰεσβοσθὲ ἐκάθευδεν ἐπὶ τῆς κλίνης αὐτοῦ, in verse 7, being very clumsy after καὶ αὐτὸς ἐκάθευδεν ἐν τῇ κοίτῃ. (2) The differences between the LXX and Hebrew cannot be entirely accounted for by the ordinary causes of textual corruption. (3) It is at least very remarkable that the Masoretic text, as it stands, should form such a complete doublet, if it is nothing but a corruption of the true text preserved *ex hypothesi* in the LXX rendering. It seems therefore far more reasonable to regard the former as the combination of two alternative forms, similar to those already adduced in 1 Sam. iii. iv. and v. The geographical note about the Beerothites introduced in verse 3, and still more the story of Mephibosheth's lameness in verse 4, show that this portion of the narrative has undergone a later revision. The LXX reading of verse 6 is probably due to the completion by conjecture of what was only legible here and there, and the repetitions of the Hebrew narrative probably helped to mislead the translators. Of course there may be some slight corruptions in the Masoretic text, as in לקחי חטים and the pointing of הנה ; but these do not affect the general question.

It remains to add a few important passages, in which the LXX seems to suggest a more probable reading than that of the Masoretic text. There can hardly be any doubt that in 1 Sam. i. 5 we should read אפס, the origin of the LXX πλήν, instead of the unintelligible word אפים. In verse 15 ἡ σκληρὰ ἡμέρα is evidently a translation of קשת יום, which is exactly parallel to קשה יום in Job xxx. 25, and preferable to קשת רוח, which would mean, not 'sorrowful,' but 'obstinate.' The LXX reading of vi. 19 is far from certain, but it at least helps us out of a great moral difficulty; and yet is not likely to have arisen out of any intention of the translators to do so, being quite unlike any of the insertions which are elsewhere found in that version. It will be seen that, according to the reading of the LXX, the death of the people of Bethshemesh was directly due to a local quarrel, and is only indirectly referred to Divine agency. It has a further probability from the fact that its omission in the Masoretic text may have arisen from *homœoteleuton*. In ix. 25, 26 for וידבר, וישכמו we should probably read וירבד (cf. Prov. viii. 16) and וישכב (or וישכבו): 'And he made a bed with Saul upon the roof, and he (or they) slept.' This agrees better with verse 26. In x. 27 ויהי כמחדש, to which the LXX points (cf. Gen. xxxviii. 24), is a much more intelligible reading than ויהי כמחריש. The words should, as in the LXX, begin the next chapter: 'And it came to pass, after a month's time or so.' In xii. 11 we may safely alter ברן into ברק, it being evident that Samuel is speaking of some well-known judge, such as Barak. In xiv. 18 the LXX אפד is better than ארון, the Ark being never used as the vehicle of an oracular response, and being in all probability nowhere near Saul at the time. In xiv. 21 there is much to be said in favour of עבדים for עברים, the people alluded to being probably the slaves, who took advantage of their chance of escaping from their Philistine masters[1]. The LXX ἐργάβ (ἀργάβ) in xx. 19, 41 is probably a transliteration of an original Hebrew ארגב, which in verse 19 has been corrupted into הנגב, in verse 41 into האבן. The word, which appears only in the Gileaditish Argob, would mean 'a mound.' In xxiii. 6 the additional clause, καὶ αὐτὸς μετὰ Δαυίδ, gets rid of the difficulty arising from the fact that David could not have been at Keilah at the time of Abiathar's escape. In xxvii. 10 the reading אל-מי (ἐπὶ τίνα) makes good sense, and avoids such a doubtful construction as אל-פשטתם; but possibly we may do better to adopt the reading אן, which is favoured by the Targum and Syriac. In 2 Sam. vi. 2 ἐν ἀναβάσει is sometimes explained as a translation of an original בעלתה (cf. 1 Chron. xiii. 6), supposed to have dropped out of the text

---

[1] In 1 Sam. xiii. 3, on the other hand, העברים is certainly correct.

from its resemblance to בעלי יהודה, which, according to this view, is correctly translated by τῶν ἀρχόντων Ἰούδα. If, however, we omit in Chronicles אל־קרית יערים, which is evidently one of the paraphrastic additions characteristic of that book, we get בעלתה אשר ליהודה, corresponding to בעלי יהודה of Samuel, showing that the latter (probably a corruption of בעל יהודה) is evidently the name of the place to which the ark was taken, the previous מן probably being inserted by some scribe who understood it, as did the LXX translators, of the princes who brought the ark. It is more probable therefore that ἐν ἀναβάσει and τοῦ ἀναγαγεῖν are alternative renderings of בהעלות. In 2 Sam. xv. 18 we have a long insertion describing the movements of David's followers, which at first sight appears to have been omitted from the Masoretic text by *homoeoteleuton*. But on closer examination it is evident that the passage is made up of three alternatives, partly following, partly included in, and partly overlapping each other. That is to say, in verse 18, Καὶ ἔστησαν ἐπὶ τῆς ἐλαίας ἐν τῇ ἐρήμῳ καὶ πᾶς ὁ λαὸς καὶ παρῇσαν ἐπὶ χεῖρα αὐτοῦ· καὶ πᾶς ὁ Χελεθί, καὶ πᾶς ὁ Φελεθί corresponds to καὶ ἔστησαν ἐν οἴκῳ τῷ μακράν. Καὶ πάντες οἱ παῖδες αὐτοῦ ἀνὰ χεῖρα αὐτοῦ παρῆγον, καὶ πᾶς Χελεθί καὶ πᾶς ὁ Φελεθί, and Hebrew ויעבירו...הפלתי of verses 17, 18, the latter resembling the Hebrew text, the former differing from, and therefore probably representing, the original LXX. Again, παρεπορεύετο ἐχόμενος αὐτοῦ, καὶ πάντες οἱ περὶ αὐτόν, καὶ πάντες οἱ ἁδροί, καὶ πάντες οἱ μαχηταὶ ἑξακόσιοι ἄνδρες corresponds obviously to ἀνὰ χεῖρα αὐτοῦ παρῆγον (παρῇσαν ἐπὶ χεῖρα αὐτοῦ), καὶ πᾶς [ὁ] Χελεθί, καὶ πᾶς ὁ Φελεθί, καὶ πάντες οἱ Γεθαῖοι οἱ ἑξακόσιοι ἄνδρες and the Hebrew איש...עברים, and was probably the effort of a later translator to render the Hebrew into more idiomatic Greek. This is shown from the Greek idioms ἐχόμενος αὐτοῦ, οἱ περὶ αὐτόν, and the translations (strange enough) of the names Cherethites and Pelethites, which are otherwise left untranslated by the LXX; but there is no reason to think that this translator had before him a different Hebrew text. The only remaining questions with regard to reading are whether we should adopt, with the original LXX, צית המדבר instead of בית המרחק in verse 17, and transpose כל־העם and כל־עבדיו in verses 17 and 18, or read one of these alternatives in both verses. In 2 Sam. xvii. 3 it can hardly be doubted that the LXX gives us a far more intelligible and forcible reading. The Masoretic text is probably due partly to a small omission by *homœoteleuton*, partly to a faulty pointing and division of words. The original Hebrew probably was nearly as follows:

כשוב הכלה אישה רך נפש איש אחד אתה מבקש.

In xviii. 22 εἰς ὠφέλειαν is clearly an explanation, and according to Gesenius the true explanation, of the Hebrew מצאת, and appears at first sight to be a remarkable exception to the literalness we almost universally meet with in the translation of these books. But it is very probable that the word πορευομένῳ, which follows, is really an alternative, being a translation of מצאת, and, if so, most likely the original LXX reading. This view is all the more probable from the fact that the following καὶ εἶπε (ויאמר) is evidently an alternative of τί γὰρ ἐάν (ויהי־מה), which is very awkward here, and probably got in from the preceding verse, where the LXX has no alternative reading.

There are several passages in which the LXX seems to point to a corrupt Masoretic text, even though it does not suggest an altogether satisfactory emendation, as in 1 Sam. ix. 24, xiii. 21, xiv. 14, 23-26. The LXX reading of 2 Sam. xxi. 1 presents peculiar difficulties. The word ἀδικία (B) cannot easily be explained as a marginal gloss, or an alternative reading. Most probably therefore it is a corruption of διὰ τό (A), and the clause διὰ τὸ αὐτὸν θανάτῳ αἱμάτων (על אשר במות הדמים) is an alternative, and probably the original rendering of the last phrase, and an early corruption of our present Hebrew text.

We may briefly sum up the results of our inquiry as follows: (1) If we leave out from the LXX what are obvious additions, and select, in cases of alternatives, that which *differs most* from our present Hebrew text, and make due allowance for errors likely to arise from the difficulties of translation by persons inexperienced in decyphering badly written or badly worn MSS., and not critically acquainted with the language they were translating, we shall be able to regain for the most part a Hebrew text many centuries older than that of our Hebrew Bibles. (2) By comparing this with the Masoretic text we can see clearly that both the latter and the LXX have been subject to several, and precisely similar, causes of corruption. (3) This comparison, by the help of the ordinary canons of textual criticism, enables us to recover in several cases the original reading of the Hebrew. (4) Even when the LXX does not enable us to restore the true Hebrew text, we can sometimes, by the wide differences between the two, conclude almost with certainty that a reading is corrupt, and save ourselves the useless labour of trying to force a meaning out of a passage which, as it stands, has none. (5) Lastly, we can in some degree learn the way in which such books as those of Samuel have gradually grown out of earlier narratives, in many cases handed down, it is probable, by oral tradition.

III.

ON THE DIALECTS SPOKEN IN PALESTINE IN THE TIME OF CHRIST.

[Ad. Neubauer.]

It has always been held that the language of the Jews in Palestine after their return from the Babylonian captivity, down to the conquest by the Arabs of Palestine, was partly the modernised Hebrew (as it is to be found in the Mishnah, in the Hebrew parts of the Talmud, and in the Midrashim), partly an Aramaic dialect intermixed with Hebrew words and forms. Were these two dialects spoken simultaneously by all classes and in all provinces of Palestine, or has one dialect given way to the other, and if so, at what epoch? It will be our endeavour in the course of the present essay to supply an answer to these questions. But before proceeding to our investigations with the help of the scanty documents at our disposal, we must allude to the opinions which have been held during the last hundred years on the language spoken by Jesus and his immediate disciples.

Isaac Voss[1] was the first to say that it was absurd to suppose that Judea alone could have escaped the fate of the provinces conquered by the armies of Alexander the Great, and have preserved its own language instead of adopting that of the conquerors; and he concluded accordingly that Greek was the only language spoken in Palestine since Alexander. Voss

[1] *De oracvl. Sibyll.*, p. 290; *Resp. ad iterata P. Simon. object.*, p. 375; *Resp. ad obj. theol. Legd.*

was closely followed by Diodati[1], who sought to prove that the mother language of the Jews in the time of Jesus was Greek, known under the name of the Hellenistic language. Bernard De Rossi[2] devoted a special monograph to refute Diodati, in which he proves that the language of the Jews at the time of Jesus, which he himself and the apostles spoke, was no other than the mixed dialect which De Rossi calls Syro-Chaldee; according to him the Hellenistic language was not current in Palestine. De Rossi's dissertation was reproduced in German, with notes, by Pfannkuche[3], who accepts its conclusions entirely. Of course the impossibility of the idea that Greek was the only language of the Jews in Palestine was ere long realized, and a compromise was proposed by Prof. Paulus[4], of Jena, who held that the current language of the Jews in Palestine at the time of Jesus was indeed an Aramaic dialect, but that Greek was at the same time so familiar in Palestine, and more especially in Galilee and Jerusalem, that Jesus and his disciples had no difficulty in using it in their public speeches whenever they found it convenient. The arguments of Prof. Paulus, which we cannot reproduce in their entirety, but some of which we shall have to mention later on, were refuted by Silvestre de Sacy[5] without great difficulty. The two dissertations of

---

[1] *Dominici Diodati J. C. Neapolitano de Christo graece loquente exercitatio*, Neap., 1767.
[2] *Della lingua propria di Cristo e degli Ebrei nazionali della Palestina da' tempi de' Maccabei*, Parma, 1772.
[3] *Ueber die palästinische Landessprache in dem Zeitalter Christi und der Apostel, ein Versuch, zum Theil nach de Rossi entworfen*, von Heinrich Friederich Pfannkuche (in vol. viii. of Eichhorn's *Allgemeine Bibliothek der biblischen Litteratur*, pp. 365 to 480). English translation, by John Brown, D.D., in Clark's *Biblical Cabinet*, 1832, vol. ii. pp. 1 to 90.
[4] *Verosimilia de Judaeis Palaestinensibus, Jesu atque etiam Apostolis non Aramaea dialecto sola, sed Graeca quoque Aramaizante locutis*. Particula prima et altera, Jenae, 1803. These two dissertations have become very scarce. I have not been able to see them. The contents of them are known to us by De Sacy's dissertation. See the following note.
[5] S. de S. (Silvestre de Sacy), *Littérature orientale*, in S. i. pp. 125 to 147 of *Magazin encyclopédique*, etc., rédigé par A. L. Millin, Paris, 1805.

Prof. Paulus and the remarks of Hug[1] on the Greek language in Palestine Dr. Roberts[2] elaborated into a volume, the first part of which is entitled, 'On the language employed by our Lord and his disciples;' Dr. Roberts' conclusion, which is summed up by Dr. Böhl[3] in the following words, 'Christ spoke for the most part in Greek, and only now and then in Aramaic,' differs but slightly from that of Paulus. It would take us too far to recount the opinions of the various authors who have written 'Introductions' to the study of the New Testament, and who naturally allude to our subject; we can only draw attention to special monographs and articles. Of recent date may be mentioned the essays of M. Renan[4], Dr. E. Böhl[5], and Prof. Franz Delitzsch[6] relating to the language of Jesus; they all range themselves beside De Rossi and De Sacy, maintaining that the language of the Jews in Palestine was a kind of Hebrew.

If it could be admitted that the Jews during the Babylonian exile had gradually forgotten, or willingly given up the *Jehudith* language (as Isaiah[7] calls it, in opposition to the *Aramith* of the Assyrians) for the Babylonian Aramaic dialect[8], the question about the language spoken by them in Palestine at the time of Hillel and Jesus could be settled

---

[1] *Einleitung in den Schriften des neuen Testaments*, von Joh. Leonhard Hug, 3te Aufl., Th. 2, p. 44 seqq.

[2] *Discussions on the Gospels, in two parts.* Part I. *On the language employed by our Lord and his disciples.* Part II. *On the original language of St. Matthew's Gospel, and on the origin and authenticity of the Gospels.* By Alexander Roberts, D. D., 2nd ed., 1864.

[3] *Forschungen nach einer Volksbibel zur Zeit Jesu und deren Zusammenhang mit der Septuaginta-übersetzung*, von Eduard Böhl, Wien, 1873, p. 3.

[4] *Histoire générale et systême comparé des Langues sémitiques, première partie. Histoire générale des Langues sémitiques*, 3rd ed., Par., 1863, p. 224 seqq.

[5] See note 3.

[6] *Saat auf Hoffnung*, Jahrg. xi, Heft 4, p. 195 seqq., von F. D. (Franz Delitzsch), and in *The Hebrew New Testament of the British and Foreign Bible Society. A contribution to Hebrew philology*, by Prof. Franz Delitzsch, Leipzig, 1883, pp. 30 and 31.

[7] Isaiah xxxvi. 11; 2 Kings xviii. 26.

[8] See *Biblisches Realwörterbuch*, etc., ausgearbeitet von Dr. Georg Benedict Winer, article *Sprache* (3rd ed., 1848, Bd. ii. p. 499).

without difficulty: it would be of course a dialect approaching that of the *Targumim*. There are, however, objections to this view. In the first place, it is scarcely credible that the short period of the Babylonian exile would have been sufficient for a nation to completely change its dialect, even when both are of the same family of languages, as is undoubtedly the case with Hebrew and Aramaic. Had the Jews not brought back their own dialect to Palestine, and had they spoken Aramaic instead of *Jehudith*, there would have been no occasion for Nehemiah[1] to say, 'And their children spake half in the speech of Ashdod and could not speak in the Jews' (Jehudith) language, but according to the language of each people.' On the other hand, the language in which the prophets of the exile, as well as Ezra and Nehemiah, address themselves to the Jews is still good Hebrew, and in some respects even classical Hebrew. The greater part of those who returned to Jerusalem must have therefore spoken Hebrew, most likely intermixed more or less with Aramaic words, but not so transformed grammatically as to be termed Aramaic. It is therefore doubtful whether the words, 'So they read in the book in the Law of God distinctly, and gave the sense, and caused them to understand the reading[2],' apply, as stated in the Talmud[3], to the beginning of a Targum. As in many other instances, the Rabbis in so explaining had in view their own time, when the reading of the Targum was a general custom (first century B. C., or even later[4]). 'Giving the sense of the Law[5]' may mean, and probably does mean, 'giving an exegetical interpretation,' which at all events was necessary for the people in general. The Hebrew of the book of Esther,

---

[1] Nehemiah xiii. 24.

[2] *Ibidem*, viii. 8.

[3] See for the passages, *Targum Onkelos*, herausgegeben und erläutert von Dr. A. Berliner, Berlin, 1884, Th. ii. p. 74.

[4] See *ibidem*, p. 89, and *Die Gottesdienstliche Vorträge der Juden, historisch entwickelt*, von Dr. Zunz, Berl., 1832, p. 8.

[5] Nehemiah viii. 8.

which was beyond question written after the captivity, and very likely for general reading and not only for a few *literati*, represents the language spoken by the Jews who returned to Jerusalem. The same language (though certainly deteriorated) we find also in the books of Chronicles. It is possible that a minority of the ten tribes who joined the exiles, on their return to Palestine, having been associated much longer with Aramaic-speaking populations, had forgotten the Hebrew tongue, if they had ever spoken it at all. The Ephraimitic Jews, who undoubtedly formed a majority of the Samaritans, knew but little Hebrew at the time when the exiles returned to Palestine[1]. But for this Aramaic-speaking minority, Ezra and Nehemiah could have scarcely arranged a Targum in the busy time of re-establishing the Mosaic institutions amongst the new comers. Consequently, we must conclude that at the time of Ezra and Nehemiah the Hebrew was still spoken generally in Judea, and more especially in Jerusalem.

Although there is a great gap between the Old Testament (excepting Esther, Chronicles, and Ecclesiastes[2]) and the Mishnah (we mean the earliest parts[3] of the Mishnah, which date from the second century B.C.) as regards documents in the spoken language by the Jews (none of the Apocryphal books existing in the original language), we may still affirm, following the best critics, that the book of Sirach was

---

[1] See *Biblisches Realwörterbuch*, etc., ausgearbeitet von Dr. G. B. Winer, article *Samaritaner* (3rd ed., 1848, Bd. ii. p. 372), and *Fragments of the Samaritan Targum*, by J. W. Nutt, London, 1878.

[2] That Ecclesiastes is a work of the time of the second Temple is now generally admitted, e. g. by Prof. Delitzsch and Dean Plumptre.

[3] Such is the early part of the tractate *Aboth* or sayings of the Jewish fathers (see Dr. Ch. Taylor's edition, Cambridge, 1877); a part of the tractate of *Yoma* or the ceremonies of the Day of Atonement (see J. Derenbourg, *Essai de Restitution de l'ancienne rédaction de Massèchet Kippourim, Revue des Études juives*, t. vi. p. 41 seqq.); and many other parts (see the excellent dissertation by Dr. D. Hoffmann, with the title of *Die erste Mischna und die Controversen der Tannaim*, Berlin, 1882; *Jahres-Bericht des Rabbiner-Seminars zu Berlin pro* 5641, 1881–1882).

written originally in Hebrew¹. The Talmud, it is true, quotes sayings from this book in Hebrew and in Aramaic², but it is beyond doubt that the latter are translations from the Hebrew, made at a later time, when Aramaic became the language of the majority. The same was the case with the book of Tobit, of which an Aramaic version has been published lately from an unique MS. in the Bodleian Library³. From the books of Maccabees we do not find a quotation in the Talmudical literature. The title 'Roll of the Hasmoneans,' given by a Rabbi of the tenth century A.D.⁴, may refer to a Hebrew or an Aramaic original. Indeed, the 'Rolls of Fasting Days' is the title of a treatise written in Aramaic⁵. Origen⁶ gives another title for the original of the book of Maccabees, viz. Σαρβηθ Σαρβανὲ ἐλ, on the meaning of which critics do not agree. Some take it as Aramaic, meaning either the revolt of the rebels of God⁷ or 'genealogy or history' of the prince of the children of God⁸; others explain it from the Hebrew 'Book of the family of the prince of the sons of God⁹.' However, even if the title were Aramaic, it would not prove that the book itself was originally written in this dialect. The Aramaic, as in the case of Sirach, might be a later translation from the Hebrew. The few words to be found on the coins of the Hasmoneans are Hebrew¹⁰. We

---

¹ See *Real-Encyklopädie für protestantische Theologie und Kirche*, etc., herausg. von Dr. J. J. Herzog und Dr. G. L. Plitt, Leipzig, 1877, article *Apocrypha* by E. Schürer, Ed. i. p. 484 seqq.).

² See *Rabbinische Blumenlese*, von Leopold Dukes, Leipzig, 1844, pp. 67 to 84.

³ *The Book of Tobit, a Chaldee text*, etc., ed. by A. Neubauer, Oxford, 1878.

⁴ מגילת בית חשמונאי. See הלכות גדולות (סי' סופרים), by Simeon of קיירא (Kayyar?), ed. Venice, 1548, fol. 141 d.

⁵ מגילת תענית. See *Essai sur l'histoire et la géographie de la Palestine d'après les Thalmuds*, etc., par J. Derenbourg, partie i. p. 439 seqq.; *Geschichte der Juden*, von H. Graetz, vol. iii (3rd ed.), p. 597 seqq.

⁶ See Eusebius, *Hist. Eccl.* vi. 25.

⁷ שרבת ברני אל. A. Geiger, *Urschrift*, etc., Breslau, 1857, p. 205.

⁸ שרבת. Jahn and Grimm (see Curtiss, *The name Machabee*, Leipz., 1876, p. 30).

⁹ ספר בית שר בני אל. See J. Derenbourg, *op. cit.*, p. 450 seqq.

¹⁰ See *Coins of the Jews*, by Frederic W. Madden (vol. ii. of *The International Numismata Orientalia*, London, 1881).

read on them לגאולת ירושלם, 'freedom of Jerusalem,' and not לגאולתא or לפורקנא די; but there are also words which are not biblical, such as חרות, 'freedom.' Had the spoken language been at that time an Aramaic dialect, and not the modernised Hebrew, the Maccabean princes would, according to our opinion, have put on their coins either pure biblical words or Aramaic words. As they have employed neither the one nor the other, we must take it for granted that the popular language in Jerusalem at least, and perhaps also in Judea, was the modernised Hebrew. This view is confirmed by the language in which the ethical sayings, which I believe may be considered as a popular literature, are written[1]. In the collection known as the *Pirqé Aboth*, 'sayings of the fathers[2],' in which every saying is recorded with the name of its author, we find that from the earliest, which is reported in the name of the men of the great synagogue, down to those connected with the name of Hillel, they are all written in the modernised Hebrew with a gradual increase of new words. In the case of Hillel only do we find sayings both in Hebrew and Aramaic.

Similarly the aggadico-homiletical literature on the Pentateuch and the prophetical lessons, to be found in the *Mekhilta*[3], the *Pesiqta* of the Haftaroth[4], and the

---

[1] When Moses desired to do miracles before Pharaoh, he, according to the Talmud, told him: 'Art thou going to bring straw to Aphraim, pottery to Kefar-Hanayah [now Kefar Anan; see our *Géographie du Talmud*, Paris, 1868, p. 179], wool to Damascus, magicians to Egypt [i. e. coals to Newcastle]?' תבן אתה מכניס לעפריים קדירות לכפר חנניה נוזוין ברמשק חרשין במצרים (*Midrash Bereshith Rabba*, ch. 86; *Bab. Talmud*, Menahoth, fol. 85 a. See Dukes, *Rabb. Blumenlese*, No. 650; Moïse Schuhl, *Sentences et Proverbes du Talmud et du Midrasch*, Paris, 1878, No. 322).

[2] פרקי אבות. *Sayings of the Jewish Fathers*, etc., by Charles Taylor, M.A., Cambridge, 1877.

[3] *Mechilta* (מכילתא) *de R. Ismael*, herausgegeben mit Noten, Erklärungen, Indices und einer ausführlichen Einleitung versehen von M. Friedmann, Wien, 1870. This book contains expositions on Exodus.

[4] The *Pesiqta* (פסיקתא, sections?) seems to have been in the first instance composed for the prophetical lessons (Haftaroth) read on special Sabbaths before and after the 9th of Ab (the day of the destruction of Jerusalem). This redaction still exists in the MS. of the Bodleian Library, Opp. Add. No. 97

Sifré[1], are nearly throughout in modernised Hebrew. Homiletic expositions, however, are usually addressed to the people in general, and not to *literati*. Again, the casuistical decisions deposited in the Mishnah (the greater part of which was written from 200–5 B.C.[2]), the *Thosifta*[3] and the *Sifré*[4], are written (excepting a few passages) in modernised Hebrew[5]. And certainly these are not all written for the schools. The prescriptions for the ceremonies of the Sabbath and feast-days[6], and of the prayers[7], served as a guide to the people in general; and even the Temple ceremonies[8], addressed only to the priests, must have been suited also for unlearned priests[9], who no doubt understood the modernised Hebrew as their usual language. The discussions between the Sadducees and the Pharisees, which we believe are reported in the Mishnah *verbatim*, are also in modernised Hebrew[10]. The witnesses for determining the new moon were examined by the Sanhedrin in modernised Hebrew[11]. The advice which

---

(our Catalogue, No. 152). Another enlarged redaction of it is attributed to R. Kahna, edited from the then known MSS. by S. Buber, Lyck, 1868. And a third form is entitled פסיקתא רבתי, 'the great Pesiqta,' edited critically by M. Friedmann, Wien, 1880. The prefaces to both these Pesiqtas are highly instructive. We cannot discuss here the relation of these three redactions one to the other. Compare also the excellent chapter on the subject by L. Zunz, in his book *Die Gottesdienstlichen Vorträge der Juden historisch entwickelt*, Berlin, 1832, pp. 226 seqq. and 239 seqq.

[1] The *Sifré* (ספרי) contains, like the Mekhilta, expositions on Numbers and Deuteronomy. Last and best edition by M. Friedmann, Wien, 1864.

[2] See p. 43, note 3.

[3] תוספתא. Literally, additions to the Mishnah or an enlarged Mishnah. See the edition of Dr. Zuckermandel, 1877 to 1882.

[4] ספרא. This book, also called *Thorath Kohanim* (תורת כהנים), contains expositions on Leviticus. The best edition is that by H. Weiss, Wien, 1862.

[5] See Z. Frankel, *Hodegetica in Mishnam*, etc. (in Hebrew), Lipsiae, 1859, p. 304 seqq.

[6] Contained in the part of the Mishnah called *Moëd*.

[7] Contained chiefly in the tractate *Berakhoth*.

[8] Contained in the tractate *Yoma*.

[9] כהן עם הארץ. It is even supposed (*Mishnah*, Yoma, i. 6) that the high priest could be unlearned.

[10] *Yadayim*, iv. 4 to 8.

[11] *Mishnah* (ed. Lowe), Menahoth, x. 5 אמר להם בא השמש אומרים הין בא ...השמש...אקצור והם אומרים לו קצור אקצור; *Rosh hash-Shanah*, ii. 9 הנגה ראית או הנוה...ראיניהי נוסעו ובליל צבורי

king Jannaeus gives to his queen Salome to make peace with
the Pharisees is in Hebrew[1]. The colloquial conversation in
the schools was in modernised Hebrew[2]. Popular songs in
the Temple and outside are to be found in the same dialect[3].
It is told in the Talmud that the damsels who went out on the
Day of Atonement in the vineyards, rejoicing to have passed
the great feast, exclaimed in Hebrew: 'Young man, lift up
thine eyes and see whom thou choosest. Set not thine eyes
on beauty, set them rather upon family and birth[4].' Miriam,
daughter of Bilgah, who was an adherent of the Greeks
during the Maccabean wars, is reported to have apostrophised
the altar in Hebrew, saying: 'Λύκος, Λύκος, thou hast de-
stroyed the wealth of Israel, and hast not stood by them in
the hour of their sorrow[5]!' The gallows on which Nicanor's[6]
head and feet were suspended, bore, according to the Talmud,
a Hebrew inscription in the following terms[7]: 'The mouth
which spoke in guilt, and the hand which stretched out

---

[1] *Bab. Talm.*, Sotah, fol. 22 b. אל תתיראי מן הפרושים ולא ממי שאינם פרושים אלא מן הצבועים שדומים לפירושים שפעשיהן מעשה זמרי ומבקשים שכר כפנחס.

[2] It is said in the Jerusalem Talmud (*Pesaḥim*, vi. 1, fol. 33 a) that the elder of the family Bethera (at the time the presidents of the Sanhedrin; see Graetz, *Geschichte der Juden*, vol. iii. p. 214) had forgotten the rule (*halakhah*) about the sacrifice of the Passover when it fell on a Sabbath. Some of the disciples reminded them that there was the Babylonian Hillel, who frequented the schools of Shemayah and Abtalyon, and who certainly would be able to tell them what was to be done. Then we read the following sentence: אמרו יש כאן בבלי אחד והלל שמו ששימש את שמעיה ואבטליון ידע אם פסח דוחה את השבת אם לאו אישר שיש ממנו תוחלת שלחו וקראו לו אמרו לו שמעיה סימיך כשהל ארבעה עשר להיות בשבת אם דוחה את השבת...יבוא עלי כך שכיחני כשמעיה ואבטליון.

[3] On the last day of the feast of the Tabernacles (the day of the water-drawing festival, St. John vii. 37), the priests not only recited prayers and psalms, but pronounced also the following words: אבותינו היו במקום הוה אהוריהם אל היכל יי ופניהם קדמה והמה משתחוים קדמה לשמש אנו ליה וליה עינינו (*Mishnah*, Sukkah, v. 5).

[4] *Mishnah*, Taanith, iv. 12 שא עיניך בחור וראה מי אהה בורר אל התן עיניך בנוי תן עיניך במשפחה.

[5] *Tosifta*, Sukkah, ch. 4 אתה החרבת את נכסיהם של ישראל ולא הצמדתה לקום לוקום עד מתי אתה בשעה צרן; *Bab. Talm.*, Sukkah, fol. 56 b; להם בשעה צרן כבלה כמונן של ישראל ואי אתה עומר להם בשעה הרחק.

[6] Josephus, *Antiquities*, XII. x. 5.

[7] *Jer. Talm.*, Taanith, ii. 13 הפה שדבר באשמה והיר שפשטה בגאוה.

with pride.' Deeds were also drawn up in modernised Hebrew[1]. When Simeon the son of Shetah recalled to the Sanhedrin his colleague, Judah son of Tabaï, who took flight to Alexandria in the time of the persecution of the Pharisees under king Jannaeus, he wrote in Hebrew the following: 'From me Jerusalem, the holy town, to thee Alexandria, my sister. My husband dwells in thee, and I remain desolate[2].' No comparison can be drawn between the Latin of the middle ages and the modernised Hebrew, the Latin having never been read by the people, whereas the Talmudical literature contains popular elements from the earlier times.

That the Aramaic dialect was used simultaneously with the modernised Hebrew cannot be doubted. During the dominion of the Seleucidae, when Syriac became the official language in Asia[3], many Jews made themselves acquainted with the ruling language, and technical terms were naturally borrowed by the Jews in general, as was later the case with Greek under the Romans. The Mishnah mentions vessels in the Temple[4] with Aramaic inscriptions, but also with Greek inscriptions[5]. A tradition states that Johanan the high priest heard a voice of heaven (*Bath qol*) coming from the

---

[1] *Bab. Talm.*, Rosh hash-Shanah, fol. 18 b נשׂיא בך יבך לפלוני כהן גדול אל עליון, referring to the time of the Maccabees.

[2] *Bab. Talm.*, Sotah, fol. 47 a מני ירושלים עיר הקדש לכי אלכסנדריא אחותי. בעלי שרוי בתוכך ואני יושבת שוממה. Further illustrations could easily be adduced, but we think they would be superfluous. We shall quote only one other instance. Agrippa I. was known as a fervent observer of the ritual ceremonies, unlike his ancestors. It is said in the Mishnah *Sotah*, vii. 8) when he read in the Temple the section of the king (Deut. xvii. 14 seqq.) and arrived at the passage (v. 15), 'Thou mayest not set a stranger over thee, which is not thy brother,' he shed tears (he having been of the Idumean race). The wise men (חכמים) pacified him, saying, 'Do not fear, Agrippa, thou art our brother,' אל תירא אגריפס אחינו אתה אחינו אתה אחינו אתה. See also J. H. Weiss, *Zur Geschichte der jüdischen Tradition* (in Hebrew), Wien (1871), i. p. 113, a valuable work, of which three volumes have appeared.

[3] *Les Apôtres*, by M. Renan, p. 228.

[4] *Sheqalim* vi. 6 תקלין חדתין תקלין עתיקין, 'shekels of this year and of last year.'

[5] *Ibidem*, iii. 2 אלפא ביתא גמא, α, β, γ. The word Alpha is also often used in the Mishnah in the sense of *first*. Tekoa is the Alpha for oil (see *Géographie du Talmud*, p. 129). Michmash is Alpha for flour (*ibidem*, p. 154).

sanctuary, saying in Aramaic, 'The young men who waged war against Antiochus are victorious[1].' Immigrations from Babylonia and from the northern parts of Palestine, where Aramaic dialects were spoken, contributed most likely to the spread of Aramaic in Jerusalem. Judea seems to have preserved a purer Hebrew, as compared with Galilee[2]. A striking instance is reported in the Talmud[3], illustrating the dialect of Judea. The word הרובה was used in Judea in the sense of ארוסה, 'betrothed,' the root bearing the same sense in Leviticus xix. 20. At the same time, probably, the use of Targums became general, and Aramaic began to be employed in liturgical formulae, such as the *Qaddish*[4], 'sanctificat,' and the first sentence of the introduction to the *Haggadah*, or the history of the exodus of Egypt, recited on the Passover evening[5]. Of course the precise date of the composition of these prayers cannot be given, but most likely they belong to the time when the Babylonian Hillel acquired his great influence in the schools. Letters which Gamaliel (the elder) addressed to the inhabitants of upper and lower Galilee, on the fixing of the new moon, are also in Aramaic[6]. A gradual immigration of Greek-speaking Jews from Egypt and Asia Minor introduced *Greek* to Jerusalem; and the use of it was further stimulated by contact with the Roman officials, and in an even greater degree by the Graeco-mania of Herod and his immediate successors.

We find accordingly, in the last century B.C., the following probable results concerning the languages spoken in the Holy Land: (1) In Jerusalem, and perhaps also in the greater part of Judea, the modernised Hebrew and a purer Aramaic

---

[1] יצחו שליא דאנחנו קרבא באנטוכיא. *Jer. Talm.*, Sota ix. 13 (fol. 24 b).

[2] See p. 51.   [3] *Bab. Talm.*, Qiddushin, fol. 6 a.

[4] קדיש, used in daily and festival prayers.

[5] הגדה, beginning כהא להמא עניא, 'like that was the bread of affliction.' See, however, Lundshuth, סדר מראשית (Berl., 1855), p. iii, who believes it to be of Babylonian origin.

[6] לאחנא בני גלילאה עילאה ואחנא בני גלילאה תתאה שלומכון יסגא לעלם מהודענא לכון... (*Tosifta*, Sanhedrin, chap. 2).

dialect were in use among the majority of the Jews. (2) The Galileans and the Jewish immigrants from the neighbouring districts understood their own dialect only (of course closely related to Aramaic), together with a few current Hebrew expressions, such as proverbs and prayers. (3) The small Jewish-Greek colony and some privileged persons spoke Greek, which was, however, a translation from the Hebrew rather than genuine Greek, in a word, a Judeo-Greek jargon. All these dialects, more or less intermingled, continued to be used till the time when the schools were gradually transferred to Galilean towns[1] (about 150 A.D.), when the Galileo-Aramaic dialect appears in *halakhic* discussions and also in *aggadic* dissertations. At this time we hear of Judah the saint pronouncing the following opinion : 'Of what use is the *Sursi* (Syriac in a wide sense) in the Land of Israel? Let us use either the Holy language or Greek[2].' The Holy language here means the modernised Hebrew or the language in which the Mishnah and contemporary books[3] are written. Much stress is indeed laid upon the knowledge of it. The passage 'Speaking to (of) them[4]' is applied to show that a father ought to teach his son the Holy language as his first language[5]. Another saying is, 'He who inhabits the Land of Israel and speaks the Holy language is certain to be an inheritor of the world to come[6].' This modernised Hebrew has never died out amongst the Jews, and it is still employed in our days in exegetical and casuistical commentaries, and even in correspondence, as the only means of general communication amongst the Jews scattered throughout the world[7].

[1] The schools were transferred from Yabneh in Judea to Ousha, Shefaram, Sepphoris, and Tiberias in Galilee.
[2] *Bab. Talm.*, Sotah, fol. 49 b בארץ ישראל לשון סורסי למה או לשון הקדש או לשון יונית.
[3] See pp. 45 and 46.   [4] Deut. xi. 19.
[5] *Sifré*, sect. עקב, § 46 ed. Friedmann, p. 83 a).
[6] *Jer. Talm.*, Sheqalim iii, end. See Dukes, *Nachbiblische Geschichte der hebräischen Sprache*, Heft I; *Die Sprache der Mischnah*, p. 10.
[7] See our report on *Talmudical and Rabbinical Literature* (fifth annual address of the President to the Philological Society, 1876, p. 37 seqq.)

The Aramaic dialect, known as *Arami* in a general sense, is also called the language of Jerusalem[1] in opposition to the Babylonian dialect. We have already had an example of the name *Sursi*[2]. The Galilean dialect is specially mentioned as having an indistinct pronunciation of the gutturals (which was, and still is, characteristic of the Samaritans), and also as a dialect in which syllables were swallowed in such a way that the meaning of words and phrases often became doubtful to a southern Jew. The Talmud has many amusing anecdotes about this dialect, of which we may quote a few[3].

A Galilean went about calling out, 'Who has *mar* to sell?' Whereupon he was asked, 'Fool of a Galilean, what dost thou want; an ass (*ḥamor*) to ride upon; wine (*ḥemar*) to drink; wool ('*imar*) for a dress, or a sheep skin (*imar*) to cover thyself withal[4]?' This negligence in the pronunciation of gutturals we find also in other localities near Galilee. It is related in the Talmud that the inhabitants of Bethshean (Scythopolis), of Haipha and Tabaon (Tab'ain?) were not admitted to recite the prayers publicly in the synagogue, because they pronounced *aleph* like *ain*, and *vice versa*[5]. In Judea, it is said, the study of the law was preserved because care was taken there for the right pronunciation; whilst in Galilee, where the pronunciation was neglected, the study of law did not exist[6]. The Talmud refers most likely to the fact that there were no schools for casuistic discussion at an early period in Galilee. Another example given in the Talmud illustrates the contraction of several words into one, by which the meaning of a sentence was completely altered.

---

[1] See Dukes, *op. cit.*, p. 3.

[2] See above, p. 50, note 2.

[3] *Bab. Talm.*, Erubin, fol. 53 *b*.

[4] דההוא בי גליל דהוה קאזיל ואמר להו מאן אמר למאן אמרו ליה גלילאה שוטה המר למירכב או חמר למישתי עמר למילבש או אימר לאיתכסאה.

[5] *Ibidem*, Megillah, fol. 24 *b* אין מורידין לפני התיבה לא אנשי בית שאן ולא אנשי בית חיפה ולא אנשי בנעונין כמני שקורין לאלפין עיינין ולעיינין אלפין.

[6] *Ibidem*, Erubin, fol. 53 *b*.

A Galilean woman inviting a friend to take a glass of milk with her, said to her, *tokhlikhlebi* (may a lion devour thee!), contracting in this fashion the three words *thei okhlik helba*[1]. It is probable that Jesus, through better education, or by a personal effort, pronounced sounds more in accordance with the Judean manner, since we do not find any allusion in the Gospels to his having been mocked, as was the case with Peter, on account of his Galilean pronunciation. It may be of interest to allude here to two other particulars respecting Galilee, mentioned in the Talmudic writings. We are told, firstly, that persons sometimes have two names, the one as used in Judea, and the other in Galilee[2]. In fact, we find that some of the Apostles had two names, a Hebrew one and a Galilean or a popular one, for instance, Simon and Cephas. The same was the case with the Maccabees, but what was exceptional in Judea was probably a general rule in Galilee. Secondly, it is stated in the Talmud, that Galileans were wandering preachers, and excelled especially in the aggadic or homiletic interpretation of the biblical texts, which was often expressed in the form of a parable[3]. This fact may partly explain how the popular teaching of Jesus had such success in Jerusalem, where this mode of interpretation seems to have been exceptional. The aggadic interpretations were individual interpretations, whilst the halakhah (dogmatic or casuistic rules) were mostly quoted as traditional. Jesus, however, spoke in his own name, even in his halakhic teaching, contrary to the practice of the schools. That is the meaning probably of what is said of him,

---

[1] *Come, I shall give thee to eat milk.* *Bidua* לביא for תאי איכליך תיכליך חלבא. See for other passages, *Winer's Chaldäische Grammatik für Bibel und Targum*, ed. Fischer, Leipzig, 1882, p. 32.

[2] *Tosifta*, Gittin, ch. 8.

[3] See *La Géographie du Talmud*, p. 185. We quote one instance only: כד דריש ההוא גלילאה... בר רעיא רעיא על ינסא עביר לנוייא שמיתא. In allusion to bad administrators imposed as a punishment on a town, it is said, as a Galilean explained, when the shepherd gets angry with his flock he gives them a blind sheep as leader. Comp. Matt. xv. 14; Luke vi. 39.

that he taught 'with authority, and not as the scribes,' who appealed to traditions[1].

The Aramaic dialect of the north (Sursi and Galilean) was the popular language in the last century B.C. It is called the language of the ἰδιώτης[2] in opposition to the learned or Holy language. Proverbs written in it are introduced with the words 'proverb of the ἰδιώτης[3],' or 'as people say[4].' When Hillel gives an explanation in the popular language, it is said, 'Hillel explains in the language of *the common people*[5].' In the New Testament it is called *Hebraisti*[6], and in the Apocrypha and Josephus the language of the country[7]. It was in this dialect that the latter at first wrote his historical work. Although Josephus says that the Jews could understand the Syrians, the Jewish Aramaic was nevertheless a distinct dialect in some respects, as may be seen from the words λαμά[8] (in Syriac *lemana*[9]), Βοανεργές[10] (in Syriac *bene ra'ma*[11]), and of the form Ἐφφαθά[12], recorded as having been uttered by Jesus, who, as is now generally admitted, addressed himself to his disciples and to his audience in the popular dialect. This appears not only from the Aramaic words left in the Gospels by the Greek translators (which will be enumerated below for completeness' sake), but more especially from his last words on the Cross[13], which were spoken under circumstances of exhaustion and pain, when a person would naturally make use of his mother tongue,

---

[1] Matthew vii. 29.
[2] Dukes, *Die Sprache der Mishnah*, p. 11.
[3] משל הדיוט.
[4] אמרי אינשי very frequent.
[5] *Bab. Talm.*, Baba Mezia, fol. 104 a.
[6] Ἑβραϊστί; τῇ Ἑβραΐδι διαλέκτῳ, John v. 2; Acts xxi. 40; xxii. 2.
[7] Ἡ πάτριος φωνή, 2 Macc. vii. 21, 27; xii. 37; Josephus, *De Bello Jud.*, Prooem. i; V. vi. 3; *Antiq.*, XVIII. vi. 40.
[8] Matthew xxvii. 46.
[9] ܠܡܢܐ.
[10] Mark iii. 17. See also p. 56.
[11] ܒܢܝ ܪܥܡܐ.
[12] Mark vii. 34. See p. 56.
[13] Matthew xxvii. 46; Mark xv. 34.

and from the fact that it is mentioned that he spoke to
St. Paul in Hebrew[1]. It is a weak argument to say that
had Jesus always spoken in the popular dialect, viz. the
Galileo-Aramean, there would have been no occasion for
the author of the Acts to state that he spoke to St. Paul
in Hebrew; and yet this is one of the chief arguments of
writers on the other side[2]. The contrary is the case: the
author of the Acts, not remembering the Hebrew words
spoken to St. Paul, or not being able to supply them from
his own knowledge of Hebrew, was obliged, in order to be
believed, to state that Jesus spoke to St. Paul in Hebrew.
We shall see later on how little the Jews knew Greek, and
how much less they cared to know it; so that St. Paul, in
order to gain a hearing, was obliged to speak to them in
their Aramaic dialects[3]. Would anyone venture seriously
to maintain that St. Peter spoke Greek when he ad-
dresses himself to the 'men of Judea and all that dwell
in Jerusalem[4],' and that, too, at Pentecost, when all the
prayers were offered in Hebrew? How would the Medes,
Elamites, and Arabians have understood if he had spoken
Greek? What else do the words 'are not all these which
speak Galileans?' mean but that the Apostles usually spoke
to the people in the Galilean dialect? Why should the men
of Cappadocia, Pontus, Asia, Phrygia, Pamphylia[5], etc. be
astonished that the Apostles spoke Greek, if it had been
their usual language? Why should the chief captain[6] wonder
that St. Paul could speak Greek, if the Jews were generally
known to be familiar with it? Is not the watchword Μαρὰν
ἀθά[7], which passed to the Greek-speaking populations of
Asia Minor, a sufficient proof that the speech of the first

---

[1] Acts xxvi. 14.
[2] See Dr. Roberts' *Discussion*, etc. (full title, p. 41, note 2), p. 74 seqq.
[3] Acts xxi. 40; xxii. 2.
[4] Acts ii. 14.
[5] Acts ii. 9 seqq.
[6] Acts xxi. 37.
[7] 1 Corinthians xvi. 22. See pp. 57 and 73.

Christians was Aramaic? Not to speak of the evident Semitic diction[1] contained in the Gospels of St. Matthew and St. Mark, who, as is stated by the early fathers, and as is now generally admitted, made use of collections and sayings written in Palestine by the first Christians. What language did Jesus speak when he said[2], 'Whosoever shall say to his brother *raca*, shall be in danger of the council: but whosoever shall say *moreh*, shall be in danger of hell-fire,' but the popular dialect, in which *raca* (*reqa*) was a weaker expression than *moreh*[3], for it is no unusual phænomenon for a foreign word to have a stronger meaning than the native one?

The following is the list of the Semitic words preserved in the writings of the New Testament[4]:—

St. Matt. iii. 7   Φαρισαῖος = פְּרִישָׁא.

iv. 10, etc.   σατανᾶς = סָטָנָא.

v. 22   ῥακά = רָקָא[5].

v. 22   γέεννα = גֵּהִנָּם.

vi. 24   μαμμωνᾶ = מָמוֹנָא.

xii. 24   Βεελζεβούλ = בַּעַל זְבוּל[6].

xxi. 9   Ὡσαννά = הוֹשַׁע־נָא or אוֹשַׁע־נָא.

[1] It is impossible to quote the whole literature on that subject. It will be sufficient to refer to Lightfoot's *Horae Hebraicae*, and to Dr. Edersheim, *Life and Times of Christ*, London, 1884, 2nd edition.

[2] Matthew v. 22.

[3] *Ibidem*. This word became a standing expression in the Mi'rash for 'fool.' See the *Athenaeum*, 1881, p. 779 (No. 2834), where Dean Stanley's suggestion that *moreh* is derived from the Hebrew is contradicted.

[4] We give the list of these words according to the method of Pfannkuche, viz. according to their occurrence in the various books of the New Testament. Prof. E. Kautzsch in his *Grammatik des Biblisch-Aramäischen*, etc., Leipzig, 1884, gives an alphabetical list of the Aramaic words occurring in the New Testament writings. We have added from his list the words composed with βαρ (רב, p. 57).

[5] רֵיקָא is used in the Talmud as empty and stupid, just as בּוּר, *pit*. See *Neue Beiträge zur Erläuterung der Evangelien in Talmud und Midrasch* von Aug. Wünsche, Leipzig, 1878, p. 47. The confusion of Tsere (Segol) and Pathah is possible. Qaraitic MSS. point indifferently with the one or the other.

[6] זְבוּל seems to be a dialectal form of זְבוּב (זבוּרָא), *bee*. In some places there was a Baal of the flies and in others of the bee. Compare Isaiah vi. 18.

St. Matt. xxiii. 7 ῥαββί = רַבִּי.

xxvi. 2 πάσχα = פִּסְחָא.

xxvii. 33 γολγοθά = גָּלְגָּלְתָּא[1].

xxvii. 46 Ἠλί, ἠλί[2], λαμὰ σαβαχθανί = אֵלִי אֵלִי לְמָא שְׁבַקְתַּנִי.

St. Mark iii. 17 Βοανεργές = בְּנֵי רְגֶשׁ or בְּנֵי רַעַשׁ[3].

v. 41 ταλιθὰ κοῦμι = טְלִיתָא קוּמִי.

vii. 11 κορβάν = קָרְבָּן.

vii. 34 ἐφφαθά = הִפָּתַח[4].

x. 51 ῥαββουνί = רְבּוּנִי[5].

xiv. 36 Ἀββά = אַבָּא.

St. Luke i. 15 σίκερα = שִׁכְרָא.

St. John i. 43 Κηφᾶς = כֵּיפָא.

iv. 25 Μεσσίας = מְשִׁיחָא.

v. 2 Βηθεσδά = בֵּית אַשְׁדָּא[6].

xix. 13 Γαββαθά = גַּבְּתָא.

Acts i. 19 Ἀκελ δαμά = חֲקַל דְּמָא[7].

ix. 36 Ταβιθά = טְבִיתָא[8].

---

[1] On the omission of the second λ, see Kautzsch, *op. cit.*, p. 11.

[2] The variant Ἐλωΐ (Mark xv. 34) represents the Aramaic form אֱלָהִי, which might be the original form pronounced by Jesus.

[3] The guttural pronunciation of ע is represented by γ.

[4] The aspiration of ה was neglected by the Galileans.

[5] This form is used in the prayers for God. The title of רבן is applied first to Gamaliel the elder.

[6] אשדא is the possible original of 'pool.' Compare אשד, Numbers xxi. 15 and elsewhere.

[7] The field of blood. The reading δαμάχ is analogous to Σιράχ for סירא (Kautzsch, *op. cit.*, p. 8); δαμάχ scarcely represents the word דמך, to sleep, to die, since the substantive death is always expressed by the word מותא. For field of death (why not rely upon the translation of the time, which is to be found in the Acts?) ought to be δαμχά, דמכא. To suppose a participial form דָּמֵךְ (Kautzsch, *op. cit.*, p. 172) is forced.

[8] Feminine form of צְבִי (צבי). Compare *Mishnah*, Berakhoth, ii. 7, and p. 60.

1 Cor. xvi. 22 Μαρὰν ἀθά = מָרָן אָתָא.

Apoc. ix. 11 'Ἀβαδδών = אֲבַדּוֹן.

xvi. 16 'Ἀρμαγεδών = הַר מְגִדּוֹן.

Proper names compounded with the word bar (בר), 'son,' belong also to the vocabulary of Aramaic words in the New Testament. The following occur:—

Βαραββᾶς = בַּר אַבָּא, St. Matthew xxvii. 16.

Βαρθολομαῖος = בַּר תַּלְמַי, ibid. x. 3.

Βαριησοῦς = בַּר יֵשׁוּ, Acts xiii. 6.

Βαριωνᾶ = בַּר יוֹנָה, St. Matthew xvi. 17.

Βαρνάβας = בַּר נַבָּא, Acts iv. 36.

Βαρσαββᾶς = בַּר סָבָא, ibid. i. 23.

Βαρτιμαῖος = בַּר תִּימָא, St. Mark x. 46.

It is possible that the two passages quoted from a gospel in the following story in the Talmud might turn out to be original Aramaic words in the New Testament.

The passage seems to us of such importance for the New Testament literature, that we have thought it worth while to reproduce it in its entirety [2]: אימא שלום דביתהו דרבי אליעזר אחתיה דרבן גמליאל הואי הוה ההוא פילוסופא בשיבבותיה דהוה שקיל שמא דלא מקבל שוחדא בעו לאחוכי ביה עיילא ליה שרגא דדהבא ואזול לקמיה אמרה ליה בעינא דניפלגו לי בנכסי דבי נשי אמר להו פלוגו לה א׳׳ל כתיב בתורה דיהיב לן קו׳׳בה במקום ברא

---

[1] The words certainly mean, Our Lord come or has come (see p. 73). To take it as the transliteration of מוהרם אתה (Lowe and others before him) is against the rules of transliteration. Besides, anathema would be הרם or מוהרם without the word אתה.

[2] We give an eclectic text according to the variations reported in Rabbi Raphael Rabinovicz's *Variae Lectiones in Mishnam et in Talmud Babylonicum*, etc., Shabbath, fol. 116a, b. See also *The Fragments of Talmud Babli Pesachim*, etc., edited with notes by W. H. Lowe, Cambridge, 1879, pp. 67 and 68, and *Religionsgeschichtliche Studien* von Dr. M. Güdemann, Leipzig, 1876, p. 67 (Die Logia des Matthäus als Gegenstand einer talmudischen Satyre).

ברתא לא תירות א"ל בן יומא דגליתון מארעיכון איתנטילת
אורייתא דמשה ואיתיהיבת ביה עון גליון ¹ וכתיב ביה
ברא וברתא כחדא ירתון למחר הדר עייל ליה איהו
חמרא לוביא אמר להו שפילי ליה לסיפיה דכתבא ²
וכתיב ביה אנא לא למיפחת מן אורייתא דמשה אתיתי
אלא לאוספי על אורייתא דמשה אתיתי וכתיב בה
במקום ברא ברתא לא תירות אמרה ליה נהור נהורך
בשרגא ³ א"ל ר"ג אתא חמרא ובטש לשרגא.

'Emma Shalom, the wife of Rabbi Eliezer, was the sister of Rabban Gamaliel. There was a philosopher[4] in the neighbourhood who had the reputation that he would not take a bribe. They wished to have a laugh at him, so she brought to him a golden candlestick, came before him, and said: "I wish to have a portion of the property of my father." The philosopher said: "Divide it." R. Gamaliel said to him: "It is written in the Law given to us by God, *Where there is a son, a daughter shall not inherit.*" The philosopher answered him: "From the day you were removed from your land the Law of Moses was taken away and the *Evangelion*[5] given, and in it is written, *The son and the daughter will inherit alike.*" Next day, R. Gamaliel in his turn brought to him a Libyan ass. The philosopher said to him: "I came to the end of the book[6], where it is written, *I am not come to take away*

---

[1] According to another reading, considered by Dr. Güdemann (*op. cit.*, p. 71) as the older one, איריתא אחריתי.

[2] According to another reading דעין גליון.

[3] In the editions בשרגא.

[4] Philosopher is taken in controversial passages in the Talmud for a Christian doctor. By a corrupt reading of the Munich MS. we should read episcopus for philosopher (see Löwe, *op. cit.*, p. 68).

[5] According to the other reading 'another Law.'

[6] According to another reading of the *Evangelion*. Dr. Güdemann (*op. cit.*, p. 92) concludes from these words that the Logia ended with the passage following. We abstain from deciding one way or another. Anyhow, Dr. Güdemann's dissertation on the subject is worth consideration. Why no notice has been taken of it by Hilgenfeld (see p. 59, note 5), nor by Mr. Löwe, we do not know.

from the Law of Moses, but[1] *to add to the Law of Moses am I come, and it is written in it, Where there is a son, a daughter shall not inherit."* Emma said to him: "Let thy light shine in the candlestick[2]." R. Gamaliel said: "The ass has come and knocked down the candlestick."'

This passage has all the appearance of genuineness. Gamaliel is the grandson of Gamaliel the elder, and Eliezer is the famous Eliezer, son of Hyrcanos, disciple of R. Johanan ben Zakkai, who was often in communication with Judaeo-Christians. Of course the passage, 'Where there is a son, a daughter shall not inherit,' refers to Numbers xxvii. 9, and may be the words of a halakhah, now lost. The words 'It is written in the Law' may thus introduce a tradition ascribed to Moses as part of the revelation given to him on Sinai[3]. The words ascribed to the Gospel (or, according to the other reading, 'to the other Law'), viz. 'The son and the daughter will inherit alike,' are compared with Luke xii. 13[4]; and 'I am not come to take away from the Law of Moses,' etc., is supposed to be taken either from the Gospel according to the Hebrews[5], or from the Logia of St. Matthew[6].

---

[1] Reading אלא, or even without it (see J. H. Weiss, *Zur Geschichte der jüdischen Tradition*, i. p. 233, note 1), if we take the word לאוסיף in the sense of completing, which is the meaning of adding to it, according to the notion of the Rabbinical schools; הייבתא, for instance, means the complete Mishnah with the additions, but not additions to the Mishnah. If we were allowed to translate למיפחת by 'to destroy,' lit. *to lessen*, which is possible, the Talmudical sentence would correspond to the words of St. Matthew v. 17 οὐκ ἦλθον καταλῦσαι, ἀλλὰ πληρῶσαι. In the ordinary sense 'of taking away and adding' the reading of ולו, 'nor,' is justified by a Rabbinical authority of the seventeenth century (see Lowe, *op. cit.*, p. 68).

[2] We read בשרגא for בשרגא.

[3] הלכה למשה מסיני occurs often in the Talmudical literature. See Z. Frankel, *Hodegetica in Mishnam*, p. 20.

[4] See Güdemann, *op. cit.*, p. 75, where the word τίς is ingeniously explained.

[5] See A. Hilgenfeld, *Evangeliorum secundum Hebraeos*, etc., ed. altera, Lipsiae, 1884, p. 15; E. B. Nicholson, *The Gospel according to the Hebrews*, London, 1879, p. 146 seqq., where the date 71-3 for the Talmudical story is arbitrary. Of course, according to the reading of the old edition which we have adopted in our translation (see above, p. 58, note 2), the saying is taken from the Logia, but it might have been also in the Gospel according to the Hebrews.

[6] By Dr. Güdemann, see above, p. 57.

Adopting the following conjecture, Dr. Güdemann argues for the Logia. He takes the word חמרא (ass) in the sense of 'bushel[1].' Gamaliel presented to the philosopher a bushel with gold or silver, which put out the light of the candle. This, according to Dr. Güdemann, would be an allusion to the passage 'Neither do men light a candle and put it under a bushel, but on a candlestick.' In fact, in another Talmudical passage we find an analogous story, where it is said that a man presented two bushels of gold (בירות = μόδιος).

We have purposely abstained from any comparison of the *logia* and other of Jesus' sayings with those occurring in the Talmud, the dates of the latter being uncertain, and the wording mostly being different. We shall only quote one passage out of the *Midrash rabboth*[2], which represents the genuine language of that time. On the passage, Prov. xviii. 21, 'Death and life are in the power of the tongue,' the following history is applied: R. Simeon ben Gamaliel said to his servant Tabi, 'Go and buy for me in the market good provisions.' He went out and bought for him a tongue. Then Simeon told him, 'Go and buy for me bad provisions,' and Tabi bought again a tongue. Simeon said, 'When I tell you to buy good provisions, you buy a tongue; and when I tell you to buy bad provisions, you buy a tongue also.' Tabi answered, 'From the tongue cometh both, good and bad; it cannot be better when it is good, and it cannot be worse when it is bad.'

מות וחיים ביד לשון ר"ג אמר לטבי
עבדיה פוק זבין לי צדו טבא מן שוקא נפק וזבן ליה ליש[ן]
א"ל פוק זבין לי צדו בישא מן שוקא נפק וזבין ליה ליש[ן]
א"ל כד אנא אימא לך צדו טבא את זבן לי ליש[ן] וכד אנא

---

[1] Hebrew חֲמָר (*op. cit.*, p. 84), which stood in the Semitic text for the word μόδιος, and became חמרא by some ignorant copyist. לוּבָא Libyan is an addition, no doubt. In the Talmudical parallel passages we find instead of חמרא the words דיה של זהב, 'a young ass of gold,' which is a more impossible object to be presented. Dr. Güdemann notices also that the parallel passage has instead of כבש, 'knocked over,' the word כבה (כבה), 'extinguished.'

[2] On Leviticus, ch. xxxiii (according to the Bodl. MS., No. 2335).

אימא לך צדו׳ בישא את זבן לי לישן א״ל מיניה בתרי מיניה דטבא ומיניה דבישתא כד היא טבא לית טבא מיניה וכד בישתא לית בישתא מיניה. Compare the Epistle of St. James iii. 8–10.

The language of the Palestinian Talmud (or, as it is commonly called, the Talmud of Jerusalem), which consists of discussions by natives of Galilee, and which is really a Galilean composition, represents, according to our opinion, the language which the disciples of Jesus spoke and wrote. The gutturals are constantly in this dialect interchanged, ע is written for ח, א for ה, which is thus often not pronounced at all, as we have seen in the word 'Ἐφφαθά[2]. Very often the א and the ה are omitted altogether: we find, for instance, מר for אמר; R. Ba for R. Abba (whence the name Rabba); Lazar for Eleazar, as in the name of Lazarus in the Gospels. The labial letters are pronounced in the Jerusalem Talmud more softly than in the Babylonian. Instead of ב and פ they use ru; for כ the Galilean Rabbis have often b. For כ we find ג; thus, the locality כזיב is in the Jerusalem Talmud גזיב. Even ל and נ are interchanged, as in Antolinus instead of Antoninus[3]. From this we may perhaps explain the name נקאי[4], given to one of the disciples of Jesus in the Talmud, and usually regarded as = Nicodemus. This name, however, is written in the Talmud Naqdimon. It is more probable that by נקאי is meant St. Luke (Luqa), whom the Rabbis treated as a disciple of Jesus. Two words are often united into one in the dialect of the Jerusalem Talmud. For אית אינן, 'they are,' we read אתינן; הבינו for הכין היא, 'so it is;' בישנין for בית שאנין, 'inhabitants of Beth Shean.' We have seen the same occur above in the mouth of a Galilean woman[5]. The vocabulary of the Jerusalem Talmud is peculiar as compared with that of the

---

[1] MS. thrice צבי. [2] See above, p. 56.
[3] See Z. Frankel, *Introductio in Talmud Hierosolymitanum* (in Hebrew), Vratislaviae, 1870, p. 8.
[4] *Bab. Talm.*, Sanhedrin, fol. 43 a. [5] See above, p. 51.

Babylonian Talmud. If, therefore, any attempt be made to translate New Testament texts into their original idiom, the language chosen for the purpose must be the dialect of the Talmud of Jerusalem [1].

Josephus has also Aramaic words in his Greek work. Thus he remarks that the Hebrews call red, Ἀδωμά (אדומא); priest, χαραίας (כהניא); Pentecost, Ἀσαρθά (עצרתא); a lame man, χάγειρας (חגירא). He has also the words *Abba* and φάσκα[2]. That he makes a distinction between the Hebrew (or rather Syro-Aramaic) and the Babylonian-Aramaic dialect results from the passage where he says concerning 'Abanet' (אבנט), *a belt*, 'we have learnt from the Babylonians to call it Ἐμίαν,' which corresponds to המין in the Onqelos Targum, a word which occurs in the same sense in the Babylonian Talmud[3].

As to the Greek spoken by the Jews in Palestine, in spite of the passage quoted above[4], to the effect that in Palestine either the Holy language or the Greek should be spoken, few, we believe, had a substantial knowledge of it. Let us examine how, and at what period, Greek could have become universal (according to Dr. Roberts' view), or indeed, even prominent in Palestine.

If the Greeks are mentioned in the Old Testament under the name of *Yawan*, there was certainly no intercourse during the period of the first Temple between Ionians and Jews. At the time of Alexander the Great, Jews settled in Egypt, Asia Minor, and probably also in Greece. These we shall find mentioned under the name of Hellenists. Their connexion with the mother-land was maintained by their going to Jerusalem for feast-days, and by their sending offerings

---

[1] Contrary to Prof. Delitzsch's opinion, who says (*The Hebrew New Testament*, etc. [see p. 41, note 6], p. 31). 'The Shemitic woof of the New Testament Hellenism is Hebrew, not Aramaic. Our Lord and his apostles thought and spoke for the most part in Hebrew.'

[2] See Siegfried, *Zeitschr. für die Alttest. Wissenschaft* (by B. Stade), 1883, p. 32 sqq.); and Kautzsch, *Grammatik des Biblisch-Aramäischen*, etc., p. 7.

[3] פרק, Erubin, fol. 104 b.   [4] See above, p. 50.

and sacrifices to the Temple¹. But we may infer that they still all spoke, more or less, their native Hebrew dialect, for no mention is made of interpreters being required for them either in the Temple or outside of it. No doubt some of them settled later in Jerusalem, and at the time of Jesus, amongst the 480 synagogues which Jerusalem then possessed², there would naturally be a Hellenistic one. History does not record that Alexander or his immediate successors had constrained the conquered nations to adopt the Greek language. That in new towns like Alexandria, Seleucia, Ctesiphon, and others, Greek was prevalent cannot be doubted, since the settlers were Greeks, but the lower class, representing labourers, servants, and even soldiers, could not have been all brought over from Greece, but were taken from the surrounding towns and villages; these would still continue to use their own dialects, and would acquire only a scanty knowledge of Greek. Such is the case now in Belgium with French and Flemish, in Alsace with French and German. To say that Greek was universally spoken, and that therefore Palestine could have been no exception to the rule, is at all events exaggerated. Antioch and other Syrian towns would not give up Syriac, as will be seen further on³. The Phœnician towns still knew Phœnician, as may be inferred from the coins with double inscriptions, Phœnician and Greek⁴. In Palmyra we find provisions for taxes payable to the Romans drawn up in Greek and Palmyrene⁵. In Egypt, Coptic survived till the twelfth century A.D. In Armenia, Armenian is even now spoken. From the Acts, ii. 9–12, we see that the Parthians, Medes, Elamites, the dwellers in Mesopotamia, and in Judea, Cappadocia, etc. spoke languages other than Greek. Indeed,

---

[1] See Graetz, *Geschichte der Juden*, vol. iii. p. 35.
[2] *Ibidem*, p. 391.
[3] See below, p. 70.
[4] Renan, *Histoire des Langues sémitiques*, p. 196.
[5] M. de Vogüé, *Journal asiatique*, 1883, i. p. 231 seqq.; ii. p. 149 seqq. Sachau, *Zeitschr. der deutschen morg. Gesellschaft*, 1883, p. 562 seqq.

Bernhardy[1] states that the Greek spoken in Asia Minor was not more than a kind of jargon. Pfannkuche[2] observes rightly, 'A conquered nation suffers the deprivation of its national language, and the obtrusion of another *totally different* from its own, only when the conqueror overturns the previously existing organization of the state, transports the greater part of the inhabitants, and gives their former abodes to foreign colonists, who inundate the whole country, and must be far more numerous than the remaining original inhabitants. This is the only condition which makes the complete extinction of a national language possible, but that condition never existed under the mild sway of the Romans in Palestine.' To this the following note is appended by the translator of Pfannkuche: 'The translator does not recollect any instance in history where even that condition has proved effective. The political organization of the ancient Britons has been overturned over and over again, and still they preserve their ancient language in its different dialects; so the Basks theirs; Italy, at all events, suffered the obtrusion of no foreign tongue, although its own was modified. The Mantshu Tartars, I apprehend, entirely overturned the political organization of China; but the conquerors did not introduce their own language, although far preferable to that of the natives, and more apt to the adequate expression of thought . . . The political organization of Prussian Poland was completely overturned, and many efforts made to introduce German, and still the Poles preserve their language. In short, I must doubt whether any political measure, though ever so violent, can completely extirpate the national language of any country.' We may add in the case of Poland under Prussia that there is compulsory education and general military service, both of which are most powerful factors in extinguishing a language. Other not less striking

---

[1] Quoted by Dr. Bahl in his *Forschungen*, etc. (see full title above, p. 41, note 3), p. 64.

[2] English translation (see above, p. 42, note 3), p. 31.

examples, from modern times, may be quoted. How little have the Alsatians, especially the rural population, adopted the French language in the course of nearly two centuries of French rule, in spite of their being satisfied with the French government, in spite of the frequent intercourse between Alsatians and French, and the institution of High Schools where French was exclusively taught. It is natural, therefore, that the Jews with their general spirit of exclusiveness and with their contempt for pagan worship, manners and customs, should not have hastened to exchange their native and holy language for the Greek. That a number of Greek words were introduced into the vernacular Hebrew, cannot be doubted. But they consist of names of instruments, such as we find in Daniel[1], vessels used in the Temple or at home, and also some satirical expressions[2]. What better proof can there be that Greek did not become familiar to the Jews in Palestine through their conquerors, than the fewness of the verbs which have been introduced in their vernacular, as far as we can judge, from the Mishnah, the Targumim, the Talmud of Jerusalem, and the early homiletical literature[3]? There are certainly more French words in German than Greek in the Hebrew vernacular, though it will hardly, we suppose, be imagined that the Germans adopted the French language during the occupation by Napoleon.

Such then is the conclusion which we reach from a consideration of the spoken language. The written literature suggests exactly the same inferences. No apocryphal book, as far as our knowledge goes, was composed in Greek by a Palestinian Jew. Very few sayings in Greek are quoted in the Midrashic literature, and the few which occur are referred to Rabbis who came from Greek-speaking towns, such as

---

[1] See Hartwig Derenbourg, *Les mots grecs dans le livre biblique de Daniel* (Mélanges Graux, Paris, 1883, pp. 235-244).

[2] See *Lehrbuch zur Sprache der Mischnah* von Dr. Abraham Geiger, Breslau, 1845, p. 20 seqq.

[3] See *Beiträge zur Sprach- und Alterthums-Forschung aus jüdischen Quellen* von Dr. M. Sachs, 2 Hefte, Berlin, 1852-4, i. p. 4 seqq.

Cæsarea, Antioch, and elsewhere[1]. Some Græcised names which Josephus mentions, such as Alkimos for Jehoiakim, Jason for Joshua, Antigonos and others do not indicate more than that some of the Jews affected Greek manners and customs; they prove nothing as to the bulk of the nation. Civil acts written in Greek, and Greek signatures[2], were declared valid by authority of the civil power. Did the Jews know Latin when they signed civil acts in Latin? Certainly not. However, even if we were to adopt the idea that under the friendly treatment which they received at the hands of Alexander the Great and his immediate successors, the Jews, in order to please their benefactors, endeavoured, like the other conquered tribes, to assimilate themselves to Greeks, the current in this direction would certainly have ceased with their persecution by Antiochus Epiphanes. Nor could such a short time as elapsed between Alexander the Great and Antiochus have been sufficient to introduce a foreign language amongst the mass of the nation. We may meet the suggestion by appealing to the continued existence of Welsh, in spite of the friendly rule of the English, to the imperfect Russification of Poland and Germanization of Posen and Silesia. All that the Jews in Palestine learned of Greek, so far as we can judge, was at most a few sentences, sufficient to enable them to carry on trade and to hold intercourse with the lower officials. And even this minimum certainly ceased after the Maccabean victory over Antiochus Epiphanes, for it was the interest of the Asmonean princes to keep the Jews aloof from the influence of the neighbouring dialects. The coins at that time were struck with Hebrew inscriptions[3], the official language and that of the schools was exclusively

---

[1] See Dr. Lewy's essay, entitled *Über die Spuren des griechischen und römischen Alterthums im talmudischen Schriftthum* Verhandlungen der dreiunddreissigsten Versammlung deutscher Philologen und Schulmanner in Gera vom 30 September bis 2 October, 1878, p. 77 sqq.

[2] *Tosifta*, Baba Bathra, ch. 9.

[3] See above, p. 44.

the vernacular Hebrew [1]. And what happened in Jerusalem was imitated also in Galilee, except in towns exclusively inhabited by Greeks, where the Jews, when in the minority, might have acquired a fair knowledge of conversational Greek, but not to such an extent as to enable them to speak in public, and still less to be able to interpret the Law in the synagogues. The inhabitants of Beth Shean or Scythopolis are mentioned as pronouncing Hebrew badly, and Scythopolis is considered an exclusively Greek town [2]. In fact, we may boldly state that the Greek translation of the Bible was unknown in Palestine except to men of the schools and perhaps a few of the Hellenistic Jews. On the contrary, it is said in the Talmud that when the Greek translation of the Seventy appeared, there came darkness upon the earth, and the day was as unfortunate for Israel as that on which the golden calf was made [3]. We believe that all the quotations in the early Gospels are derived from a traditional and unwritten vernacular Targum. Hence many of the differences in reading. The dominion of Herod was too brief to introduce the Greek language, and the troubles with the Romans which arose subsequently were certainly no inducement to Jews to adopt Greek. Had Greek been generally spoken and taught, why should the Talmud record a general exception in favour of Gamaliel [4], and later, in the second century, when the schools were already active in Galilee, in favour of the family of Judah the saint, the redactor of the Mishnah [5], that they should be allowed to learn Greek, because they had to conduct negotiations with the government? The Hebrew inscription on the cross together with the Greek and the Latin [6] is an evident proof that there were a great number of Jews who did not know Greek. If we are not mistaken, it is now

---

[1] See above, p. 47 seqq.
[2] See above, p. 51.
[3] Berliner, *Targum Onkelos*, ii. p. 78, note 3.
[4] Lewy, *Ueber die Spuren des griechischen*, etc. (see p. 66, note 1) p. 79.
[5] Dukes, *Die Sprache der Mischnah*, p. 7.
[6] St. John xix. 20.

generally admitted that the earliest writings of the Christians in Palestine and the neighbouring countries where they took refuge after the destruction of Jerusalem were uniformly in a vernacular Hebrew, and not in Greek [1]. Had a majority of the Jews spoken this language, some of these records must have been composed in Greek. Josephus wrote his history in Hebrew for the benefit of the Jewish nation [2], and he acted as interpreter between the Jewish defenders of Jerusalem and the Roman generals [3]. And when he remarks that the Jews cannot pronounce Greek purely, his meaning, as it appears to us, is, that they did not learn it in a classical sense, but that their knowledge consisted of barbarous Greek, such as they would hear from foreigners who came from the Greek provinces, and which was only a kind of jargon. The Roman legions themselves at Jerusalem were mostly composed of Syrians [4] whose Greek could by no means have been classical. Speaking of the Syrians, we may take them as an argument, how unready Semitic nations are in exchanging their own dialect for another not of the same family. The Syrian Christians, though likewise under the dominion of Rome, and employing a great number of Greek words in their translations of the Gospels and other writings, never gave up their own language, which is spoken to the present day [5]. The Arabs in Algeria have not yet learned much French, and the Arabs in Syria know not a sentence of Turkish, in spite of having been under Turkish rule for four centuries and professing the same religion as the Turks.

We must now briefly refer to the Jews in Egypt and Asia Minor. These had gradually forgotten their vernacular Hebrew. There were no schools to preserve the knowledge of it even amongst the better classes, and daily intercourse with the Greek population soon resulted in its being abandoned

---

[1] See Michel Nicolas, *Études sur les Évangiles apocryphes*, Paris, 1866.
[2] *Proœmium to the Antiquities*.
[3] *Wars*, V. vi. 3.
[4] *Ibidem*, V. ix. 2; VI. ii. 1. *Contra Apionem*, I. 9.
[5] Renan, *Histoire des Langues Sémitiques*, p. 263.

altogether. Indeed, tenacious as Jews were in their own land, and as they are now in the countries where they live together, yet they readily adapt themselves to the habit of a country where they are received as free citizens, and exchange their vernacular for the language spoken by the people amongst whom they dwell. Indeed, the second or at most the third generation of immigrating Jews know not a word of the language spoken by their parents. Take, for instance, the English Jews, who are either of Dutch-Spanish or of German-Polish extraction, very rarely of Italian, as was the case with the family of the late Prime Minister. They all speak English, none of them know Dutch or Spanish, and only a few German, unless they have learnt it as a foreign language. The same is the case with the French, Italian, and German Jews. Only where they are kept by themselves, as is the case in Russia and Turkey, and not admitted to offices, do they cling to the language of their ancestors. So the Russian Jews still speak the mediæval German, and the Jews at Salonica, Constantinople, and Smyrna speak the Spanish of the fourteenth century. But the Jews in Egypt, and more especially at Alexandria, had so soon forgotten their Hebrew that a Greek translation of the Pentateuch became a necessity for their synagogues before they had been settled there a single century. Possibly a Greek translation of the Pentateuch existed before it was written down (if there is any historical truth in this statement) for one of the kings of the Ptolemean dynasty. Here, to judge from the Greek style of an Aristeas, Aristobulus the author of the Sibyllines, and, above all, Philo, the Jews must have frequented Greek schools. Philo, it can be proved to demonstration, knew very little Hebrew, if indeed he knew any at all[1]. In Asia Minor, Jewish congregations are mentioned in all parts, in Bithynia, Cilicia, Pamphylia, Cappadocia, Lycaonia, Phrygia, Lydia, Galatia, and Pontus. Cyprus,

---

[1] See Siegfried, *Philo von Alexandrica*, p. 142 seqq.

Rhodes, and Crete had also many Jews. They are likewise mentioned in Greece itself, in Macedonia, Thessaly, Bœotia, Attica, and the Peloponnese[1]. All these Jews, far away from Palestine, spoke only Greek, with the exception of the few who learnt Hebrew in the schools of Jerusalem, like St. Paul, or others who were but recent immigrants from Palestine and with whom the apostle conversed in vernacular Hebrew. Indeed, very few Rabbis are mentioned in the Talmud as coming from the Greek provinces[2]. From inscriptions in the synagogues and epitaphs published by Stephanie in the memoirs of St. Petersburg[3], we see that they used freely and exclusively the Greek language. Even the common word *shalom* found in the catacombs of Rome, Naples, and later even at Venosa[4], is not met with in the inscriptions of Asia Minor. The same is the case with the tomb-inscription at Smyrna, discovered by Mr. Ramsay, and now edited by M. Reinach[5]. These Jews, no doubt, read the Old Testament in Greek, and through them the Bible became known, more or less, to the heathen, as may be seen from quotations made by the apostles in writings addressed to Gentile Christians. The Jews of Cæsarea and Antioch alone had a fair knowledge of Hebrew, so far as we can judge from the Talmud, and that was natural; Cæsarea was close to Palestine, and at Antioch Syriac was still spoken, a language which is so nearly related to the vernacular of Palestine. Those mentioned are mostly popular preachers (Aggadists), and they freely use Greek sentences, even in an absurd way[6]. The

---

[1] Acts ii. 8 seqq.   [2] See above, p. 66.

[3] *Parerga Archaeologica*, St. Petersburg, 1859, p. 200 seqq. See also *Epigraphische Beiträge der Juden* von Dr. M. A. Levy Jahrbuch für die Geschichte der Juden und des Judenthum, Leipzig, 1861, Bd. ii, article v), p. 272 seqq.

[4] See *Iscrizioni inedite o male note, greche, latine, ebraiche di antichi sepolcri giudaici del Napolitano*, edite e illustrato da G. I. Ascoli (Atti del IV congresso internazionale degli orientalisti, Firenze, 1880, vol. I, p. 239 seqq.

[5] See *Inscription grecque de Smyrne. La Juive Rufina*, by Salomon Reinach, *Revue des Études juives*, tom. vii. p. 161.

[6] See Dr. Lewy's essay (full title, p. 66, note 1) and the Supplementary Notes.

Galilean Rabbis were no longer able to pronounce against the study of Greek, having seen and heard from travellers, such as R. Aqiba and R. Meir, how important, and how widely spread the Greek language was amongst the Jews in Asia Minor. Moreover, the Greek Jews undoubtedly contributed to the support of the Rabbis and their schools in Palestine, for the Jews here were by no means rich. They had very little to hope from Babylonia, since the schools of that country became rivals of the Palestinian or rather Galilean schools. We find, therefore, in the second century R. Simon ben Gamaliel[1] saying that the Law can only be adequately translated into Greek. Another Rabbi applies the words of Genesis ix. 27, 'Japhet shall dwell in the tents of Shem,' to the Greek language. R. Jehudah the saint, towards the end of the second century, says, 'Of what use is Syriac in Palestine? Let us use only either Hebrew or Greek[2].' Not only was it permitted at Cæsarea that the prayer *Shema*[3] might be recited in Hellenistic, but a new Greek translation of the Bible was made under the auspices of R. Aqiba by Aquila. It will not be in place here to discuss who this Aquila was; the Talmud calls him a proselyte, and it is remarkable that Onqelos the Aramean translator[4] is mentioned as having been a proselyte likewise. In any case, Aquila the translator cannot be identified with the Aquila mentioned in the Acts. Indeed, the Rabbis saw that the Jews in Asia Minor could only use the Greek translation of the Bible, which then became also current among Christians. A complete return to Hebrew being thus an impossibility, they caused a new translation to be made in the literal sense of the interpretations followed in the schools. R. Joshua and R. Eleazar[5] praised Aquila for his translation, and applied to him the passage of the Psalms: 'Thou art

---

[1] *Jer. Talm.*, Meguillah, i. 11; Berliner, *Targum Onkelos*, ii. p. 94.
[2] *Bab. Talm.*, Sotah, fol. 49 b.
[3] Frankel, *Vorstudien zur Septuaginta*, p. 58.
[4] See Berliner, *Targum Onkelos*, ii. p. 97 seqq.
[5] *Ibidem*, p. 96.

fairer than the children of men.' The Rabbis began to read Greek books, and some of them even busied themselves with Greek philosophy. It is said of Elishah ben Abhuyah (about 160 A.D.) that he preferred Greek studies to those of the law. Greek songs (Homer?) were always on his lips[1]. In another passage, R. Aqiba explains the prohibition not to read 'outside' books by the books of Homer[2]; Aqiba, as well as Elishah, pursued mystic studies, and Homer was already in the time of Anaxagoras explained allegorically[3]. Epiphanius says[4] that the Gnostics and other sects found support in Homer for all their arguments, and appealed to his writings as we appeal to the Bible. R. Meir frequently held conversations with a philosopher called in the Talmud Ennomos, of Gadarah[5], a town of the Decapolis, where, according to Strabo[6], many Greek philosophers were settled.

When the Galilean schools ceased to exist, and the Talmud of Jerusalem had been written down, we lose sight of the Jews in Palestine. Arabic takes the place of Greek, but we know from non-Jewish documents that in Byzantium the Jews used the Greek translation of the Bible in the synagogues[7]. We find Greek words in the exegetical and philosophical works of the Qaraites, who wrote on the Bosphorus in the eleventh century[8]. There exists a Greek translation of the Book of Jonah[9], made at Corfu in the

---

[1] *Bab. Talm.*, Ḥagigah, fol. 15 b אהד מאי ומי יייני לא ססך כסוםיה אםרי עליו על אהר בשעה שהיה עומד בניה המדרש ספרי םיני נושרין םהיקו Lewy, *Ueber die Spuren des griechischen*, etc., p. 80.

[2] הםירם. *Jer. Talm.*, Heleq. x. Explained also (see Graetz) by daily reading from ἡμέρα.

[3] See Zeller, *Die Philosophie der Griechen* (4th ed.), vol. i. p. 931.

[4] Haeres, i. 200.

[5] אבנוםים רגדרי for הגדרי. See Graetz, op. cit., s. iv. p. 469; identified with Οἰνόμαος Γαδαρεύς.

[6] Syria, ii. 29. [7] Graetz, *Geschichte der Juden*, vol. v. p. 435.

[8] See Steinschneider, *Catalogus Codicum Hebr. Bibl. Lugd. Batav.* (1858), MS. Warner, No. 41.

[9] MS. Opp. Add. 8, 19 our Catalogue, No. 1144°. This is probably a remnant of the old use of translating the lessons of the prophets (Zunz, *Die Gottesdienstlichen Vorträge*, Berlin, 1832, p. 8). This translation is, we believe, the earliest modern Greek text we possess in prose. We hope to publish it shortly.

twelfth century, in MSS. of the Bodleian Library and that of Bologna. This is the earliest example of modern Greek prose. In the prayer-book of the Greek rite a great number of hymns are to be found in Greek, or sometimes in Hebrew with the Greek translation[1]. A version of the Pentateuch in Greek was printed as early as 1547, together with a Spanish translation, for the use of the Jews in Turkey[2]. There are in existence documents enough for writing a grammar of Jewish Greek, which we believe would throw some light on the grammar of the Septuagint as well as of that of the New Testament writings.

[1] Sp. Pappageorgios, *Merkwürdige in den Synagogen von Corfu im Gebrauche befindliche Hymnen* (Abhandlungen und Vorträge des fünften internationalen Orientalischen Congresses, Berlin, 1882, i. p. 226 seqq.). The Bodleian Library possesses several MSS. containing hymns in Greek.

[2] Constantinople, fol. 1547. See Steinschneider, *Catalogus Librorum Hebraeorum in Bibliotheca Bodleiana*, 1852–1860, No. 122.

Supplementary Notes.

P. 50. M. Halévy (*Revue des Études juives*, t. ix. p. 10, note 2) thinks that the Talmudic *Sarsi* means the language of Ashdod, or the Nabataean dialect. According to his conjecture, the word 'bastard' (ממזר, Zach. ix. 6) refers to the Nabataeans (see below, p. 229).

P. 55 *b*. M. Rubens Duval in his review of Professor Kautzsch's Grammar (*Revue des Études juives*, t. ix. p. 144) finds Ewald's explanation of ῥακά from רקב, 'shabby' (in German, *Lump*), preferable to the ריקן suggested by Professor Kautzsch (see also Nöldeke, *Göttingische gelehrte Anzeigen*, 1884, p. 1023). We do not remember a single instance where shabby in an Oriental language would be employed as a reproach. We believe that ריקא after all is the best explanation, since this occurs in the Talmud as a reproach.

P. 57. From the form מראנא, 'our master,' occurring in the Nabataean inscriptions discovered by Mr. Doughty, M. Halévy conjectures (*Revue des Études juives*, t. ix. p. 9) that Μαρὰν ἀθά represents מראנא תא, 'our Lord, come.' Cf. ναὶ ἔρχου, Rev. xii. 20 (see also Nöldeke, *ibidem*).

Specimens to p. 70, note 6.

Jer. Talm., *Rosh hash-Shanah*, i. 3. R. Eleazar, arguing that God gives the first example of keeping the commandments, while a king of flesh and blood is arbitrary in this respect, uses the following Greek sentence: פרא בטילוס או נומוס או נריפוס, Πρὸ βασιλέως ὁ νόμος ἄγραφος (read אנרפוס). This was perhaps a current proverb.—Ibidem, *Shebuoth*, iii. 10, we read that R. Menahem stated in the name of Resh (R. Simeon ben) Laqish: if a man who sees rain coming down exclaims, קורי פלו בריבסון, Κύριε, πολὺ ἔβρεξεν (according to another reading אברובסיס), he is guilty of a vain oath.—Ibidem, *Yebamoth*, iv. 2, we read that R. Abahu (of Cæsarea) having been asked whence he knew that a child born at seven months could live, answered, 'I know it from your own language.' זינא אבמא אבמא (read אנא) זונא Ζῆτα ἑπτά, ἦτα ὀκτώ, Ζῆτα is connected fancifully with ζῆν.—We read in the *Pesiqta Rabbathi*, xl, ויאמר יצחק אל אברהם אביו הנה האיש והעצים ואיה הישה לעולה אמר לו אברהם אלהים יראה לו הישה יומי קרבנו ואם לא יה לעולה בני יה לעולה סי לעולה לישון יוניח אתה הוא הקרבן. 'Isaac said unto Abraham his father, My father.... Behold the fire and the wood: but where is the lamb for a burnt offering? And Abraham said, God will provide himself a lamb (Gen. xxii. 7, 8). God will provide for himself the sacrifice; and if not, thou (יה) shalt be the burnt offering, my son.' יה is explained as the accusative pronoun σέ (see Ed. Friedmann, p. 170 *b* and Dr. Güdemann's *vocabulary* of the Greek and Latin words occurring in this Pesiqta, a. v. יה).—Bab. Talm., *Shabbath*, fol. 31 *a*, the word הן (Job xxviii. 28), 'behold,' is connected with the Greek ἕν, and translated 'the fear of the Lord is the *one* thing which God asks from man.' הן is understood in the same sense in other passages.

IV.

ON A NEW THEORY OF THE ORIGIN AND COMPOSITION OF THE SYNOPTIC GOSPELS PROPOSED BY G. WETZEL [1].

[A. Edersheim.]

At the outset of this paper I would wish it clearly understood that my purpose is not to present an exhaustive review of the opinions entertained by scholars on the origin and composition of what are known as the Synoptic Gospels; still less, a criticism of their views. Least of all is it my object to state or defend the conclusions at which in the course of study I may have arrived. My task is much more simple and humble. On a question of such primary importance as this, every new contribution is of interest, and every proposed new solution of the difficulties claims the attention of the student. It is as promising, and in part giving, a new explanation of the origin of our Synoptic Gospels that I propose to lay before you the theory which Pastor Wetzel has advanced, with only such review of other theories as the subject demands—and, indeed, Wetzel has made [2]—and with only such criticism as may be suggested by a statement of the facts.

I need scarcely remind you that what may be called the criticism of the Gospels occupies a field both wider and narrower than that of the Gospel-narratives. The former deals with the origin, composition, and sources of the Gospels as a whole,—and with their narratives and other contents only in so far as they bear on the general question of their *origines*.

---

[1] *Die Synoptischen Evangelien*, etc., von G. Wetzel, Heilbronn, 1883.
[2] The Review by Dr. Wetzel is both comprehensive and able, and it has been followed in the present paper.

On the other hand, the criticism of the Gospel-narratives deals primarily with their contents: with the text itself, the genuineness or spuriousness of certain parts of it, and its meaning—and it enters on the question of authorship and composition only in so far as these bear on the understanding of the text itself. Naturally the two have an important bearing upon each other. Thus our understanding of the text of the fourth Gospel will be very different, if we regard it as Ephesian and of the second century, from what it would be if we treated it as the work of the Apostle John. Similarly our view of divergences or accordances in the Synoptic Gospels, or of the insertion in, or omission from, one or the other of them of certain narratives or traits—and with it our explanation of the text—will be greatly influenced according as we regard these Gospels as either redactions, *Bearbeitungen*, of one original Gospel ('Ur-Evangelium'), or else as supplementations—or it may be amplifications, or even rectifications—by the two other Evangelists of the first and oldest Gospel, which they had before them; or, finally, as all springing alike from a common tradition in the Church.

As regards the Synoptic Gospels, with which we are at present exclusively concerned, the very name indicates the character of the problem. Formerly, the expression Synopsis of the Gospels simply meant a bird's eye view of the Gospel-history, derived from what we now call a harmony of the Gospels. But in our modern *usus* the term Synoptic Gospels indicates the common, general character and contents of the first three Gospels as distinguished from the fourth. And this, as regards the subject-matter of these three narratives, and their general selection of, and mode of reporting, events and discourses—in short, their general character, style, and treatment of the Gospel-history. The designation, which seems to have been introduced by Griesbach, has, as Canon Westcott notes, been brought into general use by Neander. Thus the term Synoptic Gospels raises at once the twofold question: (1) Whence the striking agreement in these three Gospels—first, in the selection of the matter; secondly, in the succession of the narratives; thirdly, in the mode of their presentation—and this not only as regards thoughts but even the wording? (2), and equally strikingly, whence their remarkable divergences in these three respects?

In other times, indeed, there was a short and easy way of dealing with such questions. You simply cut the knot by the sword of verbal inspiration, or dictation of the sacred text. The Evangelists had not derived their materials from one another, nor from a common original, nor from the *consensus* of tradition in the Apostolic circle, but alike the thoughts and the words had been dictated to them from above—and all that we had now to do was to ascertain how they were to be harmonised. But modern criticism can no longer be satisfied with such foreclosing, rather than answering, of the question. I am not now referring to negative, but to positive and believing criticism. While thankfully retaining (I speak, of course, on my own part) what we hold to be intrinsically true and scientifically capable of ample defence—our belief in the Divine inspiration of the Gospels, we think of their writers, not as impersonal machines, but as inspired men, who in the preparation of their narratives availed themselves of the usual sources of historical composition, and whose writings (as regards their human aspect) are subject to all the ordinary canons of historical criticism. And having arrived at this general conclusion, we can address ourselves fearlessly, although with even more than usual reserve and caution, to the study of the literary origin of the Gospels, well assured that the results of the fullest historical investigation will establish the truth of Holy Scripture, and that anything that may seem to the contrary must be due to hasty inferences, or to insufficient consideration of both sides of the question, or else to want of such information, as, if we possessed it, would remove our difficulties.

On what theory, then, of their composition are we to account for the threefold agreement and the threefold differences between the Synoptic Gospels? Before stating the theory of Dr. Wetzel let me give a brief historical synopsis of the attempted explanations.

In general these may be arranged in three groups, to each of which, as well as to their subdivisions, the names of certain critics attach. I would call them: the mutual dependence-hypothesis; the original Gospel- or original documents-hypothesis; and the original tradition- or oral Gospel-hypothesis. Let us examine each in briefest manner.

Firstly, according to the mutual dependence-hypothesis, the affinity between the different Gospels is explained by their mutual use. Here the question would arise, What is to be regarded as the chronological order of the three Gospels? Six different answers have been proposed, according as you place one or the other Gospel first in the order of time. The various arrangements of the Gospels are as follows:

a. According to some, St. Matthew comes first; from him St. Mark; and from both St. Luke. So St. Augustine, Bengel, Credner, Hilgenfeld, Hengstenberg. And here this other question arises, whether it was the Hebrew or the Greek Gospel of St. Matthew (the latter: Hug)?

b. Others arrange the order thus: St. Matthew, St. Luke, St. Mark. So Griesbach, De Wette, Theile, Strauss, Gfrörer, Schwegler, Baur, Delitzsch, Bleek, Anger, Köstlin, and Keim.

c. Others begin with St. Mark. Thus: St. Mark, St. Matthew, St. Luke. So Storr, Thiersch, Reuss, Meyer, Tholuck, Tobler, Plitt, Weiss.

d. Or else: St. Mark, St. Luke, St. Matthew. So Herder, Lachmann, Br. Bauer, Hitzig, Holtzmann, Volkmar.

e. Lastly: Some place St. Luke first. Thus: St. Luke, St. Matthew, St. Mark. So Heubner, Rödiger, Schneckenburger.

f. Or else: St. Luke, St. Mark, St. Matthew. So Vogel.

I ought to add that at least one writer (Saunier) supposes the dependence to have been, not on a written copy of the Gospels, but on memory.

From this classification you will observe, first, that there are few names in favour of the absolute priority of St. Luke, and among them only those of Schneckenburger and Rödiger which claim special attention. Secondly, that as between the priority of St. Matthew and St. Mark authorities are somewhat evenly divided, the balance being in favour of the priority of St. Matthew, although of late the weight of opinion has turned in favour of the priority of St. Mark; and that, in support of each view, you have distinguished names on the positive, as well as the negative side of criticism. Thirdly,—and I trust the inference will not be regarded as cynical,—that, since learned opinions are so evenly divided on the subject, there can scarcely be any decisive evidence as to the priority of either one or the other Gospel, or indeed in favour of this hypothesis generally, which the Germans call the *Benützungs-Hypothese*.

Secondly. According to the second hypothesis, which I have called the original Gospel- or original documents-hypothesis, the Synoptic Gospels all rest on one original Gospel, which, however, is no longer extant, and to which various additions were afterwards made. This theory was first broached by that original exegete, Eichhorn. Eichhorn supposed that the common sections in the three Gospels were taken from this *Ur-Evangelium*, the differences and specialities of each being accounted for by the later additions already mentioned. You will notice that this scarcely satisfactorily accounts for such questions as these, why two Evangelists record an event which is omitted by the third, or why one records what the other two omit. Again, as there are differences (though only in detail) even in those accounts which are common to all the three Gospels, it was further assumed that this original Gospel and the additions to it had been written in Hebrew, and then differently translated into Greek—the writers, or rather those who finally redacted our Synoptists, having in their version of the original Gospel and of its additions also made use of the existing translations.

Although I have to remind myself and you that the object

of this paper is not to make detailed criticism, I cannot help expressing the feeling that, like many other explanations—theological, exegetical, and philosophical—this does not so much spring out of the facts, as it is rather adapted to them. It seems not like the natural covering of a plant, but like a garment made to measure, fitted on and altered to suit the figure. For the sake of completeness let me add, that this *Ur-Evangelium*, or derivation-hypothesis, has been differently presented. Some critics maintain:

a. That the original Gospel was the Aramæan (or Hebrew) St. Matthew, which contained the sections common to all the Gospels (Heilmann), or else that the matrix of all was a translation of it into the Greek (Bolten).

Before proceeding, I should perhaps say that this second might be combined with the first hypothesis. For you may hold that the Evangelists were dependent on each other, and yet that their writings were derived from an original which was the basis of that one existing Gospel, on which the others were severally dependent. Thus, according to Baur, there was an original Matthew; from this, the canonical Matthew; from this again, the original Luke; from the two latter, Mark; and finally, the canonical Luke. This gives five documents. Weiss, on the other hand, has it, that from the Apostolic original Gospel (*Ur-Matthæus*) came Mark, and from both, Luke and the canonical Matthew (independently of each other)— our St. Matthew being not Apostolic at all. Ewald marks not less than nine formations, of which St. Luke is the last.

b. There are critics, such as Hilgenfeld and Schwegler, who hold by an original Gospel of the Hebrews.

c. Eichhorn, as we have seen, speaks of a Greek translation of it and of certain additions to it.

d. Lastly, in this direction, we have the view which assumes the existence of various sources—notes, records, etc.—which served as the original basis of the Gospels. So Schleiermacher.

Thirdly. We now turn to the third, commonly known as the tradition-hypothesis, or, as Canon Westcott has happily designated it, that of the oral Gospel. It had best be presented in the form originally given it by Gieseler. That scholar reminds us that oral tradition, rather than written composition, was in accordance with the genius of the ancient Hebrews. Similarly, he suggests, the Evangelical history had for a time been orally transmitted, and by frequent repetition assumed a peculiar type, which was afterwards presented in the written Gospels. I have hitherto purposely omitted all reference to living English divines. But there need not be any reserve in stating that this is the view advocated by Canon Westcott, in his *Introduction to the Study of the Gospels*. He speaks of an oral Gospel, which formed the basis and substance of Apostolic teaching, as traced in the Acts and Epistles, centring 'in the crowning facts of the Passion and Resurrection of the Lord, while the earlier ministry of Christ was regarded chiefly in relation to its final issue.' In these respects, he supposes, 'the Synoptic Gospels exactly represent the probable form of the first oral Gospels.' 'In their common features they seem to be that which the earliest history declares they are, the summary of Apostolic preaching, the historical groundwork of the Church.' Then, as regards the probable order of precedence of the forms of the narratives, he ranges them: as St. Mark, St. Luke, St. Matthew, although he adds that 'it is, of course, possible that an earlier form of the Apostolic tradition may have been committed to writing at a later period.'

It must be admitted that this theory is not only attractive, but that *prima facie* it contains evident elements of truth. The Gospel-history, specifically that of Christ, would naturally be the great centre of interest, alike to Christians and unbelievers (and hence the subject of preaching): and it would continue such, the more, that so few had personally known Christ, or followed Him for any length of time, and that even this small band was continually decreasing by death. All the more earnest would be the desire to possess an authentic record of the great facts of Christ's life and death. But it is another question whether this desire would not have led to, and indicated the necessity, not of an oral, but of a written Gospel. Besides, to my mind, this theory, if standing alone, would leave a number of questions unanswered, some of them of deepest importance. Whence—if the oral Gospel be the sole basis—whole sections peculiar to only one Gospel, such as the Peræan section in St. Luke, or even the history of the forerunner of Christ, not to speak of much else, say, in the proœmium of the third Gospel? Besides, these sections, by their language and style, make, at least upon my mind, the impression of separate documents lying at the foundation of the narrative—some strongly Hebraic or local, such as the introductory portions of St. Luke. Similarly, the tradition-theory, if alone, does not account for the opposing phenomenon of the occurrence of not only similar but identical portions, not merely in the discourses (where perhaps it might have been preserved in tradition), but in the historical parts of the Gospels[1]. To these must be added such considerations as that evidently Christ and His Apostles spoke in Aramæan. Whence then, on the tradition-hypothesis, the verbal agreements in the Greek? Again, on the tradition-hypothesis, whence such a phenomenon as that St. Mark alone has scarcely anything peculiar to himself and distinctive? Further, whence the accordance in the arrangement of the material in the three Gospels which is far greater than the differences? whence also this, that out of the many miracles and events in the life of Christ, the three Synoptists mostly choose the same for their narration? If it had been derived exclusively from an oral Gospel we would have expected here rather differences.

To this review of the various opinions held you will perhaps allow me to add a brief criticism. It appears to me, that

[1] Wilke here makes an apt distinction between what he calls that in the narratives which might depend on the memory of the writer such as certain facts and speeches', and that which would depend on his reflection (Gedachtnissmässig; Reflexionsmässig'. But there is literal agreement in the latter also between the three Evangelists.

neither of the three theories mentioned is sufficient, alone and by itself, to explain all the facts of the case. Besides the difficulties already stated, this has to be added about the tradition-hypothesis, that if, as we must believe, there were various sources or *media* of this tradition (not one, but several narrators) we should scarcely expect that the issue would be *one* oral Gospel. Rather would the tendency of such traditions be to diverge. On the other hand, besides the attractiveness of the tradition-hypothesis, this element of great importance attaches to it—to which even such negative critics as Wittichen have been obliged to give due weight—that accord in the different Gospels establishes and presupposes a consensus of earliest Apostolical tradition, with which historical criticism has to deal as a fact that cannot be overlooked nor set aside.

I must here venture to express the opinion that no theory of the origination of the Gospels can be satisfactory, unless it go hand in hand with (I had almost said, be preceded by) an inquiry not only into the general purpose of the Gospels as written documents, but into the specific object of each individual Gospel. I am aware that I am here treading, or at least approaching, dangerous ground. It may be that I am making concessions to the Tübingen school—to what is known as the *Tendenz-Kritik*, which traces in almost every narrative of the Gospels design and purposes: the manifestation of an internecine war within the Church, or else cunning attempts at conciliation. I can scarcely express in too strong language my dissent from this *Tendenz-Kritik*, alike on ethical, critical, and literary grounds. Yet there is this underlying truth in it, that alike the Gospel-narrative and its different narrations must in their varied selection have had some *raison d'être*. Such a *raison d'être* would, if ascertained, also give them, whether viewed in their combination or separately, a bond of unity. And it is in the recognition of this unity and rationalness that the charm of the theory of the Tübingen school lies, since it seeks to solve the problem by reducing the existing diversity to an underlying unity of purpose and plan.

Our reference to the *Tendenz-Kritik* leads us back to the book more immediately under review. Of late critical opinion has chiefly reverted to the theory of an original Gospel—not indeed one of our present canonical Gospels, but an *Ur-Evangelium* outside the canon. And here the difference between critics lies mainly in this, whether this *Ur-Evangelium* was an original Matthew or an original Mark. Brief remarks must be made on each of these two views.

First, the existence of an original Matthew is chiefly, though not exclusively, advocated by the school of tendency-criticism, that is, by those critics who discern in each Gospel a peculiar tendency, perhaps I should rather say, a party-aim and animus. Thus Schwegler puts it in this manner. Originally Christianity was what we term Ebionite. This Ebionite Christianity found expression in the Gospel according to the Hebrews, which was a Jewish-Christian party-work. From this Gospel according to the Hebrews proceeded, by a modification of its Ebionism, the Gospel by St. Matthew. Again, in opposition to the Ebionite, there was the direction, known as Pauline Christianity, which found expression in the Gospel of Marcion[1], and this Paulinism, once more modified, appears in the Gospel according to St. Luke. And the antagonisms already modified in these two Gospels were finally smoothed into a harmony in the Gospel of St. Mark. Without attempting either detailed examination or criticism of this view, it may be said that it has been rendered quite untenable, when it was shown (by Volkmar) that the Gospel of Marcion was not an original Luke, but our canonical Luke in a form suited to the views of Marcion. As regards the Gospel according to the Hebrews, most critics also consider it a corrupted retranslation of St. Matthew into Hebrew.

Secondly, I have still briefly to notice the theory which speaks of an original Mark. It was propounded in 1838 by Weisse in his *Evangelische Geschichte*. He maintained

---

[1] See the analysis of it in Westcott, *Introduction to the Study of the Gospels*, pp. 470-472.

that the first and third Gospels originated from the second, and from a collection of discourses, to which Papias is supposed to refer. This hypothesis was next developed by the supposition of an *Ur-Markus*. This chiefly by Wilke, and it is represented by Volkmar.

I am not by any means disposed cursorily to set aside this theory. Whatever may be thought of an *Ur-Markus*, it appears to me—alike from its conception, style, and language—that the Gospel by St. Mark is the oldest, as well as the simplest, and, if I may use the expression, the freshest of the three. But I must not here commit myself either to definite statements or strictures, nor even to such remarks as would require a much fuller treatment than I can attempt at present.

The theory in question was adopted and modified by Holtzmann in 1863, in his work *Die Synoptischen Evangelien*. He traces two sources in our Gospels. He considers that the principal of these was the *Ur-Markus*, which he designates A, and which he supposes to have related the deeds of Christ, the miracles, etc. The second he designates Λ', and supposes to have been a collection of discourses by St. Matthew. Our canonical Mark omits a number of things from document A; the two other Gospels have used besides A, also Λ: St. Luke more than St. Matthew. The view of Holtzmann was substantially adopted by Weizsäcker—although he somewhat differently describes the two sources A and Λ. Another slight modification of this view was made by Weiffenbach in his work *Die Papias-Fragmente über Markus und Matthäus*, 1878. Suffice it to say, that he places before the *Ur-Markus* yet another, an *Ur-Ur-Markus*. This original Mark really contained the notes taken by Mark from the preaching of St. Peter—a kind of diary, without chronological order or arrangement. Next, these notes were arranged, and this is the *Ur-Markus*; or, as Weiffenbach calls it: 'the narrative Synoptic foundation-work' ('die erzählende Synoptische Grundschrift'). Thence the canonical Mark was derived, and from the *Ur-Markus*, along with the discourses of St. Matthew, the other two Gospels.

It is this Markus-Hypothesis which Dr. Weltzer subjects to a detailed examination in the work which I am introducing to your notice. He proceeds to do so (1) by a discussion of the import of the well-known testimony of Papias (Euseb. *Hist. Eccl.* iii. 39): (2) by a consideration of what in Germany are called the *Doubletten* in the Gospels, that is, such discourses and narratives as are supposed to appear in one and the same Gospel in a twofold recension. Holtzmann, however, holds that such certainly exist only in three, or at most four, instances, viz.: (*a*) St. Mark iv. 25; *Doubletten* of it: St. Matt. xiii. 12 = St. Luke viii. 18 = St. Matt. xxv. 29 = St. Luke xix. 26; (*b*) St. Mark viii. 34, 35; *Doubletten*: St. Matt. xvi. 24, 25 = St. Luke ix. 23, 24 = St. Matt. x. 38, 39 = St. Luke xiv. 27, 33; (*c*) St. Mark viii. 38; *Doubletten*: St. Matt. xvi. 27 = St. Luke ix. 26 = St. Matt. x. 32, 33 = St. Luke xii. 8, 9; (*d*) St. Mark xiii. 9–13; *Doubletten*: St. Matt. xxiv. 8–14 = St. Luke xxi. 12–19 = St. Matt. x. 17–22 = St. Luke xii. 11, 12. (3) Weltzer considers the theory in connexion with the different quotations from the Old Testament in the Gospels, in answer to the contention that these different modes and kinds of quotation point to the different sources of the Gospels. (4) He discusses at length the reasoning of Holtzmann as to the supposed linguistic peculiarities of the two fundamental documents, A and Λ, which are said to reappear in our canonical Gospels.

I must, in conclusion, refer to the last modification of the Matthew-hypothesis, as being connected with the name of B. Weiss[1], whose writings are so well known. Indeed, his commentaries are little else than an elaborate attempt to prove in detail his theory, that all the Gospels arose out of one 'Apostolic foundation-work' (*Grundschrift*) by St. Matthew—it need scarcely be said, not our canonical Matthew. This *Grundschrift* does not, however, represent a wholly free, original product by St. Matthew, but embodies that type of narration formed in the oldest circle of Apostles. This oldest document was not

---

[1] See the criticism by Beyschlag, in the *Studien und Kritiken* for 1881, p. 571.

merely a collection of discourses, but an account of the most important teachings of Christ and of the most prominent events of His Life. With the help of this fundamental document St. Mark wrote his Gospel, availing himself also besides of communications by St. Peter. By combination of this original document with the canonical Mark the other two Gospels arose—St. Luke being wholly independent of St. Matthew.

The limits of this paper prevent further details. Nor indeed are they necessary, since what has to be said regarding the theory of Wetzel himself can be compressed into short space. Generally speaking, I can only so far agree with Wetzel as that our inquiry should start from what, as it seems to me, is the only stable historical notice we possess in regard to this question: the procemium to St. Luke's Gospel. Wetzel holds the tradition-hypothesis, but in such modified form as, I think, will scarcely recommend itself to your minds. He sets out by stating that, in the primitive Church in Jerusalem, the Hellenists especially knew little of the life and work of Jesus, since they had lived in other countries, and had only become believers on their return to Palestine, or during a visit to it. It was primarily to these Hellenists that one Apostle, either exclusively or principally, gave instruction, in their own tongue, the Greek. This Apostle was Matthew. And this explains why the first Gospel was called after him. Besides, he was best suited for that work, since his former avocations must have rendered him familiar with the Greek. Those who attended his lectures either remained in Jerusalem, or returned to their homes in other lands. Their requirements explain the origin of the written Gospels. The hearers of St. Matthew first asked the Apostle frequently to repeat the principal portions of his lectures. And St. Matthew came to catechize his hearers on the main portions of his narration. A successive stream of hearers gave to these lectures a fixed type. And so St. Matthew came gradually to select, in these lectures, certain portions as the most important, since his hearers could not have retained all in their memories. This selection, presentation, and arrangement of events soon acquired a stereotyped form. Strictly speaking, the Apostle had wished to present a chronological narrative, and in the main he had done so. But, as he could only give his hearers a selection from the material at his command, it was natural that the chronological arrangement should sometimes have been subordinated to that of subjects (*Sach-Ordnung*). Besides, his memory sometimes failed. Hence he had inserted discourses and events, not exactly in their proper succession, but with a view to the best arrangement of the subject, and not without frequent variations of order. What the Apostle taught, that his hearers learnt—sometimes by heart (as, for example, the Lord's Prayer), at other times by taking notes of it. In this manner various Gospel-narratives came into circulation. Three out of their number (the 'many' to which St. Luke refers) deserved to be permanent. These are our Synoptic Gospels. Substantially they are the lectures of St. Matthew, but they also contain additions from other sources. Thus the history of the Infancy in the first and third Gospels—which is not related by St. Mark—was taken from other, and, as compared among themselves, diverging sources. Otherwise also St. Luke sometimes derived his narrative from other sources than the lectures which he had attended, preferring, for reasons not stated, those sources of information. Thus the lectures of St. Matthew, committed to memory, or notes taken by the hearers, together with subsidiary sources of information, constituted the materials of which our canonical Gospels are composed—and among them that of St. Mark is the simplest and oldest.

Such is the theory of Dr. Wetzel, which I have undertaken to lay before you as being the latest contribution on the subject. But, while fully acknowledging the care and learning of its author, it scarcely seems to require detailed criticism at our hands.

V.

A COMMENTARY
ON THE GOSPELS ATTRIBUTED TO
THEOPHILUS OF ANTIOCH.

[W. SANDAY.]

Zahn, Dr. Theodor, *Forschungen zur Geschichte des Neutestamentlichen Kanons*. II. Theil: *Der Evangelien-commentar des Theophilus von Antiochica*, Erlangen, 1883. III. Theil, Beilage iii, *Nachträge zu Theophilus*, 1884. Harnack, Dr. Adolf, *Texte und Untersuchungen zur Geschichte der altchristlichen Literatur*: I. Band, Heft iv, *Der angebliche Evangeliencommentar des Theophilus von Antiochien*.

THE paper[1] that follows is an attempt to present briefly, to English students of early Christian literature, some of the main points in a controversy which has recently arisen, and is still being prosecuted with great activity, between two of the most eminent of the scholars who are working at that field in Germany. The limits of space at my disposal will, I fear, make it difficult for me to do justice to the learning and closeness of reasoning which are displayed in equal measure on both sides. Dr. Zahn's argument especially is liable to suffer by compression. His own complaint[2] has truth in it, that the kind of points that he urges are not to be judged off hand on the strength of the superficial knowledge derived from compendiums of Church history or doctrine. Where the early growth and first germinal appearance of ideas are concerned, a bald abstract must needs dispense with those qualifications and gradations which make a proposition rea-

---

[1] It should perhaps be explained that this paper was read, at rather short notice, as the first of the series, when the scale and character of the Essays were still matter of experiment. It has been slightly altered, so as to include a reference to Dr. Zahn's second article, which has since appeared.

[2] *Forschungen*, iii. p. 231.

sonable and defensible that otherwise would not be so. I
cannot conceal my belief that Dr. Zahn is fighting a losing
cause. I think that he has been led away by something of
the eagerness of discovery; and it is natural that he should
hold tenaciously a position to which he has once been committed. But I believe, at the same time, that he had a case
in the first instance that was quite worth stating. I do not
doubt that his arguments are put forward in perfectly good
faith; they are stated with much ability, and with a
thoroughness and closeness that I am afraid is not common
in English controversy. The one thing that is really to be
regretted is that in its later phases so much heat should have
been imported into a discussion that ought to proceed quite
objectively. We are all liable to error; and so long as work
is sound and honest it reflects no discredit that some one else
should find out two or three new facts or hit upon a new
train of argument that upsets our own conclusions. Both
the disputants may be assured that in England, at least, our
respect for them is too firmly established to need support — which indeed it does not receive — from personal
recriminations.

Theophilus of Antioch is one of the precursors of that
group of writers who, from Irenaeus to Cyprian, not only
break the obscurity which rests on the earliest history of the
Christian Church, but, alike in the East and in the West,
carry it to the front in literary eminence and distance all their
heathen contemporaries. The contribution which Theophilus himself makes to this body of literature is not great.
Eusebius[1], and after him Jerome[2], tell us that he wrote a
book against Marcion and one against the heresy of Hermogenes, both of which are lost. A third treatise, in three
books, addressed to Autolycus has been preserved, and is
that from which our knowledge of the writer is chiefly
derived[3]. But besides these Jerome speaks of Commentaries

---

[1] *H. E.* iv. 20 f.   [2] *D. Vir. Ill.* 25.
[3] The doubts as to the identity of the author of these works, raised by Dod-

on the Song of Songs and on 'the Gospel,' which he regarded as inferior to the other works in elegance and diction.

Now a Commentary bearing the name of Theophilus of Antioch was published, in 1576, in vol. v. of the *Magna Bibliotheca Veterum Patrum*, by Margarin de la Bigne. The Commentary was in Latin, and therefore purported to be a translation. No account was given of the MS. from which the text was taken. And from that day to this, though diligent search has been made for it, the MS. has not been found. There is, however, no suspicion attaching to De la Bigne. He undoubtedly had before him a real text, which he has reproduced with a fair degree of accuracy.

A proof that the text had not been largely tampered with is seen in the treatment of the ancient headings of the four books into which the Commentary is divided. The heading of Book I is this: *S. P. nostri Theophili patriarchae Antiocheni commentariorum sive allegoriarum in sacra quatuor Evangelia*. But the heading of Book II passes from Theophilus of Antioch, whose date is 170–180 A.D., to his better-known namesake, the contemporary and bitter opponent of Chrysostom, who was bishop of Alexandria in 385–412: *S. P. nostri Theophili, archiepiscopi Alexandrini, allegoriarum in Evangelium secundum Marcum liber secundus*. And the like heading is kept, *mutatis mutandis*, for the next two books dealing with the two remaining Gospels. Zahn and Harnack agree in inferring from this that the *patriarchae Antiocheni* in the heading of the first book is a critical correction on the part of the editor, based upon his knowledge of the mention of certain Commentaries of Theophilus of Antioch by Jerome.

This brings us to the next step in the process by which the Commentary came to be attributed to Theophilus of Antioch. The direct evidence clearly counts for little or nothing. But it was upon the indirect evidence that Dr. Zahn took his stand.

well and revived by Erbes, seem to be sufficiently answered by Harnack (*Texte u. Untersuch.* i. p. 287 ff.).

Jerome not only mentions Commentaries by Theophilus of Antioch three times over, but on one occasion (*Ep.* 121 *ad Algasiam*) he quotes from the book at some length. His quotation is an exposition of the parable of the Unjust Steward, which he introduces thus: *Theophilus Antiochenae ecclesiae septimus post Petrum apostolum episcopus, qui quatuor Evangelistarum in unum opus dicta compingens, ingenii sui monumenta dimisit, haec super hac parabola in suis commentariis est locutus.* Now the passage which Jerome quotes reappears in the Commentary published by De la Bigne. This may be set down as the first fact of real significance.

Dr. Zahn took hold of a further point in the description just given of Theophilus' Commentary. Jerome speaks of its author as *quatuor Evangelistarum in unum opus dicta compingens*: and Dr. Zahn tries to show that this description corresponds to the phenomena of the printed Commentary, contending that what is implied is not so much that Theophilus first constructed a Harmony of the Gospels and then commented upon it, as that he took texts from each in somewhat irregular order. Here perhaps we may not be quite able to follow him.

But in another direction he seemed to be more successful. On the occasion to which I have referred Jerome quotes from the Commentary with distinct acknowledgment. But on examination it is found that there are a number of other passages in which the language of Jerome coincided with that of the Commentary, but without anything to show that he was quoting from a previous writer. Nor was Jerome the only writer who stood to the Commentary in this relation. Similar coincidences were found with a number of other writers, most plentifully with Arnobius junior, a Gallican presbyter or possibly bishop, about whom not very much is known, but who is set down as having lived at a date not earlier than 460 A.D.

In all these parallelisms there is no external mark of quotation, either in the printed Commentary or in the writer with whom the coincidence occurs, to show on which side the priority lay. Neither the Commentator on the one hand, nor Jerome or Arnobius on the other, made any confession of borrowing. In other words, it seemed to be a case of what we should call simple plagiarism. And the question arose, Who was the plagiarist? Previously to Dr. Zahn the current opinion had been that the Commentator wrote in the sixth century, and borrowed freely from his predecessors. Dr. Zahn undertook to show that the reverse was really the case; and he tried, by an elaborate comparison of the passages, to prove that the priority was on the side of the Commentator. Arguments of this kind are always delicate and difficult to bring to a positive conclusion. There were, however, some points that struck me as being in Dr. Zahn's favour.

In the first place I was quite prepared to believe in any degree of what we should call 'plagiarism' on the part both of Jerome and the other ecclesiastical writers in question. There is abundant evidence that the state of opinion on such a point was very different in ancient times from what it is now. That a writer should borrow from his predecessors was the natural thing rather than otherwise. And it did not by any means always follow that the borrowing would be acknowledged.

I was therefore quite ready to admit that Jerome, Ambrose, Arnobius, and the rest, might have drawn upon some older Commentary without naming it. And, on the other hand, there seemed a certain *prima facie* probability that the work printed by De la Bigne was that Commentary. Here we had only two alternatives. Either it was the original work at the base of all these later writers, or else it was a wholesale compilation. But not a word was said, either by way of introduction or incidentally, admitting any kind or degree of compilation. If the Commentary was not an original work, as it seemed to profess to be, then it could only be set down as a very bare-faced production.

I was somewhat loth to adopt this conclusion. But, without following Dr. Zahn through all his proofs, some of the instances quoted seemed to tell more or less distinctly against it. The coincidences were most abundant with Latin writers, Jerome, Ambrose, Hilary, Juvencus, not to speak of later writers, like Bede. But there were some coincidences also with the Greeks.

'Why,' the supposed Theophilus asks[1], 'was not Christ conceived by a simple virgin, but by one already betrothed?' And he gives four reasons. 'First, in order that the descent of Mary might be exhibited by the genealogy of Joseph (*ut per generationem Joseph origo Mariae monstraretur*); secondly, that she might not be stoned by the Jews as an adulteress; thirdly, that on her flight into Egypt she might have the solace of a husband; fourthly, that her birth-giving might escape the devil, by leading him to suppose that Jesus was born from a married woman and not from a virgin.' This fourth reason is ascribed by Jerome to Ignatius. It is found in other writers. And Basil the Great expressly gives it as proceeding from one of the 'ancients.' Similarly Origen, in his *Homilies on St. Luke*, refers to one of the πρεσβύτεροι an interpretation of the parable of the Good Samaritan, which Dr. Zahn contends to be that of Theophilus. His words in the Latin version are, *aiebat quidam de presbyteris volens parabolam interpretari.* And the two interpretations, though not identical, seem to be sufficiently near: the priest and Levite are (practically) the Law and the Prophets; the Samaritan is Christ. But the passage which, I confess, carried most weight with me was one in which the Commentary presented an almost *verbatim* coincidence with a letter of Cyprian's. The comment was on the words of institution in the Last Supper: Hic est corpus meum. *Corpus suum panem dicens, de multorum granorum adunatione congestum, populum suum quem assumpsit indicat adunatum.* Hic est calix sanguinis mei. *Sanguinem suum vinum appellans, de botris atque acinis plurimis expressum et in unum coactum, item congregationem nostram significat commixtione adunatae mul-*

[1] On Matt. i. 18 Zahn, *Forschungen* ii. p. 32 ff.

titudinis copulatam[1]. With this is to be compared Cyprian, *Ep.* 69 *ad Magnum*, c. 5: *Nam quando Dominus corpus suum panem vocat de multorum granorum adunatione congestum, populum nostrum quem portabat indicat adunatum: et quando sanguinem suum vinum appellat de botruis atque acinis plurimis expressum atque in unum coactum, gregem item nostrum significat commixtione adunatae multitudinis copulatum.*

Here there could of course be no doubt that we have a direct transcription of one writer by the other. And in asking oneself which had the priority it seemed natural to bear in mind the character of the composition in each case. The passage in Cyprian occurs in the course of a letter, dealing not directly with any question of interpretation, but with the question whether baptism by the followers of Novatian ought or ought not to be repeated. But on the face of it it seemed more probable that, in an exposition of Scripture coming in thus incidentally, the writer of a letter should quote from a Commentary than that a commentator should set down, without any hint of quotation, an extract from a letter. It might also be thought that the expression *populum quem assumpsit* bore a greater appearance of originality than the less intelligible and indeed rather curious *quem portabat* of Cyprian.

But *prima facie* probabilities, as this discussion tends to show, will only carry us a short way. When we turn to the parallel to which Dr. Zahn, with his usual combination of candour and learning (for a little onesidedness in reasoning is quite compatible with complete straightforwardness in the presentation of facts), himself directs us, viz. Cypr. *Ep.* 63 *ad Caecilium*, c. 13, where not only is *portabat* repeated and enlarged upon, but almost identical phraseology is used in reference to the mixing of the chalice, *quando autem in calice vino aqua miscetur, Christo populus adunatur et credentium plebs ei in quem credidit adunatur et jungitur;* though the possibility of suggestion from without

[1] Zahn, *Forschungen*, ii. p. 62.

still remains, it becomes more natural to suppose that Cyprian is working out a thought of his own; and all that we should have to assume would be a greater diligence on the part of the author of the Commentary in seeking matter for his compilation, and a little greater skill in adapting the matter so found to his purpose.

However, this is an after-thought. For the moment I contented myself with noting the coincidence, and I confess that it gave a certain bias to my judgment in favour of the Commentary. I was therefore all the more glad to find, on paying a farewell visit to the Bishop of Durham, that he too leant to a similar conclusion. That Dr. Zahn had proved his whole case that the Commentary was by Theophilus, he did not think, but he was prepared to regard it as probable that Jerome, Ambrose, Arnobius, and the rest, were quoting from the Commentary rather than the Commentary from them; in other words, that it was an early and original work.

This was the kind of view that I was inclined to hold in Sept. 1883, and I proposed to myself to test it in three ways: (1) by a more careful examination of the coincidences with early writers, such as Cyprian and Origen; (2) by trying to ascertain how far the Commentary possessed that character of unity which Dr. Zahn claimed for it, and which quite upon the surface, though with some exceptions, it seemed to possess; and (3) by examining more in detail the characteristics of the Biblical text which the Commentary presented.

The materials for this last inquiry had been laboriously collected by Dr. Zahn; and it might have had some interest, as tending to show to what stage in the history of the Latin text of the Gospels the Commentary, as it has come down to us, really belonged [1].

But whatever might have been the result of these inves-

---

[1] There are a few coincidences with *a* and *c*, both of which represent early types of text, but a reading like *primus* in Matt. xxi. 31 (Zahn, *Forschungen*, ii. p. 204) is most suspicious: the mass of Old Latin MSS. have *novissimus*, and *primus* is only found in *c*, *f*, and the printed Vulgate, which have all been corrected by comparison with the Greek.

tigations—and in the light of what we now know they could hardly have been very favourable—there would still have remained some serious difficulties in the way of accepting Dr. Zahn's hypothesis. He indeed grapples with them bravely and does his best to minimise their significance, but when all was said a stubborn residuum still remained.

The difficulties in question took the shape of apparent anachronisms. *Margarita pretiosa est trinitas sancta, quae dividi non potest, nam in unitate consistit.* The genuine Theophilus *ad Autolycum* used the term τριάς, and for the stress upon the idea of unity Zahn seeks parallels not only in the Dionysii of Rome and Alexandria, but in Clement, Tertullian, and Athenagoras.

Per caecum naturaliter non videntem et illuminatum significat humanum genus originali peccato detentum . . . ut illuminationem nostram auctori imputemus potius quam naturae. Such expressions have a suspicious ring of Augustinianism about them, which Dr. Zahn tries to lessen by quoting *originis vitium* from Tertullian.

Lapides pro paganis ait propter cordis duritiam; and *celeriter ite ad gentes, hoc est paganos.* Here *pagani* are said to stand for 'dwellers in the country,' 'rustic, uncultivated people.'

But strongest perhaps of all is the comment on Luke xvii. 34: *In lecto esse monachos significat qui amant quietem, alieni a tumultu generis humani et domino servientes, inter quos sunt boni et mali.*

It is no doubt interesting to know that in Ps. lxviii. 6 (A.V. 'God setteth the solitary in families') Symmachus translates the word for 'solitary' by μοναχοί, the LXX by μονότροποι, Aquila by μονόζωτοι, and to know further that Eusebius, in commenting upon the passage, speaks of these μοναχοί as forming a special τάγμα by the side of widows and orphans on the one hand, and prisoners on the other, while he finds a special application for each of the other renderings—because they are few they are μονογενεῖς; because their lives are uniform μονότροποι; because they are solitary μονήρεις; and because they wear a peculiar kind of girdle μονόζωνοι. It is interesting too to have it pointed out that Aphraates, writing in A.D. 337, has a somewhat similar description, but with less emphasis on the important particular of 'solitariness.' Instances like these may tend to throw back the beginnings of Monasticism to an earlier date than that at which we have been accustomed to place them. Or it is possible that the word μοναχοί may be used in a wider sense than the technical one.

A single difficulty of this kind might perhaps be got over, if very strong reasons could be shown on the other side; but four such phrases as *trinitas quae dividi non potest, originale peccatum, pagani, monachi*, must be allowed to be exceedingly formidable. And there are yet others.

It was natural that Dr. Harnack, in his searching reply to his former colleague, should insist strongly upon these anachronisms. But they do not constitute the whole of his argument. He contests the ground all along the line, and it must be confessed with marked ability. Dr. Zahn would say that our ignorance as well as our knowledge makes for the negative conclusion—that we assume that ideas and designations do not exist at a time previous to that at which we are ourselves familiar with them. Something may be deducted on that score, but not so much as is required. There is always a great temptation to controversialists to lose sight of the proportion in things. And Dr. Zahn, it is to be feared, has succumbed to that temptation. Carried away by zeal for his subject—a most honest and singleminded zeal, to which his learning has supplied abundant fuel—he has pursued fine and subtle reasonings to such an extent that the plain and simple indications have dropped out of sight. But with the average reader it is just these plain and simple indications that tell most strongly. And in criticism, as in life, they are the safest guide to follow.

Upon the whole, then, it appeared that Dr. Harnack had distinctly the best of the argument. The probabilities on his side were by far the more definite and tangible. But he was able in an appendix to throw a yet more decisive weight into the scale. Seldom, indeed, has a controversy culminated so rapidly, and seldom has a literary argument received such opportune and such striking confirmation. The preface to Zahn's volume is dated February 1883, and Harnack's reply was already written when on May 19th he received a communication from the director of the Royal Library at Brussels, which altered at a stroke the whole complexion of the problem. This was nothing less than the description of a MS. which proved to contain the very Commentary that was the subject of discussion. The MS. claimed to have been written at the instance of a certain Nomedius, who is known to have been Abbot of the Monastery of Soissons in the years 695–711; so that the MS. itself would belong to the extreme end of the seventh or beginning of the eighth century. It was not, however, the MS. from which De la Bigne had taken his *editio princeps*. It contained just what that MS. apparently wanted—the preface, in which the nature and origin of the Commentary were explained. In an elaborate phraseology, borrowed largely from Virgil, the writer compares himself to a bee which collected its honey from flowers of every kind. 'So I,' he says, 'a servant of the Lord, at your instigation have composed a spiritual work culled from the commentators (*tractatoribus defloratis opusculum spiritale composui*), a work to bring forth an ecclesiastical swarm, avoiding, like Grynæan yews, the bitter speeches of the envious. There is in it too nectar of sweetest taste caused by breath divine[1].' It seems impossible to put on this any other construction. The work is evidently composed in the most complete good faith. The compiler makes no secret of his method. If the writers of an older age are rifled of their sweets it is only that he may fill his cells with honey that he offers for the use of his contemporaries. He is careful to avoid the deadly heretical yew, but from the nectar

---

[1] *Texte*, etc., I. iv. 166 f.

that he has stored he hopes to feed and send forth a swarm of busy ecclesiastical bees.

An ounce of fact is worth a pound of theory; and this unlooked-for contribution of fact seemed as if it must put a stop to all further debate. One was tempted to go a little further down in the passage from the Georgics that the nameless editor who had given rise to so much speculation had in his mind, and see there a summary of this battle of the critics. *Hi motus animorum*—for there were even then some *motus animorum*!

> '*Hi motus animorum atque haec certamina tanta*
> *Pulveris exigui jactu compressa quiescunt.*'

But no! the thought would have been premature! The indefatigable Zahn has now brought out a third part of his series of *Forschungen*, dealing mainly with that very interesting subject of investigation—the fragmentary traces of the *Hypotyposes* of Clement of Alexandria; and in a long appendix he returns to the charge about Theophilus. It cannot be said that the *motus animorum* are assuaged; on the contrary, the heat of the combat has become such as to call forth a solemn protest from his opponent in the columns of the *Theologische Literaturzeitung*, and the old position, not very greatly contracted, is still maintained with stubborn resolution. One concession is made independently of the Brussels MS. Ten passages are identified as borrowed from Eucherius, Bishop of Lyons (c. 434–450). These passages Dr. Zahn allows to have the priority as compared with the Commentary, from the main body of which he believes them to be separated by certain characteristic differences. Whereas the coincidences with Ambrose, Jerome, and Augustine are often very free, those with Eucherius are close and exact. One of the passages is introduced by an *item aliter* (= ἄλλως, ἄλλου), which is common enough in *Catenae*, but is not found elsewhere in the Commentary. They occur in groups near each other. They deal with dogmatic questions such as were current in the time of Eucherius, and are not allegorising

Scholia like the rest of the Commentary. And, lastly, they stand alone, without any other attestation to make an earlier origin for them probable.

These sections then, and two others of less importance which he is not able exactly to identify, Dr. Zahn sets down to an interpolator some time between A. D. 450–700, leaving open the question how much further the added matter may extend. He then throws out the suggestion that the interpolator may be also the author of the preface in the Brussels MS. If so it would be an inaccurate and verbose but yet a recognisable (?) description of his procedure, and the bulk of the Commentary would still be vindicated for Theophilus.

Dr. Zahn reiterates, expands, and augments with fresh detail, a number of his previous arguments, thoroughly to test and examine all of which would require a diligence equal to his own. But meantime the old difficulties *pagani, monachi, peccatum originale,* stick in one's throat. And these, taken together with the admission as to Eucherius and the precarious nature of the distinction which it is sought to establish between the acknowledged interpolations and the rest of the Commentary, may be held to justify us in taking the Brussels preface literally as it stands, and adopting the compilation theory as at least the simplest and easiest hypothesis. I am not aware of any phenomena that stand seriously in the way of it.

VI.

THE TEXT OF THE CODEX ROSSANENSIS (Σ).

[W. Sanday.]

Gebhardt, Oscar von, *Texte und Untersuchungen zur Geschichte der altchristlichen Literatur;* I. Band, Heft iv, *Die Evangelien des Matthaeus und des Marcus aus dem Codex Purpureus Rossanensis,* Leipzig, 1883.

SOME three (four) years ago there appeared a sumptuous volume[1], by the eminent critics O. von Gebhardt and A. Harnack, containing the description of an ancient MS. of the sixth century, hitherto unused in editions of the Greek New Testament, and lost to sight and knowledge in the Cathedral Library of the town of Rossano in Calabria, not very far from the site of ancient Sybaris. The description of which I speak was, however, especially tantalising to the textual critic, because it was confined to the external characteristics of the MS. and said very little about the text. It is true that externally the MS. presented features in their way of considerable interest. In the first place it was one—and if not quite the largest, probably on the whole the most important—of several extant specimens of the *Codd. Purpurei* of the Greek Bible. These MSS. had their vellum dyed purple, and the letters seem to have been written upon it with a chemical preparation of silver and gold[2]. Jerome speaks scornfully of these purple codices as a kind of *éditions de luxe,* which he would leave for his opponents to prize for the magnificence of their outward appearance, while he himself

---

[1] *Evangeliorum Codex Purpureus Rossanensis,* Leipzig, 1880.
[2] Dr. Scrivener (*Introd.* p. 25, ed. 3) says 'stamped rather than written;' but see Gardthausen, *Griechische Palaeographie,* p. 84 f.

was content with a poorer material, if only it offered (as his own translation did offer) a purer text (*Praef. in lib. Job, ad fin.*): a maxim which, by the way, might with advantage have been taken to heart by some modern editors of Biblical MSS. The practice must from this have attained considerable dimensions in the time of Jerome. Most of the extant examples date from the sixth century. After that date they become rare in the East, which observed a greater sobriety in such matters than the West. Three of the most important MSS. of the Old Latin, *b* (Cod. Veronensis), *c* (Cod. Palatinus), *f* (Cod. Brixianus), and the famous Cod. Argenteus of the Gothic version are written in this way. Under Charlemagne and his successors silver and gold were lavishly used, but the purple dye more sparingly: in the Cod. Aureus at Stockholm alternate leaves are purple.

More important still, from the same external point of view, is a collection of miniatures, at the beginning of the volume, representing scenes from the close of our Lord's earthly ministry, beginning with the raising of Lazarus and ending with the scene in which our Lord and His accusers both appear before Pilate. After the Agony in the Garden are interpolated, in the present order, the healing of the man born blind (St. John ix), and the Good Samaritan; so that it is clear in any case that the present order is not original. And it is highly probable that Gebhardt and Harnack are right in supposing that the miniatures still preserved are only the remains of a larger collection, the rest of which have been lost. The miniatures are said to present a close resemblance to some of the mosaics at Ravenna (p. xxvii). There is only one other Biblical MS., and that also a Codex Purpureus (of Genesis, at Vienna), which contains illustrations of the same date—the sixth century. And the scarcity of these forms of art at this period gives them an additional value.

This date, the sixth century, seems to be generally accepted, so far as the information at present accessible allows, by the scholars who have examined the subject. A more precise definition may perhaps be possible, but will require a renewed examination of the MS. It is worth notice that the additional matter, the *Ep. ad Carpianum*, the κεφάλαια, etc., which the MS. contains, are written though in the same hand, in smaller characters, differing, as it would appear, somewhat considerably from the main body of the text. A similar phenomenon was observed by Tregelles in the Catena which accompanies the Codex Zacynthius (Ξ). It is found also in Cod. Guelpherbytanus I (P. Gospp.). And the beginnings of something of the same kind may be seen in the Cod. Alexandrinus, where the subscriptions to St. Matthew and St. Mark and the superscription of the latter Gospel are said to be different in style from the body of the text, though they also are probably by the same hand.

It was not, however, my intention to go particularly into these points of external description. I will only therefore summarise them briefly by saying that the MS. is written in uncial letters of silver (the three opening lines of each Gospel in gold) on a purple ground, the colour, especially on the smooth side of the leaf, being for the most part well preserved. It consists of 188 leaves of fine vellum, containing the Gospels of St. Matthew and St. Mark, damaged towards the end of the latter Gospel and ending at Mark xvi. 14 (it therefore possesses the disputed verses). The sheets are arranged in quinions (like B), with original signatures in silver uncials at the lower right hand corner[1]. The present dimensions are 30.7 centim. ($13\frac{1}{2}$ in. Scrivener) high by 26 centim. ($10\frac{1}{4}$ in.) broad. The writing is in two columns of 20 lines to a column and 9–12 letters to a line. The MS. has the Epistle of Eusebius to Carpianus, containing an account of the use of the canons which follow; a table of the Eusebian Canons; the so-called Ammonian sections, and the Eusebian Canons noted in the margin; a table of κεφάλαια or longer sections,

---

[1] There are two rather important misprints in Scrivener's account of the MS. (Introd. p. 158, ed. 3). It ends at Mark xvi. 14, not xiv. 14; and the gatherings are quinions, not quaternions.

and headings corresponding to the κεφάλαια at the top of the page. It is illuminated and mutilated; its designation is Σ.

And now to come to the inside of the MS. and the character of its text, which is the subject more especially before me. Our curiosity in respect to this has been only recently satisfied. The editors hoped, when they brought out the first instalment of their description of the MS., to have an opportunity of inspecting it at leisure either in Rome or Naples. Failing this, they were prepared to return to Rossano. And Von Gebhardt set out thither in the spring of 1882, taking with him an artist to reproduce the miniatures and a photographer from Naples to reproduce both the miniatures and specimens of the writing. His disappointment may be imagined when, upon his arrival at Rossano, all access to the MS. was refused him on the pretext that the Chapter themselves were about to publish a complete edition of it. Considering that this learned body, of some forty-eight persons, did not even know in what language the MS. was written, the prospect of an edition brought out under their auspices is not very encouraging. And the world at large would doubtless have been better pleased to see it in the practised hands of the two German scholars. Perhaps the uncomfortable disclosure just mentioned may have had something to do with the refusal. At any rate, it is to be hoped that higher influences may intervene to prevent the work being carried out by altogether incompetent persons or deferred till the Greek Kalends. But in the meantime there was nothing for it but that Von Gebhardt and his cavalcade must return with their purpose unaccomplished. And, as a consequence, we have now to be content with the original collation made by Von Gebhardt and Harnack at their first visit, hurriedly indeed, but with as much care as time permitted. The text of the MS. is printed from the collation in the third issue of the *Texte und Untersuchungen*.

I have not had time to examine with any care more than the readings of the first ten chapters of St. Matthew, and just those sections of the latter half of the Gospel which Σ (Rossanensis) has in common with its fellow purple MS. N (fragments at London, Rome, Vienna, and Patmos). But this examination, together with the classified collection of readings given by Von Gebhardt in his introduction to the text of the MS., will enable us to form a sufficient idea of its general character.

Turning, then, to the beginning of St. Matthew's Gospel, we observe at once that our MS. has the ordinary spelling of the proper names, Βούζ, 'Ωβήδ, 'Ασά, 'Αμών, and not Βοές with ℵ B k (Bobiensis) and the Egyptian versions, 'Ιωβήδ with ℵ B C* Δ Egyptt. Aeth. Arm., or the very peculiar 'Ασάφ of ℵ B C (D in Luke iii.) Egyptt. etc., and 'Αμώς of the same list of authorities somewhat strengthened. It has Σολομῶντα (v. 6) with Δ and a few others, as against Σολομῶνα, not only of the best, but of a majority of the MSS. After Δαυείδ δέ it inserts ὁ βασιλεύς with the mass of the MSS. and Textus Receptus, against ℵ B Γ, Egyptt. Cur. Pesh., k of the Old Latin, and others. In fact, so far as the genealogy is concerned, it presents a thoroughly commonplace text, relieved only by a single reading, which does not at all redound to its credit, the insertion of the name 'Ιωακίμ in v. 11, 'Ιωσίας δὲ ἐγγέννησεν [τὸν 'Ιωακίμ. 'Ιωακὶμ δὲ ἐγγέννησεν] τὸν 'Ιεχονίαν, which is obviously put in to make good an apparent defect in the genealogy; and besides that it does not tally with the express statement that the genealogy contained only fourteen generations between David and the Babylonian Captivity, is only supported by a quite weak body of authorities, M U and others, with the two later Syriac versions. In v. 18, however, Σ has γένεσις with the older MSS., against γέννησις of E K L and the later ones. But this is the solitary spark of originality throughout the chapter. In the insertion of γάρ after μνηστευθείσης, in the compounds παρα-δειγματίσαι and δι-εγερθείς, and in the insertion of τὸν [υἱὸν] αὐτῆς τὸν πρωτότοκον it keeps in the most beaten of beaten tracks.

A similar character is observed throughout chap. ii. The order Ἡρώδης ὁ βασιλεύς in v. 3, ἔστη for ἐστάθη in v. 9, ὑπό for διά Ἱερεμίου in v. 17, the insertion of θρῆνος καί before κλαυθμός in the quotation that follows, and the form Ναζαρέθ all duly appear. In one point φαίνεται κατ᾽ ὄναρ in v. 19 Σ goes with ℵ B D Z and the older versions against the later authorities, and in v. 22 it omits ἐπί (in the phrase βασιλεύει ἐπὶ τῆς Ἰουδαίας) with ℵ B, some cursives, and Eusebius.

In chap. iii, of the readings I have noted eight agree with the common text, while ποταμῷ is inserted after Ἰορδάνῃ (in v. 6) with ℵ B C* M Δ in what the strong attestation proves to be a right reading, though otherwise it might be suspected, and in v. 8 καρπὸν ἄξιον is read instead of καρποὺς ἀξίους of the Textus Receptus, but only with the great majority both of MSS. and versions.

It will be observed in the last chapter that Σ stumbles just as a commonplace MS. may be expected to stumble. It completes what seem to be defective expressions, adding αὐτοῦ after ἡ τροφή, τὸ βάπτισμα. It fills in the missing proper name ὁ δὲ Ἰωάννης, for the sake of clearness. It removes an asyndeton in v. 2, and substitutes καί for a rather tautological δέ in v. 16. The same sort of phenomena may be observed persistently. In chap. iv. there is an insertion of ὁ Ἰησοῦς just of this character, ἵστησιν and λέγει assimilated to surrounding presents in vv. 5, 9, and ἐπὶ [παντὶ ῥήματι] substituted for ἐν because of ἐπ᾽ ἄρτῳ preceding. To the credit side may be placed the insertion of an article before ἄνθρωπος and omission of a superfluous subject in v. 18, but in each case with overwhelming authority. When Σ is right it takes care, as a rule, to have a substantial backing.

In the Sermon on the Mount it has increased opportunities of going wrong with the multitude, and it makes good use of them. Here are some of its more conspicuous blots. I can only regard in this light the insertion of the Doxology after the Lord's Prayer, against the general consent of all authorities older than the fourth century, with the exception of the Old

Syriac, the Thebaic or version of Upper Egypt and *k* of the Old Latin, the last two in variant forms. We must now add the *Doctrine of the Twelve Apostles*, but also with a variation. Without wishing to underrate this last accession to the evidence, it cannot be held to counterbalance the great preponderance of ante-Nicene authority. The long insertion in v. 44 from the parallel passage in St. Luke naturally finds a place. Glosses like [πᾶν πονηρὸν] ῥῆμα and ἐλεημοσύνην for δικαιοσύνην in vi. 1 are adopted. Additions like ἐν τῷ φανερῷ in vi. 4, 6 come in to heighten the antithesis; and the various corrections of style by which the later text is characterized are almost all represented. It is noticeable that one reading, ἀντιμετρηθήσεται for μετρηθήσεται in vii. 2, found in Σ, though it has gained a footing in the Textus Receptus, has only cursives and some Old Latin MSS. in its favour. Here, as in a number of other cases, Σ heads the list for the debased text.

Summing up the result for the three chapters Matt. v–vii, I find that there are thirty-six places in which Σ joins the Textus Receptus in what is probably a wrong reading. There are several instances in which Σ joins a long array of weightier authorities in deserting the Textus Receptus. In v. 39 it strikes out a bolder course, ὅστις σε ῥαπίζει (pres.) εἰς (for ἐπὶ) τὴν δεξιὰν σιαγόνα. For the first two variations from the Textus Receptus Σ is allied with ℵ B alone of uncials. For σιαγόνα, without σου, it has the solitary support of ℵ (with cursives and some MSS. of the Old Latin). Again in the reading προσέχετε δέ in vi. 1, Σ joins a small group, ℵ L Z 33, Memphitic version, which I see is followed (with δέ in single brackets) by Westcott and Hort. On the surface one might have been disposed to set it down as rather an Alexandrine correction of style by removing the asyndeton. In vii. 9, 10 ὃν ἐὰν αἰτήσῃ followed by καὶ ἐὰν αἰτήσει, Σ has just stopped short of adopting the whole of the amended text: αἰτήσει is a single relic of the original reading. In the narrative verses at the end of chap. vii. Σ has rightly the simple verb ἐτέλεσεν and οἱ γραμματεῖς αὐτῶν, but in both cases with a strong backing.

The audacity of v. 39 and vi. 1 has no other parallel in these chapters.

The remaining chapters, viii–x, offer merely a repetition of the same phenomena. Faults of the kind already noticed are plentiful, especially supplementary and explanatory insertions. Once or twice, as in viii. 32 ἡ ἀγέλη without τῶν χοίρων, and ix. 13 ἁμαρτωλούς without the addition of εἰς μετάνοιαν, the temptation has been resisted. But in these cases there is a strong supporting phalanx in the background. The same, or nearly the same, holds good of the two other most important right readings which Σ presents in these chapters, Γαδαρηνῶν in viii. 28, and ἐσκυλμένοι καὶ ἐριμμένοι in ix. 36.

It is hardly necessary to go into further detail. A precisely similar character pervades all the later sections that I have examined. And it is abundantly confirmed by the instances collected by Von Gebhardt. The latter gives several interesting lists. First, two, containing in all some 86 distinct readings, in which Σ is in error with little or no support. Then a list in which Σ joins what had hitherto been singular or subsingular readings of ℵ 11 times in the two Gospels, of C 20 times, of D 16 times, of Δ 10 times, and of Φ, the hypothetical uncial which forms the common stock of the cursives 13, 69, 124, 346, 13 times. In this company the other cursives 1, 28, 33, 81, 157 are often included. Besides, 1 is in agreement twice, 33 and 157 each four times, either alone or with a few other subordinate authorities.

Next Von Gebhardt works out a problem which is of special interest. I have said that the MS. which presents the closest external resemblance to Σ is N, the other leading Codex Purpureus of the Greek Testament. It is therefore an obvious question to ask, How are they also related as regards their text? The answer is not uncertain. The two MSS. have the closest resemblance. N, it will be remembered, is a series of fragments amounting in all to about 334 verses in the Gospels of St. Matthew and St. Mark. In these there are as many as thirty-three hitherto singular readings of N in which Σ joins. And there are thirty-four others in which N and Σ go together, not indeed alone, but with little further support. From these instances Von Gebhardt justly infers that the two MSS. are near descendants of the same common exemplar. In fact he thinks that both may have been copied from it directly.

Lastly, he gives a list of readings in which Σ joins with a comparatively small group of the oldest MSS. These are in all fifty-two for the whole two Gospels with 1749 verses, which certainly cannot be considered a large proportion. Perhaps the most interesting of these readings are: in St. Matthew viii. 28 Γαδαρηνῶν just mentioned, with B C* M and virtually ℵ* Δ, the graphic ἐπέσπειρεν for ἔσπειρεν in the parable of the Wheat and the Tares with ℵ^b B alone of uncials (well supported, however, by the Latin authorities and Fathers), Ἰωσήφ for Ἰωσῆς or Ἰωάννης as the name of our Lord's brother in xiii. 55, κακῶς ἔχει for κακῶς πάσχει with ℵ B L Z in xvii. 15, οἰκετείας for θεραπείας with B I L and others in xxiv. 45. In St. Mark iv. 21, Σ also has that curious clerical error ὑπὸ for ἐπὶ τὴν λυχνίαν with ℵ B* Φ 33. In iv. 28 Dr. Hort contends for the peculiar reading πλήρης σῖτον (πλήρης being treated as indeclinable) on the strength of C* only with two lectionaries and partial support from B D and one cursive. Σ now presents the same reading as C*. With the exception of ταλιθὰ κοῦμ for κοῦμι and τὸ εἰ δύνῃ I hardly think that there is another reading of even secondary interest in St. Mark. In all such crucial texts as υἱοῦ τοῦ θεοῦ i. 1, ἐν τοῖς προφήταις i. 2, αἰωνίου κρίσεως for αἰωνίου ἁμαρτήματος in iii. 29, εὐθέως ἀκούσας for παρακούσας in v. 36, ἐποίει for ἠπόρει in vi. 20, καθαρίζον for καθαρίζων in vii. 19, καὶ νηστείᾳ in ix. 29, even the interpolation πᾶσα θυσία ἁλὶ ἁλισθήσεται in ix. 49, and in the retention of the last twelve verses, Σ goes with the crowd.

Summarising then, we should imagine that the Codex Rossanensis was just such a MS. as would delight the heart of the Dean of Chichester. In very many places it supplies the oldest extant uncial authority for the common reading. In the great majority of other cases it votes steadily on the same side. It shares to a very slight extent in the heresies of ℵ B. It is found in the long array with the great mass of later documents and Fathers. It is innocent of Origenian or Eusebian mutilation.

On all these points Σ lends its support decidedly to the defenders of the traditional text. And yet even they, we should think, must accept its alliance with some little misgiving. Of the eighty and odd manifestly wrong and scantily supported readings which it contains, many are obviously mere assimilations of the text of one Gospel to another, or due to other equally unmistakeable causes of corruption. And yet there is no difference in kind between these readings and those which form so large a part of the characteristic text of the great mass of MSS. And the suspicion must ultimately force itself upon the mind, whether, after all, this great numerical majority can be so pure as it is supposed to be, and whether, after all, the process of wholesale correction and emendation which is asserted of it has not some foundation.

As for the Codex Rossanensis it is a typical example of the representatives of this emended and corrected text. Its character is essentially eclectic. It borrows, now from one source and now from another, whatever tends to make the narrative more flowing and more complete. In his original account of the MS. Von Gebhardt laid some stress on the affinities of its text to that of the Old Latin version. To the best of my belief he does not repeat this remark in his later publication. It is true that the MS. has a little sporadic relation to the Old Latin, but hardly more than it has to other forms of ante-Nicene text. Its own fundamental text is a mosaic, like that of the many other MSS. that are allied with it. And the wonder chiefly is that a MS. of such early date should have so few readings that bear the stamp of originality.

VII.

THE CORBEY St. JAMES (ff), AND ITS RELATION TO OTHER LATIN VERSIONS, AND TO THE ORIGINAL LANGUAGE OF THE EPISTLE[1].

[J. WORDSWORTH.]

TEXT OF THE EPISTLE.
 History of the MS. Martianay. P. Dubrowsky. Rediscovery. Belsheim. V. Jernstedt. Description, contents, date.
 I. Relation to other Latin versions. Amount of agreement with Cod. Amiatinus. ff ante-hieronymian. How far did St. Jerome revise the Epistles? The Itala (and Vulgate) based on an independent version. The version quoted in the Speculum (m) also independent in its origin. Optatus' evidence ambiguous. Jerome probably used a fourth version. All are as old as the fourth century. Chromatius used our version, which is probably the oldest.
 II. Our version made from a Greek text; but from a text differing in a striking manner from the current editions. Instances of the difference. Hypothesis of two Greek versions from an Aramaic original: (A) points in favour of this in the text; (B) parallel cases establishing the *a priori* probability of such an original: our Lord's usage, St. Paul, St. Matthew, St. Peter, (Epistle to the Hebrews,) Josephus; (C) character of the Greek too classical to have been written by either of the reputed authors. Summary.

---

[1] This Essay is based upon a review which appeared in the *Guardian*, Jan. 9th, 1884, and a paper read on Feb. 11th of the same year. But it has been entirely rewritten, and I hope much improved. The author has to thank his colleagues and Dr. Hort for some very kind help in rendering it less incomplete and inaccurate. The reader is also referred to Dr. Sanday's paper at the end of the volume for further considerations on the relation of the text to other Latin versions. Dr. Hort proposes to edit the Epistle critically and has made large preparations for the purpose. He is not inclined, I may remark, to accept my hypothesis as regards the Aramaic original.

Explicit epistola Barnabe ·.· Incip epistĺ Iacobi feliciter ·.·

I.¹ Iacobus dei et dn̄i ih̄u x̄p̄i seruus XII tribus quesunt in dispersione salī · ²Omne gaudium existimate fratres mei quando in uarias temptationes incurritis ³scientes quod probatio uestra operatur sufferentiam ⁴sufferentia autem opus consummatum habeat ut sitis consummati & integri in nullo deficientes ⁵& si cui nestrum deest sapientia petat a deo quia dat omnibus simpliciter & non inproperat & dabitur illi · ⁶p&at autem in fide nihil dubitans · Qui autem dubitat similis est fluctui maris · qui a uento fertur & defertur ⁷nec sper& se homo ille quō accipi& aliquit adño · ⁸homo duplici corde inconstans in omnibus uiis suis · ⁹glori&ur autem frater humilis in altitudine sua ¹⁰locuples autem in humilitate sua quō sicut flos feni transi& ¹¹ori&ur enim sol cum ęstu suo & siccat fenum & flos eius

I. ¹ *Ad initium lineae I· in mg., et sic* U[is] ii. 20, O[mnis] iii. 1, N[umquid] iii. 12, *et* S[i] iv. 11.

Fol. 89 B. cadit & dignitas facie ipsius perit sic & locuples in actu suo
marcescit · ¹²Beatus uir quia sustinuerit tem*p*tationem
quō probatus factus accipi& coronam uite quam promitt& eis
qui eum diligunt · ¹³Nemo qui temptatur dicat quō a deo
temp
tatur de*us* autem malor*um* temptator non est · temptat ipse ne
minem ¹⁴unusquisque autem temptatur a sua concupiscentia
abducitur & eliditur · ¹⁵Deinde concupiscentia conci
pit & parit peccatu*m* · peccatum autem consu*m*matum adquirit
mortem · ¹⁶Nolite errare fratres mei dilecti ¹⁷om*n*is datio
bona & omne donu*m* perfectu*m* desursum descendit a patre lu
minum aput quem non est permutatio uel modicu*m* obumbra
tionis ¹⁸uolens peperit nos uerbo ueritatis ut simus
primitie conditionu*m* eius ¹⁹scitote fratres mei dilecti · sit
autem
omnis homo uelox ad audiendum tardus autem ad loquen
dum · tardus autem ad iracundiam · ²⁰iracundia enim uiri
iustitiam
dei non operatur · ²¹Et ideo exponentes om*nes* sordes &
abundantia*m* malitie · per clemenciam excipite genitu*m*
uerbu*m*
qui potestis saluare animas ue*s*tras ²²estote autem factores uer
bi & non auditores tantum aliter consiliantes ²³quia si q*uis* au
ditor uerbi est & non factor hic est similis homini res
picienti faciem natali sui in speculo ²⁴aspexit se & recessit

---

¹² quia m. p., quis corr. eadem manu. temptationem *credo*, a Meruinigira;
temptetionem Belsheim; temptictionem Jernstedt.

¹⁷ perfectum MS., sed pf in rasura.

²¹ clemencia m. p., sed eadem corr. potestis MS. sine rasura. Belsheim
credit -is crasum a m. p. sed deceptus est puncto, a calami lapsu, sub -i- littera
(Jernstedt.).

et in continenti oblitus est qualis erat ²⁵ qui autem respexit Fol.21.90.
in [l]egem consummatam libertatis & perseuerans non audi
ens obliuionis factus sed factor operum hic beatus erit in
operibus suis · ²⁶ si qu[is] autem putat se religiosum esse Non in
frenans linguam suam sed fallens [co]r suum, huius uana est re
ligio · ²⁷ Religio autem munda & inmaculata apud dominum
hæc est uisitare orfanos & uiduas in tribulatione eo
rum seruare se sine macula a seculo · II. ¹ Fratres mei
Nolite in acceptione personarum habere fidem dñi nostri ihu
xp̄i honeris · ² si autem intrauerit in synagogam uestram
homo · anulos aureos in digitos habens in ueste splen
dida · intr& autem pauper in sordida ueste ³ respiciatis autem
qui uestitus est ueste candida & dicatis tu hic sede bene
& pauperi dicatis tu sta aut sede illo sub scamello meo
⁴ diiudicati estis inter uos facti estis iudices cogitationum
malorum · ⁵ Audite fratres mei dilecti nonne deus elegit pau
peres seculi locupletes in fide & heredes regni quod expro
misit diligentibus eum · ⁶ Uos autem frustratis pauperem
nonne diu[it]es potentantur in uobis & ipsi uos tradunt
ad iuditia ⁷ nonne ipsi blasphemant in bono nomine
quod uocitum est in uobis ⁸ Si tamen lege consummamini

---

²⁵ regem m. p., legem corr.

²⁶ quis corr. ex que, Iernstedt. Contra Belsheim. In cor, co- est in rasura, ubi uidetur fuisse hu-. Nimirum omissurus erat cor suum scriba, sed cum scripsisset hu- animaduertit errorem (Iernstedt).

II. ¹ acceptione m. p., acceptatione corrector, fortasse non m. p., Iernstedt. Contra Belsheim.

⁶ diues m. p., diuites corrector (ut 26, et II. 1).

Fol. 00. B. regale secundum scripturam · Diliges proximum tuum tanquam te benefaci
tis · ⁹ si autem personas accipitis peccatum operamini a lege traduc
ti tamquam transgressores ¹⁰ qui enim tota lege seruauerit peccaue
rit autem in uno factus est omnium reus · ¹¹ Nam qui dixit non
moechaberis · dixit & no[n] occides · si autem non moecha
beris
occideris autem factus est transgressor legis · ¹² sic loquimini &
sic facite quasi a lege liberalitatis iuditium sperantes · ¹³ iuditium
autem non miserebitur ei qui non fecit misericordiam · super
gloriatur autem misericordia iuditium · ¹⁴ Quit prodest fratres
mei
si quis dicat se fidem habere opera autem non habeat ·
numquit potest fides eum sola saluare ¹⁵ siue frater siue soror
nudi sint & desit eis uictus cottidianus · ¹⁶ dicat autem illis
ex uestris aliquis uadite in pace · calidi estote & satulli
non dederit autem illis alimentum corporis · quid & prodest
¹⁷ sic & fides si non habeat opera mortua est sola ¹⁸ sed dicet
aliquis tu operam habes ego fidem habeo ostende mihi fidem
sine operibus · & ego tibi de operibus fidem · ¹⁹ tu credis quia
unus deus · bene facis · & demonia credunt & contremescunt
²⁰ Uis autem scire ó homo uacue quoniam fides sine operibus
uacua
est · ²¹ Abraham pater noster nonne ex operibus iusti
ficatus est · offerens Isaac filium suum super aram · ²² uides
quoniam fides

---

¹¹ moech-, n es e facta. non secundum fuit noci, confusione orta ex uerbo sequenti. Post autem sec. punctum addidit corrector.
²⁰ U· extra lineam.

communicat cum operibus suis & ex operibus fides confirmatur ; **Fol. 22. 01.**
²³ & impleta est scriptura dicens · Credidit abraham domino &
esti
matum est ei ad iustitiam & amicus dei uocatus est · ²⁴ Uidetis
quoniam
ex operibus iustificatur homo & non ex fide tantum ²⁵ similiter
& raab fornicaria nonne ex operibus iustificatus est cum
suscepiss& exploratores ex · XII · tribus filiorum israhel & per
aliam uiam eos ciceciss& · ²⁶ sicut autem corpus sine spiritu
mortuum est
sic fides sine opera mortua · est · **III.** ¹ Nolite multi magistri
esse
fratres mei scientes quoniam maius iuditium accipiemus ·
² multa autem
erramus omnes · si quis in uerbo non erat hic erit consum
matus
uir · potens est se infrenare & totum corpus · ³ Si autem
equorum frenos in ora mittimus ut possint consentire
& totum corpus ipsorum conuertimus · ⁴ ecce & naues tam mag
ne sunt & a uentis tam ualidis feruntur · reguntur autem
paruulo gubernaculo & ubicumque diriguntur uolump
tate eorum qui eas gubernant ⁵ sic & lingua paruulum mem
brum
est & magna gloriantur · Ecce pusillum ignis in quam
magna silua incendium facit ⁶ & lingua ignis seculi iniquita
tis · lingua posita est in membris nostris que maculat totum
cor
pus & inflammat rotam natiuitatis & incenditur a gehenna
⁷ Omnis autem natura bestiarum siue uolatilium repentium &
natantium

²⁶ opera m. p., operae corr. = opere.
III. ⁴ uolumptate m. p., uoluntate corr.   ⁷ O- extra lineam.

Fol. 91 B. domatur & domita est · nature autem humane ⁸linguam nemo
hominum domare potest · inconstans malum plena ueneno
morti
fera ⁹in ipsa benedicimus dominum & patrem & per ipsam
maledicimus
homines qui ad similitudinem dei facti sunt ¹⁰ex ipso ore
exit bene
dictio & maledictio · Non dec& fratres mei haec sic fieri
¹¹num
quit fons ex uno foramine bullit dulcem & salmacidum ·
¹²Numquid potest fratres mei ficus oliuas facere · aut uitis ficus
sic nec salmacidum dulcem facere aquam · ¹³Quis sapiens et disci
plinosus in uobis demonstrat de bona conuersatione ope
ra sua in sapientie clementiam · ¹⁴si autem zelum amarum
habetis
& contontionem in precordiis uestris quit alapamini men
tientes contra ueritatem ¹⁵non est sapientia que descendit
desursum sed terrestris animalis demonetica · ¹⁶ubi autem
zelus & contentio inconstans ibi & omne prauum nego
tium ¹⁷dei autem sapientia primum sancta est · deinde pacifica
& uerecun
die consentiens plena misericordie & fructum bonorum
sine diiudicatione inreprehensibilis sine hypocrisi ¹⁸fructus
autem institiae in pace seminatur qui faciunt pacem · **IV.** ¹Unde
pugne et unde rixe in uobis nonne hinc ex uoluptatibus uestris
que militant in membris uestris ²concupiscitis & non habebitis
occiditis & zelatis & non potestis impetrare · rixatis

⁸ *Post* linguam *punctum est, fortasse a scriba digito deletum.*
¹² N- *extra lineam.*
¹¹ fructum *pro* fructuum *MS.*
IV. ² rixatis + & pug- *m. p., deinde erasum.*

& pugnatis & non habetis propter quod non petitis ³ p&titis Fol.23.92.
& non acci
pitis propter hoc quod male petitis ut in libidines uestras ero
getis ⁴ for
nicatores · nescitis quoniam amicitia seculi inimica dei est ·
Quicumque
ergo uoluerit amicus seculi esse inimicus dei perseuerat ⁵ aut
putatis quoniam dicit scriptura ad inuidiam conualescit spi
ritus qui
habitat in uobis ⁶ maiorem autem dat gratiam · propter quod
dicit · deus
superbis resistit · humilis autem dat gratiam ⁷ subditi estote deo
resistite autem zabolo · & fugi& a nobis ⁸ accedite ad dominum &
& ipse ad uos accedit · Mundate manus peccatores & sancti
ficate corda uestra duplices corde ⁹ lugete miseri & plorate
risus uester in luctum convertatur & gaudium in tristitiam
¹⁰ humiliate uos ante dominum & exaltabit uos · ¹¹ Nolite
retractare de alterutro frater · Qui retractat de fratre
et iudicat fratrem suum retractat de lege & iudicat legem ·
Si autem iudicas legem · non es factor legis sed iudex ¹² unus
est legum
positor & iudex qui potest saluare & perdere · Tu autem quis és
qui iudicas proximum · ¹³ Iam nunc qui dicunt hodie aut cras
ibi
mus in illam ciuitatem & faciemus ibi annum & negotiamur ·
& lucrum faciemus ¹⁴ qui ignoratis crastinum · ¹⁵ Quæ autem
uita
uestra momentum enim est · per modica uisibilis · Deinde &
exter
minata propter quod dicere uos oport& · si dominus uoluerit

¹¹ S. *extra lineam.*
    Inter ¹¹ et ¹² lineola addita est a m. recenti inter iudex (index *lapsu* Belsh.)
et unus.   ¹² + = est.   ¹³ uita *in rasura.*

Fol. 92. B. & uincmus & faciemus hoc aut illud · ¹⁶ nunc autem gloriami
ni in superbia uestra omnis gloria talis mala est ¹⁷ scienti
bus autem
bonum facere & non facientibus peccatum illis est V. ¹ iam
nunc locuple
tes plorate ululantes in miseriis uestris aduenientibus ² Diuiti
ę uestrę · putrierunt res uestrę · tiniauerunt ³ aurum uestrum ·
& argentum
eruginauit & erugo ipsorum erit uobis in testimonium & man
ducabit carnes uestras tanquam ignis tesaurizastis & in
nouissimis
diebus ⁴ & ecce mercedes operariorum qui arauerunt in agris
uestris
quod abnegastis clamabunt & uoces qui messi sunt ad aures
domini
sabaoth introierunt ⁵ fruiti estis super terram & abusi estis
cibastis cor
da uestra in die occisionis ⁶ damnastis & occidistis iustum non
resistit uo
bis ⁷ patientes ergo estote fratres usque ad aduentum domini
ecce agricola
expectat honoratum fructum terre patiens in ipso usquequo
accipiat matutinum & serotinum fructum · ⁸ Et uos patientes
estote confortate precordia uestra · quoniam aduentus domini ad
propiauit · ⁹ Nolite ingemescere fratres in alterutrum ne in iu
ditium incidatis ecce iudex ante ianuam stat ¹⁰ accipite expe
rimentum fratres de malis passionibus & de pacientia · Prophe
tas qui locuti sunt in nomine domini · ¹¹ ecce beatos dicimus qui
sustinuerunt · sufferentiam iob audistis & finem domini uidistis
quoniam misceraliter dominus misericors est ¹² ante omnia autem
fratres mei

¹⁵ & faciemus *MS.*; aut facimus *Bal-heim.*
V. ³ *In man- pars n- abrasa est.*   ⁸ *In* propiauit p- *est in rasura.*

nolite iurare neque per celum neq; per terram. nec alteru Fol.24.03.
trum
iuramentum sit autem aput uos est est non est non est.
ne in iuditium incidatis ¹³anxiat aliquis ex uobis or&. hilaris
est. psalmum dicat ¹⁴ & infirmis est aliquis in uobis uoc&
presbyteros & orent super ipsum ungentes oleo in nomine
domini
¹⁵ & oratio in fide saluabit laborantem & suscitauit illum dominus
& si peccata fecit remittuntur ei. ¹⁶Confitemini alterutrum
peccata uestra & orate pro alterutro ut remittatur uobis.
Multum potest p&itio iusti frequens. ¹⁷ Helias homo erat
similis nobis & oratione orauit ut non pluer& & non plu
it in terra annis tribus & mensibus sex. ¹⁸ Sed iterum
orauit & celum dedit pluuium & terra germinauit fructum
suum. ¹⁹ Fratres mei si quis ex uobis errauerit a ueritate & ali
quis eum reuocauerit ²⁰ qui reuocauerit peccatorem de erro
ris uia saluat animam de morte sua & operi& multitu
dinem peccati. EXPLICIT EPISTOLA
IACOBI FILII ZAEBEDEI ⁖ ⁖ ⁖

---

¹³ or & *MS.*, *sed m. recentior ligauit.*

¹⁴ infirmis *m. p.*, -mus *corrector.*

¹⁶ *In* potest petitio, -t p- *sunt in rasura et inter eas duae tresue literae crasae. Conicio primitus fuisse* potest est (*Iernstedt.*).

²⁰ peccatorem ... animam *MS.*; peccatorum ... annimam *Belsheim.*

THE manuscript which is the subject of this Essay is not a new discovery like the Codex Rossanensis, nor can it boast anything like so great antiquity. It was written probably not before the tenth century, and the text contained in it has been before the world nearly 200 years. It was in fact one of the first old Latin texts of the New Testament which was ever printed. Yet its peculiarities have I think been much overlooked and deserve attentive consideration [1].

In the year 1695, Dom Jean Martianay, of the congregation of St. Maur, best known as the principal editor of the Benedictine St. Jerome, published a small duodecimo volume of New Testament texts, which has now become extremely scarce [2]. I have not been able to discover a single copy of this book in Oxford, and I believe that the little volume of notes, forming a sort of appendix to it, which I was fortunate enough to meet with in Paris, is scarcely less rare. Martianay's texts were the Corbey St. Matthew usually called ff$_1$, to which he added a marginal collation of the same Gospel from the St. Germain Bible (g$_1$), and the Corbey St. James (ff) which is our immediate subject. It will be unnecessary to occupy time with a discussion of the character and fate of the two MSS. of St. Matthew on which I have written at some length in the introduction to my edition of the latter, in the first number of our *Old-Latin Biblical Texts* [3]. With regard however to the parentage of two out of Martianay's three MSS, it is just worth while to mention that the most important portion of the great monastic Library of Corbey

---

[1] Drs. Westcott and Hort have no notes on select readings of St. James in either volume of their edition, except incidental references. Tischendorf however incorporates many readings of ff in his apparatus.

[2] *Vulgata antiqua Latina et Itala versio Evangelii secundum Matthaeum e vetustissimis eruta monumentis illustrata Prolegomenis ac notis nunc que primum edita studio et labore D. J. Martianay, Pres. Ben. C. S. Mauri, Parisiis apud Antonium Lambin, 1695.*

[3] *The Gospel according to St. Matthew from the St. Germain MS. (g$_1$) now numbered Lat. 11553 in the National Library at Paris*, &c. Oxford, 1883. The Corbey MS. of St. Matthew is now at St. Petersburg, where it is numbered Ov. 3 (p. 326).

or Corbie on the Somme near Amiens (the parent house of Corbey or Corvey on the Weser) was transferred to St. Germain des Prés at Paris in or about the year 1638, and incorporated with that very valuable collection. It naturally shared the fortunes of the St. Germain Library in the troublous times of the French revolution, and was largely pillaged. The two Corbey MSS. edited by Martianay fell at this crisis into the hands of Peter Dubrowsky, secretary of the Russian Embassy at Paris, who transferred them, with the greater part of his other acquisitions, to the Imperial Library at St. Petersburg in or about 1805. But as no sufficient catalogue of this library is accessible, it was long unknown whether these two books still existed. The present home of our MS. was first mentioned (as Dr. Hort informs me) by Muralt in 1848[1]. The information was repeated by Oehler in 1856, in his edition of Philastrius, and latterly by Gebhardt in his editions of Barnabas (1875-6) and by Mr. F. T. Bassett in his Commentary on this epistle. Mr. John Belsheim, a Norwegian scholar, who has done good service in the publication of such texts, was, however, unaware of its existence when he transcribed the Corbey St. Matthew in 1880. When he published his edition of the Gospel he therefore reprinted Martianay's text of St. James as an appendix. But soon after hearing that the MS. was still accessible he took another journey to St. Petersburg, and published the Epistle directly from the original in the course of last year (1883).

The book in question when it was in the Corbey and St. Germain libraries contained four treatises, viz. Philastrius on Heresies (folios 1-69), Pseudo-Tertullian on Jewish Meats (ff. 70-77), the unique Latin version of 'Barnabas' (ff. 77-89), and lastly our Epistle (ff. 90-93). At present, however, Philastrius is bound separately and the two volumes are now

---

[1] Ed. de Muralt, *Bulletin de la Classe Historico-philologique de l'Acad. des Sciences de Pétersbourg*, tom. v. no. 1, 1848. Oehler, *Corpus Haereseologicum*, vol. i. p. ix., 1856.

numbered Qv. I. 38, and Qv. I. 39. In the Corbey Library the MS. first bore the pressmark 635, and in Dom Poirier's catalogue (made about A.D. 1791) it was numbered 717.

The MS. thus consists of ninety-three leaves of parchment in quarto form, being about twenty-four centimeters high and nineteen broad. Each page of the Epistle, except the first and last, contains twenty-one lines. Mr. Belsheim has preserved the original pages and lines, but has not given what is in my opinion more important, namely, the original punctuation, and I have therefore reprinted the text exactly as it stands in the MS. This I am enabled to do by the kindness of Professor V. Jernstedt, of the University of St. Petersburg, who made a careful collation of it in October, 1884.

The date assigned by Dr. Alfred Holder is of the tenth century. Others had previously conjectured it to be of the eighth or ninth. I cannot myself form any opinion worth speaking of, and I have not as yet been able to obtain a photograph, but the great number of the contractions seems rather to suggest the later date.

The object of this paper is chiefly to determine the character of the text in its relation—firstly, to other Latin versions, and secondly, to the Greek of the Epistle. In treating the latter of these topics I shall advance an opinion with regard to the original language of the book.

I. *Relation of the text to other Latin versions.*

We first naturally ask what is the relation borne by it to St. Jerome's revision. In considering this question we have the advantage of Sabatier's collections of patristic quotations in his great work, *Bibliorum Latinorum Versiones Latinae antiquissimae*, in which he reprinted Martianay's text. I have also collated the Epistle with the Codex Amiatinus. This examination shows that there is no verse of it in which there is not some agreement with the Vulgate, and none in which there is not some difference from it. Occasionally the agreement extends to a whole clause or even to two clauses of from ten to fifteen words in length—though there is only one instance of an agreement of as many as fifteen continuous words, and that at the commencement of the book[1]. The agreements on the whole exceed the differences in amount; but the latter are almost always in the more striking and difficult parts of the sentence, while the agreements are in the simple and commonplace words and phrases. It is hardly an exaggeration to say that there is no single important noun or verb in which the Corbey MS. agrees with the Vulgate. There can therefore, I think, be no reasonable doubt that the text before us is wholly Old Latin or ante-Hieronymian, not *mixed* or constructed on a Vulgate basis. Whatever agreement there is will then be due to the use of our text by St. Jerome, or some of his predecessors, as material for a revision, not to mixture on the part of the scribe of our MS.

Before considering the relations of our text to other Latin versions in detail a few remarks of a general kind may not be out of place. St. Jerome's work on the New Testament was, it must always be remembered, wholly one of revision, not of translation, and he was by no means the first or the last reviser that the Latin Church has known. His method of procedure is only directly revealed to us by some words in his letter to Damasus prefixed to his edition of the Gospels (in A. D. 383). From them and from a comparison of various types of MSS. we infer that he chose the Latin text which had the greatest authority in Italy, and emended it where it was very incorrect with the aid of ancient Greek MSS. and probably of other Latin versions. The basis of St. Jerome's work is therefore provisionally called the Itala—to distinguish it from African and other Old-Latin texts—this being the name given by St. Augustine to the text which he commends in a single passage of his book on Christian doctrine (ii. 15). In the Gospels it is now generally looked for in the MSS. of Brescia

---

[1] 'Iacobus dei et domini [+ nostri] ihesu christi seruus xii tribus que [tribubus quae] sunt in dispersione salutem. Omne gaudium existimate fratres mei.' The words in square brackets are the readings of the Codex Amiatinus.

and Munich—*f* and *q*. In the other books we must, I suppose, regard it as chiefly represented by the writings of St. Augustine and the Freisingen and Gottweig fragments. Jerome's emendation of the Gospels was clearly hurried and perfunctory, and he shrank from giving offence by introducing changes which he knew would be popularly denounced as 'needless.' He left, however, a preface which expressly describes what he had done in that portion of the New Testament. As no such prefaces exist for the other books, it has been sometimes doubted whether he carried his revision any further. This doubt is, however, overborne by other evidence, and we are bound to believe, on his own authority, that he revised the whole New Testament, though he may have treated the other books even more superficially than the Gospels[1].

When we come to inquire concerning the special history of St. James in the Western Church we are at once confronted with the difficulty of its apparently late reception by Latin writers. It is never quoted by Tertullian or Cyprian, nor, I believe, by St. Ambrose[2]. St. Hilary quotes it

---

[1] Vallarsi's collection of evidence on this point is the best with which I am acquainted: see his edition, vol. x. p. xix. foll. The passages bearing on it are Jerome's own *Catalogue of his Works* and the following four *Epistles*, 112 (*to Augustine*), 71 (*to Lucinius*), 106 (*to Sunnia and Fretela*), and 27 (*to Marcella*). It is remarkable that in the last letter Jerome refers to three passages which he had emended from the Greek, and that all of them are from St. Paul's Epistles, viz. Rom. xii. 11, where he read 'serving *the Lord*,' 1 Tim. iii. 1, '*fidelis sermo*' (for *humanus*), and ib. v. 19, 'Against an elder receive not an accusation *except before two or three witnesses*,' where Cyprian and Ambrosiaster omit the saving clause altogether. Jerome indeed writes here *ne receparis*, while my Vulgate MSS. have *noli recipere*, but he is probably quoting from memory.

[2] The two passages supposed by the Benedictine editors to be references to St. James in the genuine works of St. Ambrose (tom. i. pp. 1071 and 1312) are both probably to other passages of Scripture. The first is *in Psalm* cxviii, *sermo* 8, § 42, 'Vinculis enim peccatorum suorum unusquisque constringitur, sicut ipse legisti: ligat nos vinculis carnis illecebra,' and is supposed = James i. 14. But without a doubt the reference is to Prov. v. 22, see Sabatier on that place, where this and other old renderings of the verse are given. The second *in Lucam* ii. § 91, 'Purificate igitur vos, ut apostolus dicit; quia purificavit se ille pro nobis, qui purificatione non eguit' is much more likely to be a reference to 1 John iii. 3 and 5 than to James iv. 8. The supposed references in Novatian *de Trinitate* iv. and viii. are equally unsafe, and so are those in Anon. *ad*

apparently only once and that in refuting Arian arguments[1]. Its patristic use did not become common till the next generation, that of St. Augustine and St. Jerome, who cite it frequently, the latter especially in controversy with Jovinian (A.D. 393) and the Pelagians (A.D. 416?)[2]. It is a remarkable fact that St. Augustine's quotations (representing our supposed Itala) are nearer the Vulgate than St. Jerome's[3].

Granting, then, that this Itala, when further revised, became the Hieronymian Vulgate, are we justified in supposing that it was based directly on our Corbey version? Certainly not. Our Corbey version may have been, and probably was, a subsidiary source of the Itala, but the latter must have been chiefly drawn from a wholly different translation. We are led to this conclusion not only by the differences between *ff* and the patristic quotations, but by the singular character of the book as it appears in the Vulgate. The current text of St. James has a colour of its own, which forbids us to regard it as a mere composite, smoothed down to the Hieronymian level. It differs in method of translation almost as much from other books of the New Testament as it does from our *ff*. This may be shown by the following table, based on a note of

Novatianum de Lapsis (Galland. iii. p. 374 D) and S. Zeno Veron. *de spe fide et caritate* (Gall. v. p. 111) and *Tractatus* i. 9. 2, *de avaritia* (ib. p. 122).

[1] Hil. *de Trin.* iv. 8, p. 830, 'quia et Iacobus apostolus dixerit apud quem non est demutatio ' = i. 17.

[2] The Dean of Chichester, who has kindly sent me a long list of references from his great storehouse, adds that there are as many as 123 quotations from this Epistle in St. Jerome and 389 in St. Augustine.

[3] The Epistle, though early known and received in the Eastern Church and by such Greek Western writers as Irenaeus, was apparently not received as Scripture by the Latin Church till comparatively late. When St. Jerome wrote his *de Scriptoribus Ecclesiasticis* (s. v. *Iacobus*) in 392, he implies that it had only recently acquired authority. 'Iacobus qui appellatur frater Domini, cognomento Iustus... unam tantum scripsit epistolam, quae de septem Catholicis est, quae et ipsa ab alio quodam sub nomine eius edita asseritur, licet paullatim tempore procedente obtinuerit auctoritatem.' Perhaps (as Dr. Hort has suggested to me) its association in this volume with three other uncanonical writings may imply that the archetype of our book was written before it became canonical in the West. It was, however, acknowledged by the Council of Carthage in 397, in the first Canon of Holy Scripture perhaps ever promulgated by such an assembly. See Westcott, *On the Canon of the New Testament*.

K

Dr. Westcott's in his book *On the Canon of the New Testament* (note p. 261 foll. ed. 1875):—

CHAP.	GREEK.	VULGATE ST. JAMES.	ELSEWHERE IN VULGATE.	CORBEY ST. JAMES.
i. 5.	ἁπλῶς	affluenter	(simplicitas)	simpliciter
i. 7.	οἰέσθω	aestimet	(existimo)	speret
i. 16, 19; ii. 5.	ἀγαπητοί	dilecti or dilectissimi	carissimi 20 times, but dilecti 1 Cor. xv. 58, and dilectissimi Heb. vi. 9. Cf. Rom. i. 7; xvi. 9.	dilecti
ii. 6.	ἠτιμάσατε	exhonorastis	(inhonorare or contumelia afficere)	frustrastis
i. 21; v. 15, 22.	σῶξειν	salvare	(salvum facere, salvus esse or fieri)	salvare
ii. 23.	ἐπληρώθη	suppleta est	(implere)	impleta est
iii. 17.	ἁγνή	pudica	(castus and once sanctus, 1 John iii. 3)	sancta
i. 21.	ἀποθέμενοι	abicientes (so Rom. xiii. 12.)	deponere six times)	exponentes
v. 11.	μακαρίζομεν	beatificamus	(beatam me dicent, Luke i. 48)	beatos dicimus
iv. 2.	πολεμεῖτε	belligeratis	(pugnare, Apoc. ii. 16; xii. 7, etc.)	pugnatis
v. 11.	οἰκτίρμων	miserator	(misericordes, Luke vi. 36)	misericors.

The striking divergence, even in simple words, between the three Latin columns speaks for itself. We may therefore conclude with safety that the Corbey St. James is not only ante-Hieronymian, but that the Vulgate is founded (not on it, but) on an entirely different version which, for the sake of distinctness, I will call the Itala-Vulgate.

We have thus produced evidence for two early Latin versions of our Epistle. A third equally distinct is known to us by the quotations in the *Speculum* (m),—a late African text, though probably not St. Augustine's. As these are not accessible to everyone I print them from Mai (with Dr. Sanday's help), giving the Vulgate and Corbey parallels[1].

[1] Dr. Hort has recently made the important discovery that MS. Libri 16 of the Ashburnham collection (deposited for a few months in the British Museum) contains thirteen leaves of a better MS. of the Speculum than that used by Mai, and 'at least older than any which Weihrich knows of for his forthcoming edition for the Vienna Academy. Moreover, they (with two leaves now lost) make up the Fleury [Floriacensis] 10 and 12, occasionally cited by Sabatier. There can be no doubt about the identification, though Sabatier's inaccuracy is unpleasantly illustrated by it' (Letter from Cambridge, 4 Oct., 1884). M. Delisle has recently described this discovery in a paper headed *Le plus Ancien MS. du Miroir de St. Augustin*, Paris, 1884. The only passage from St. James contained in these leaves is iv. 11–13³ (c. 31 of the Speculum). Dr. Hort has noticed two variations from Mai in these verses, viz. '*nobis* (for *uos* detrahere,' and '*qui autem*' (for *enim*). He adds: 'Mai's text, unchecked by other MSS., cannot safely be treated as more than an approximation' (Letter of 14 Oct., 1884).

SPECULUM (m).	VULGATE (COD. AM.).	CORBEY MS. (ff).
I. ¹⁹ Sit uero omnis homo citatus audire, et tardus loqui, piger in iracundia. ²⁰ Iracundia enim uiri iustitiam Dei non operatur.	¹⁹ Sit autem omnis homo uelox ad audiendum, tardus autem ad loquendum et tardus ad iram. ²⁰ Ira enim uiri iustitiam Dei non operatur.	¹⁹ Sit autem omnis homo uelox ad audiendum, tardus autem ad loquendum, tardus autem ad ira undum. ²⁰ Iracundia enim uiri iustitiam Dei non operatur.
²⁶ Si quis putat superstitiosum se esse, non refrenans linguam suam, sed fallens cor sum (sic), huius uana religio est. ²⁷ Sanctitas autem pura et incontaminata haec est aput Deum patrem, uisitare orfanos et uiduas in angustia ipsorum et inmaculatum se seruare a mundo	²⁶ Si quis autem putat se religiosum esse, non refrenans linguam suam, sed seducens cor suum, huius uana est religio ²⁷ Religio autem munda et inmaculata apud deum et patrem haec est, uisitare pupillos et uiduas in tribulatione eorum, et inmaculatum se custodire ab hoc saeculo.	²⁶ Si quis autem putat se religiosum esse non refrenans linguam suam, sed fallens cor suum, huius uana est religio ²⁷ Religio autem munda et inmaculata apud Dominum haec est, uisitare orfanos et uiduas in tribulatione eorum ; seruare se sine macula a seculo
II. ¹³ Iudicium enim sine misericordia his qui non fecit misericordiam ; quoniam misericordia praefertur iudicio. ¹⁴ Quid prode est, fratres, si fidem quis dicat in semet ipso mauere, opera autem non habent? Numquid potest fides (sic) sola saluare eum? ¹⁵ Si frater aut soror nudi fuerint et defuerit eis cottidianus cibus; ¹⁶ dicat autem eis aliquis uestrum : Ite in pace, et calefacimini, et satiemini, et non det eis necessaria corporis, quid prode est haec dixisse eis ? ¹⁷ Sic et fides quae non habet opera, mortua est circa se.	¹³ Iudicium enim sine misericordia illi qui non fecerit misericordiam; superexaltat autem misericordia iudicio. ¹⁴ Quid proderit, fratres mei, si fidem quis dicat se habere, opera autem non habeat ? Numquid puterit fides saluare eum ? ¹⁵ Si autem frater aut soror nudi sint et indigeant uictu cottidiano, ¹⁶ dicat autem aliquis de uobis illis ; Ite in pace, calefacimini et saturamini, non dederitis autem eis quae necessaria sunt corporis quid proderit ? ¹⁷ Sic et fides si non habeat opera mortua est in semetipsa.	¹³ Iudicium autem non miserebitur ei, qui non fecit misericordiam. Supergloriatur autem misericordia iudicium. ¹⁴ Quit prodest, fratres mei, si quis dicat se fidem habere opera autem non habeat ? Numquid potest fides eum sola saluare ? ¹⁵ Siue frater siue soror nudi sint et desit eis uictus cottidianus, ¹⁶ dicat autem illis ex uestris aliquis ; Vadite in pace, calidi estote et satulli ; non dederit autem illis alimentum corporis ; quid et prodest ? ¹⁷ Sic et fides si non habet opera, mortua est sola.
²⁶ Sicut enim corpus sine spiritu mortuum est, sic et fides sine operibus mortua est.	²⁶ Sicut enim corpus sine spiritu mortuum est, ita et fides sine operibus mortua est.	²⁶ Sicut autem corpus sine spiritu mortuum est, sic fides sine opera mortua est.
III. ¹ Nolite multiloqui esse, fratres mei ; quia maius iudicium accipietis ; ² multa enim omnes delinquimus. Si quis in uerbo non deliquid (sic) hic perfectus uir est, potest fraenare totum corpus et dirigere. ³ Quare ergo equis frena in ora mittuntur, nisi in eo ut suadeantur a nobis, et totum corpus circumducamus? ⁴ Ecce et naues quietam (i.e. quae tam) immensae sunt, sub uentis duris feruntur, et circum ducuntur a paruissimo	¹ Nolite plures magistri fieri fratres mei, scientes quoniam maius iudicium sumitis. ² In multis enim offendimus omnes, Si quis in uerbo non offendit, hic perfectus est uir * potest etiam circumducere freno totum corpus. ³ Si autem equis frenos in ora mittimus ad consentiendum nobis, et omne corpus illorum circumferimus. ⁴ Ecce et naues cum magnae sint, et a uentis ualidis minentur, circumferuntur a modico	¹ Nolite multi magistri esse fratres mei, scientes quoniam maius iuditium accipiemus. ² Multa autem erramus omnes. Si quis in uerbo non errat ; hic erit consummatus uir. Potens est se infraenare et totum corpus. ³ Si autem equorum frenos in ora mittimus ut possint consentire, et totum corpus ipsorum conuertimus. ⁴ Ecce et naues tam magnae sunt, et a uentis tam ualidis feruntur, reguntur autem paruulo

* Hieron. *Contra Pel.* 17, Si quis in uerbo non peccauit, hic perfectus est uir.

SPECULUM (m).	VULGATE (COD. AM.).	CORBEY MS. (ff.).
gubernaculo, ubi impetus dirigentis uoluerit. ⁵ Sic et lingua pars membri est, sed est magniloqua. Et sicut paruus ignis magnam siluam incendit. ⁶ Ita et lingua ignis est: et mundus iniquitatis per linguam constat in membris nostris, quae maculat totum corpus, et inflammat rotam (rotum m. 1) geniturae et inflammatur a genitura. ⁷ Omnis enim natura bestiarum et auium et serpentium et beluarum maritimarum domatur et subiecta est naturae humanae: ⁸ linguam autem hominum domare nemo potest, nec retinere a malo, quia plena est mortali ueneno.	gubernaculo ubi impetus dirigentis uoluerit: ⁵ ita et lingua modicum quidem membrum est, et magna exaltat. Ecce quantus ignis quam magnam siluam incendit ⁶ Et lingua ignis est: uniuersitas iniquitatis lingua constituitur in membris no-tris, quae maculat totum corpus et inflammat rotam natiuitatis nostrae inflammata a gehenna. ⁷ Omnis enim natura bestiarum et uolucrum et serpentium ceterorumque * domantur et domata sunt a natura humana: ⁸linguam autem nullus hominum domare potest. Inquietum malum, plena ueneno mortifero †.	gubernaculo et ubicumque diriguntur uoluntate eorum qui eas gubernant. ⁵Sic et lingua parumulum membrum est, et magna gloriantur. Ecce pusillum ignis, in quam magna silua incendum facit, ⁶ Et lingua ignis seculi iniquitatis. Lingua posita est in membris nostris, que maculat totum corpus et inflammat rotam natiuitatis et incenditur a gehenna. ⁷ Omnis autem natura bestiarum siue uolatilium, repentium et natantium domatur et domita est. Nature autem humanae ⁸ linguam nemo hominum domare potest. Inconstans malum, plena ueneno mortifera.
¹³ Quis prudens et sciens uestrum? Monstret de bona conuersatione opera sua in mansuetudine et prudentia.	¹³ Quis sapiens et disciplinatus inter uos? Ostendat ex bona conuersatione operationem suam in mansuetudinem sapientiae.	¹³ Quis sapiens et disciplinosus in uobis? demonstrat de bona conuersatione opera sua in sapientie clementiam.
IV. ¹ Unde bella? unde rixae in uobis? nonne de uoluntatibus uestris quae militant in membris uestris, et sunt uobis suauissima?	¹ Unde bella et lites inter uos? Nonne ex concupiscentiis uestris quae militant in membris uestris §?	¹ Unde pugne et unde rixe in uobis? Nonne hinc? ex uoluptatibus uestris que militant in membris uestris?
⁷ Humiliate uos Deo, et resistite diabolo, et a uobis [fugiet?] *proximabit Deo et proximauit uobis.	² Subditi igitur estote Deo, resistite autem diabolo, et fugiet a uobis, ⁸ Adpropinquate Deo et adpropinquauit uobis.	⁷ Subditi estote Deo resistite autem zabolo, et fugiet a uobis. * Accedite ad Dominum et ipse ad uos accedit.
¹⁰ Humiliamini in conspectum Domini et exaltabit uos.	¹⁰ Humiliamini in conspectu Domini et exaltauit uos.	¹⁰ Humiliate uos ante Dominum et exaltabit uos.
¹¹ Fratres nolite nos [uobis Flor.] detrahere. Qui enim [autem Flor.] uituperat fratrem suum et iudicat legem uituperat et iudicat. Si legem iudicas, iam non factor legis sed iudex es. ¹² Unus est enim legum dator et iudex, qui potest saluare et perdere. Tu autem quis es qui iudicas proximum?	¹¹ Nolite detrahere alterutrum, fratres mei. Qui detrahit fratri aut qui iudicat fratrem suum detrahit legi et iudicat legem. Si autem iudicas legem, non es factor legis sed iudex. ¹² Unus est legislator et iudex, qui potest perdere et liberare. Tu autem quis es qui iudicas proximum?	¹¹ Nolite retractare de alterutro, frater. Qui retractat de fratre et iudicat fratrem suum, retractat de lege et iudicat legem. Si autem iudicas legem, non es factor legis sed iudex. ¹² Unus est legum positor et iudex, qui potest saluare et perdere. Tu autem quis es qui iudicas proximum?
V. ¹ Agite nunc diuites plangite uos ululantes super miserias uestras quae superuenient.	¹ Agite nunc diuites plorate ululantes in miseriis quae aduenient uobis.	¹ Iam nunc locupletes plorate ululantes in miseriis uestris aduenientibus.

* No Vulgate MS. as yet collated reads *cetorum*, though one at Paris (Walker's κ) has *cetorum*. But St. Jerome probably wrote *cetorum*.

† Hieron. *Contra Pel.* 17, Linguam autem hominum nullus potest domare; inconstans malum, plena ueneni mortiferi.

§ Hieron. *Contra Pel.* 17, Unde bella et unde rixae inter uos? Nonne ex uoluptatibus quae militant in membris uestris?

SPECULUM (m).	VULGATE (COD. AM.).	CORBEY MS. (ff.).
² diuitiis uestris Putruerunt et tiniauerunt uestes uestrae, ³ Aurum et argentum uestrum quod reposuistis in nouissimis diebus aeruginauit et aerugo errum in testimonium uobis erit et comedit carnes uestras sicut ignis.	² Diuitiae uestrae putrefactae sunt et uestimenta uestra a tineis comesta sunt, ³ Aurum et argentum uestrum eruginauit, et erugo eorum in testimonium uobis erit et manducabit carnes uestras sicut ignis.	² Diuitiae uestrae putrierunt, res nestrae tiniauerunt, ³ aurum uestrum et argentum eruginauit et erugo ipsorum erit uobis in testimonium et manducabit carnes uestras tanquam ignis.
⁵ Et uos deliciati estis super terram et luxoriati estis: creastis autem corda uestra in die occisionis.	⁵ Epulati estis super terram et in luxuriis enutristis corda uestra in diem occisionis.	⁵ Fruiti estis super terram et abusi estis. Cibastis corda uestra in die occisionis.

Coincidences between one or other of the three columns are not rare, but very rarely indeed do all three agree even in simple phrases or sentences. The amount and character of the agreement are such as to suggest that both the Speculum and the Corbey text were in the hands of St. Jerome or the editor of the text used by Augustine.

The substantial distinctness of all the three is, however, clearly proved by such triplicate renderings as: ii. 13, praefertur, superexaltat, supergloriatur; 15, et defuerit eis, et indigeant, et desit eis; 16, calificimini et satiemini, calificamini et saturamini, calidi estote et satulli; 17, mortua est circa se, m. e. in semetipsa, m. e. sola. iii. 1, multiloqui, plures magistri, multi magistri; 2, delinquid, offendit, errat (*Jerome* peccauit); 3, circumducamus, circumferimus, conuertimus; and many others, in all about thirty-five.

That there may have been even more versions than three in the Latin Church is not, I think, at all improbable; in fact I believe it to be almost certain, and that without pressing ambiguous evidence, such as that of Optatus (*De Schism. Donat.* i. 5). Sabatier gives the words 'nolite per opinionem iudicare fratres uestros' as a rendering of James iv. 11, but he does not notice that Optatus refers them to the Epistle of St. Peter. Needless to say no such words occur in either of St. Peter's Epistles, and they may be a bungling reminiscence of the passage of St. James confused with other passages such as Is. xi. 3 and Rom. xiv. 10; but they are not near enough to the words μὴ καταλαλεῖτε ἀλλήλων ἀδελφοί to rank as a version of them, and must not therefore be pressed into our service on this occasion.

But apart from Optatus, St. Jerome's own quotations of the Epistle are, as I have already intimated, farther from the Vulgate than St. Augustine's, and I am inclined to think that they represent his use of a distinct version at one period of his life. Without going more deeply into this question at present, I would indicate Sabatier's collections as sufficient to make this point easily verifiable. The reader may compare i. 13 with *Adv. Iovin.* ii. 3; i. 16, 20 = *ib.* i. 39; i. 22 = *ib.* ii. 3; ii. 10, iii. 2, iii. 8, iv. 1, etc. = *Contra Pelag.* 17 [1]. This version we will call 'Hieronymian,' to distinguish it from the 'Itala-Vulgate' or 'Itala.' Our four versions will then be the Corbey, the Itala-Vulgate, the Speculum, and the Hieronymian, without counting that of Optatus, and possibly Hilary.

It is important to establish this multiplicity of versions, not only for the sake of showing the early diffusion of this particular book in the West, but also as a contribution to the question, which has been often mooted, whether the Old Latin texts of the New Testament are all to be traced to one original. The more the subject has been investigated the more clear does it become that the sources were many rather than one; though absolutely unmixed and original versions have very rarely come down to us. St. Jerome long ago asserted this in general terms in the well-known passage of his preface to the Gospels: 'Si enim Latinis exemplaribus fides est adhibenda respondeant quibus: tot enim sunt paene quot codices.' We must look to Dr. Sanday to go more thoroughly into the question of the number of what can be called separate translations.

[1] Some of these quotations have already been given as notes to the comparison of the Speculum. Unfortunately the longest do not coincide with the extracts of that compilation. Two others of some length may be given here:—i. 16 (*Adv. Iov.* i. 39), 'Omne datum bonum et omnis perfecta donatio desursum est descendens a patre luminum apud quem non est differentia aut auersionis obumbraculum. Volens genuit nos uerbo ueritatis ut simus primitiae creaturarum eius;' and i. 22 *ib.* ii. 3', 'Estote factores uerbi et non auditores tantum. Si quis auditor est uerbi et non factor iste similis est uiro qui considerat uultum natiuitatis suae in speculo. Considerauit illud et statim recedens oblitus est qualis sit.'

Of the four versions which we have traced of St. James three of course have been already shown by implication to be at least as old as the fourth century, the Hieronymian, the Itala-Vulgate, and the Speculum.

The Corbey version comes to us in a late MS., but its antiquity might be inferred to be considerably earlier than the Council of Carthage (A.D. 397), from the fact of its association with uncanonical literature. This inference is fortunately substantiated by two quotations in the works of Chromatius, Bishop of Aquileia, the friend of Ruffinus and St. Jerome, and the supporter of St. Chrysostom. The reader will judge from the following parallel:—

Corbey St. James.	Chromatius, *Tract. in Ev. S. Matt.*
i. 12. Beatus uir qui sustinuerit temptationem quoniam probatus factus accipiet coronam uite quam promittet eis qui eum diligunt.	xiv. 7. Beatus qui sustinuerit tentationem quoniam beatus (*lege* probatus) factus accipiet coronam uitae quam promittit Deus iis qui eum diligunt.
i. 15. Deinde concupiscentia concipit et parit peccatum. Peccatum autem consummatum adquirit mortem.	ix. 1. Concupiscentia parit peccatum. Peccati autem concupiscentia adquirit mortem.

The senseless repetition in i. 12 of 'beatus ... beatus,' and in i. 15 of 'concupiscentia ... concupiscentia' shows either that Chromatius is very badly edited or that he quoted from a very bad MS., but the substantial agreement of his citations with the Corbey version is apparent in the use of the unique phrase 'adquirit mortem,' the origin and meaning of which is extremely obscure. The Greek ἀποκυεῖ θάνατον throws little light upon it.

The conclusion, then, of this part of the subject is that the Corbey version is at least as old as the fourth century, and that it is, in its origin, distinct from three others which were known in the Western Church at the same date[1]. Its employment as subsidiary to the Itala probably implies a greater antiquity than that assignable to the rest.

II. We must now pass to the second part of our subject: *Relation of the Corbey version to the Greek text of the Epistle, and its bearing on the question of the language in which St. James originally wrote.*

That the version is made from a Greek text of some kind is clear; that it is from a text in many respects differing from that received by any modern editor is also evident. The first proposition is proved, amongst other things, by the use of such quasi technical terms as *conditio* = κτίσμα in i. 18; *traducti* = ἐλεγχόμενοι, ii. 9; *disciplinosus* = ἐπιστήμων, iii. 13, which we may say without offence belong to the 'jargon' of Latin interpreters from the Greek[2]. Something of the same

---

[1] I have not entered into a discussion as to the Latin style of the version. There is a certain rude force and eloquence in it, not altogether marred by the numerous anacolutha. The vocabulary is rich in remarkable words, as becomes a translation from an Epistle which contains so many uncommon phrases (see note below, p. 149). It seems worth while to give a rather full list of the rarer words, including those which are found occasionally in other books. It may be possible to trace the local affinities of some of them—especially if some progress is made in the direction in which Sittl has recently attempted to move.

alapamini (κατακαυχᾶσθε)
animalis (ψυχική)
anxiat (κακοπαθεῖ)

bullit (βρύει)

conditionum (κτισμάτων)

datio (δόσις)
demonetica (δαιμονιώδης)
disciplinosus (ἐπιστήμων)

eliditur? (δελεαζόμενος)
exploratores (κατασκόποις)
exponentes (ἀποθέμενοι)
exterminata (ἀφανιζομένη)

fornicaria (πόρνη)
fornicatores (μοιχοί?)

germinauit (ἐβλάστησεν)

inreprehensibilis (ἀδιάκριτος)

legum positor (νομοθέτης)
liberalitas (ἐλευθερία)

natantium (ἐναλίων)

potentantur (καταδυναστεύουσιν)

retractare (καταλαλεῖν)

salmacidum (πικρόν and ἀλυκόν)
satulli estote (χορτάζεσθε)
scamello (ὑποπόδιον)

tiniauerunt (σητόβρωτα γέγονεν)
traducti (ἐλεγχόμενοι)

uisceraliter misericors (πολύσπλαγχνος καὶ οἰκτίρμων)

zabolo (διαβόλῳ).

[2] *Disciplinosus* is a very rare word, but *disciplina* = ἐπιστήμη is common enough, though not always understood by those who read translations from the

bare equivalence is noticeable in *legum positor* = νομοθέτης in iv. 12, and '*faciemus ibi annum*' in iv. 13. Another proof is afforded by the ingenious conjecture, which has occurred independently to Mr. D. S. Margoliouth and Dr. Sanday, that '*momentum enim est per modica uisibilis*' in iv. 15 is due to a confusion in the translator's mind, or in his Greek MS., between ἀτμός (ἀτμίς, editors), *vapor*, and ἄτομος, *momentum*. Similarly the dative '*naturae autem humanae*' in iii. 8 appears to me a mere mis-translation of the Greek dative.

The difference of the original text from our existing Greek MSS. must also be evident to every attentive reader, but a collection of the most important variations will bring it home to his imagination with greater distinctness.

In the following list I have not generally registered variations of tense, which are too common phenomena in the unrevised Latin versions to be of great importance for a rigorous criticism[1]; nor have I set down a number of cases of the interchange of number in nouns, which seem usually due to mere carelessness. The Greek text is generally that of Tischendorf.

i. 3. probatio uestra operatur sufferentiam   τὸ δοκίμιον ὑμῶν τῆς πίστεως κατεργάζεται ὑπομονήν.

<small>The omission of the words τῆς πίστεως agrees with B³ and Syr. philox., but they are found apparently in all other authorities (since probably here 81 = B). The words may possibly be a gloss or expansion from 1 Pet. i. 7 rightly omitted by ff.</small>

i. 14. abducitur et *cliditur*   ἐξελκόμενος καὶ δελεαζόμενος.

<small>The reader may conjecture *elicitur* or *cluditur*, but neither seems quite satisfactory. Possibly our Greek text had ἐκκρουόμενος or παρακρουόμενος in the sense of 'deluded,' 'cheated.'</small>

Greek, or *vice versa*. A good Græco-Latin glossary with reverse index, embracing Irenaeus and the early versions of the Apostolic Fathers, and the Greek translations of Latin documents and laws in the Church Historians, as well as the Scriptural matter, is still a desideratum.

[1] In the first draft of this paper I was inclined to lay stress on these variations of tense as pointing to the influence of a Hebrew original; but a careful examination of them, which Dr. Driver has kindly made for me, proves that this method of explanation will not hold good as regards these tenses. Nor had I then observed how common such variations are in other Old-Latin texts. They seem to be due to defective knowledge of Greek grammar as much as to any other cause.

i. 15. *adquirit* mortem   ἀποκυεῖ θάνατον.

This is at present unexplained. Dr. Hort suggests a western gloss ἐργάζεται; cf. Oecumenius here, and Rom. vii. 13, 2 Cor. vii. 10. Dr. Driver compares Job xv. 31 (LXX), where the similar Hebrew metaphor is obliterated.

i. 17. apud quem non est   παρ' ᾧ οὐκ ἔνι παραλλαγὴ ἢ
permutatio uel *modicum obum-*   τροπῆς ἀποσκίασμα.
brationis

Here, as is well known, ℵ* B have the apparent conflation τροπῆς ἀποσκιάσματος, and c of Scrivener adds a gloss, apparently based on a misconception of Oecumenius, οὐδὲ μέχρι ὑπονοίας τινὸς ὑποβολὴ ἀποσκιάσματος, meaning 'not even the least suspicion of an idea of shadow.' The Vulgate has *vicissitudinis obumbratio*, Jerome (*Iovin.* i. 39), *aversionis* (or *conversionis*) *obumbraculum*, and Augustine (passim) *momenti obumbratio*. It is clear to me that ff is a translation of ῥοπὴ ἀποσκιάσματος, 'a moment of shadow,' and Augustine's of ῥοπῆς ἀποσκιάσμα, 'shadow of a moment,' which is in fact the same thing, i.e. shadow lasting for a moment. This sense of ῥοπή is justified by the use in Wisdom xviii. 12 and ὁ 'Εβραῖος in Job xx. 5 = Heb. רגע. See Field ad loc. and I. p. lxxv. f. I am myself inclined to believe that either ῥοπὴ ἀποσκιάσματος or ῥοπῆς ἀποσκιάσμα is right, notwithstanding the wealth of astronomical learning which has been spent on illustrating παραλλαγή and τροπή.

i. 18. *primitiae* conditionum   ἀπαρχήν τινα τῶν αὐτοῦ κτισ-
eius   μάτων.

The word τινα is omitted also by 81 (cf. i. 3) and 95* as well as by Jerome, *Adv. Iovin.* i. 39, 'primitiae creaturarum eius.' I am inclined to think that the reading of ff is right, and that τινα is a softening of the phrase, perhaps merely for literary elegance, but more probably to avoid any idea of collision with the use of ἀπαρχή of Christ (1 Cor. xv. 20 and 23). Cp. the glosses in ff and the Sahidic in ii. 14.

i. 22. *aliter consiliantes*   παραλογιζόμενοι ἑαυτούς.

This is an unique variation. But it is to be noticed that St. Jerome, *Adv. Iovin.* ii. 3, omits the clause altogether, and possibly rightly. The sort of explanation of our reading that occurs to me is that the archetype had in the text something like *male suadentes vosmet ipsos*, with a gloss in the margin *aliter* (= otherwise read) *consiliantes*. *Consiliantes* was of course intended as a variant only on *suadentes*, but the scribe stupidly copied the two words as if they were a substitute for the whole clause. It is perhaps even more likely that the corruption arose in the Greek stage, since ἄλλως is used in Greek in such cases, and *uel*, more often than *aliter*, in Latin. It is less likely, though not impossible, that *aliter consiliantes* is a rough translation of παραλογιζόμενοι, set at first in the margin as a variant for *seducentes* or *fallentes*.

ii. 4. Diiudicati estis inter   Οὐ διεκρίθητε ἐν ἑαυτοῖς;
uos

Here ff agrees with B* alone in omitting the οὐ. Cp. v. 20 for another case. Similarly, in verse 26, the only Greek MS. which omits γάρ is B with Syr. Arm.

Aeth.; while ff and Origen represent δέ. Westcott and Hort not unnaturally read ὥσπερ τὸ σῶμα κ.τ.λ. without a particle.

ii. 7. nonne ipsi blasphe-   οὐκ αὐτοὶ βλασφημοῦσι τὸ κα-
mant *in bono nomine*, etc.   λὸν ὄνομα, κ.τ.λ.

This will be discussed below. Cf. v. 10, 15.

ii. 14. numquid potest fides   μὴ δύναται ἡ πίστις σῶσαι
cum *sola* saluare   αὐτόν;

The addition of *sola* is evidently a gloss from verse 17, in order to soften what seemed a hard expression. It is found only in the Speculum besides, but the Sahidic version adds in a similar spirit 'save him *without works*.'

ii. 25. *exploratores ex* XII   τοὺς ἀγγέλους.
tribus filiorum Israhel

Exploratores is evidently a translation of τοὺς κατασκόπους, which is found in some Greek MSS. including CK^{mg}L Syr^{sch} p^{marg} (exploratores Iosue) and Arm. Arab^c Aeth. The exact form of the gloss seems to occur nowhere else. See below.

iii. 4. The version is very free, but the sense is the same as the Greek.

iii. 6. et lingua ignis *sceuli*   καὶ [om. Tisch. with ℵ*]
iniquitatis   ἡ γλῶσσα πῦρ ὁ κόσμος τῆς
   ἀδικίας.

This verse will be discussed below. There is no reason to change *sceuli* to *sceulum* as Martianay suggests.

iii. 14. *quid alapamini....?*   μὴ κατακαυχᾶσθε.

Alapamini is merely a rare word. See the gloss in Ducange, *alapator*, καυχητής. But *quid* seems really a variant and an unique one. See on ii. 4.

iii. 16. *inconstans* ibi et omne   ἐκεῖ ἀκαταστασία, κ.τ.λ.
prauum negotium

See below.

iii. 17. *sine diiudicatione in-*   ἀδιάκριτος.
reprehensibilis

This is merely a conflation either from the use of two Latin texts or the introduction of a marginal gloss. See on i. 22.

iv. 4. *Fornicatores* nescitis,   μοιχαλίδες κ.τ.λ. ℵ* A B 13
etc.   Tisch., and μοιχοὶ καὶ
   μοιχαλίδες ℵ^c K L P and
   most others.

Fornicatores appears to be an African word. The Vulgate has here *adulteri*: both point to a reading μοιχοί, with possibly a variant πόρνοι, which is not, however, found at present alone in any Greek MS. The common reading μοιχοὶ καὶ μοιχαλίδες is, however, seemingly a conflation of the two words which were read separately in older MSS. Μοιχαλίδες being at first sight the harder reading is probably correct. I do not, however, think it refers to spiritual unfaithfulness, as some do, or that it is a feminine for masculine, like the (supposed) ποταγωγίδες, instanced by Tischendorf ad loc. The Apostle seems rather to address verse 2, referring to acts of violence, to men who do not pray at all, but are zealots, assassins, and murderers: while women pray, but ask amiss, uniting seeming devotion with incontinence and worldly ambition in a way not wholly unknown to any age. It makes little difference whether we subjoin μοιχαλίδες (with Tischendorf) to verse 3, or (as usual) prefix it to verse 4.

iv. 5. aut putatis quoniam dicit Scriptura: Ad invidiam conualescit Spiritus qui habitat in nobis? ἢ δοκεῖτε ὅτι κενῶς ἡ γραφὴ λέγει πρὸς φθόνον ἐπιποθεῖ τὸ πνεῦμα ὃ κατῴκισεν ἐν ἡμῖν;

The variants of ff are (1) omission of κενῶς, else unexampled; but cf. the varying order of the Armenian, teste Griesbach, ἡ κενῶς δοκεῖτε; (2) conualescit, which is almost inexplicable; (3) habitat = the common Greek reading κατῴκησεν, and so the Latin Vulgate and the versions; (4) in nobis, also in the Vulgate = ὑμῖν, which is apparently not now found in Greek MSS. The varying place of κενῶς in the Armenian makes it not impossible that the word is a gloss: at any rate, it is evidence, taken with the reading of ff, that some Greek MSS. omitted it. (On the Latin affinities of the Armenian, see Westcott and Hort, *G.T.* vol. 2, p. 158.) *Conualescit* would naturally be the translation of ἐνδυναμοῦται (as in Acts ix. 22; Heb. xi. 34) or κραταιοῦται, not of ἐπιποθεῖ. The whole passage is one of extreme difficulty, but the Corbey text, whether right or wrong, gives an intelligible view of it, which is at any rate worth considering. It may be paraphrased, 'Do not love the world and strive to get the better of your neighbours. It cannot be of our Christian spirit, of the Spirit of God dwelling in us, that the Scripture speaks as growing strong in envy of its neighbours. It is of the wicked that we read (Prov. xxi. 10) "The soul of the wicked desireth evil: his neighbour findeth no favour in his eyes." But the Christian spirit giveth its possessors greater grace than this. Wherefore he saith, "God resisteth the proud, but giveth grace unto the humble "(= Prov. iii. 34. Surely he scorneth the scorners: but he giveth grace unto the lowly).' There is perhaps also a tacit reference to Prov. xx. 27, 'The spirit of man is the candle of the Lord, searching all the inward parts of the belly.'

iv. 11. nolite retractare de alterutro *frater* μὴ καταλαλεῖτε ἀλλήλων ἀδελφοί.

This seems more than a simple case of interchange of number: cf. v. 9, 'nolite ingemescere *fratres* in alterutrum.' See below.

iv. 14. *momentum* enim *est* ἀτμὶς γάρ ἐστε.

The translator, as we have said, probably had ἀτμός in his copy, and confused it with ἄτομος. Dr. Hort suggests, however, *flamentum* corrupted to *momentum*. Many MSS. have ἐστιν, and it is the reading of the Vulgate.

v. 2. *res uestrae tiniauerunt*   τὰ ἱμάτια ὑμῶν σητόβρωτα γέγονεν.

See below. The Greek of ff may have been χρήματα or σκεύη instead of ἱμάτια. Dr. Hort suggests a possible loss of *ues-* before *res uestrae*.

v. 4. qui *arauerunt*   τῶν ἀμησάντων.

The contrast between ploughmen and reapers makes the picture more complete, and is one we should have expected in such an Epistle: but no extant Greek MS. or other authority has *ploughed*. Cf. however 1 Sam. viii. 12 (LXX) for the converse change.

v. 10. accipite experimen-   ὑπόδειγμα λάβετε, ἀδελφοὶ τῆς
tum, fratres, *de malis passio-*   κακοπαθείας καὶ τῆς μακροθυ-
nibus et *de patientia* prophetas   μίας τοὺς προφήτας.

v. 15. oratio *in fide*   ἡ εὐχὴ τῆς πίστεως.

These two cases stand together, and may be compared with ii. 7.

v. 16. oratio iusti *frequens*   δέησις δικαίου ἐνεργουμένη.

The Vulgate *assidua* has much the same sense. The Greek may have been ἐκτενής or ἐνδελεχής.

v. 20. Qui renocauerit, etc.   γινωσκέτω ὅτι ὁ ἐπιστρέψας,
κ.τ.λ.

Greek MSS. vary between γινωσκέτω ὅτι and γινώσκετε ὅτι. The words are omitted by the Sahidic as well as ff, and probably by Ambrosiaster and Cassiodorius.

de morte *sua*   ἐκ θανάτου.

Here again B alone of the Greek MSS. agrees with ff in adding αὐτοῦ, as does Aeth. Cp. on ii. 4.

Lastly, the subscription runs, *Explicit Epistola Iacobi filii Zaebedei*. We shall return to this presently.

In the above collection of passages we have some which clearly point to a Greek text differing from that current in any known MS. It must have had for instance the following readings, if our arguments are sound, ῥοπὴ ἀποσκιάσματος in i. 17, καθ' ἑαυτὴν σῶσαι αὐτόν in ii. 14, ἡ γλῶσσα πῦρ τοῦ κόσμου τῆς ἀδικίας in iii. 6, μοιχοί or πόρνοι in iv. 4, τὰ χρήματα or σκεύη ὑμῶν σητόβρωτα γέγονεν in v. 2—and others of which the original form is less certain, though the fact of its variation is indisputable.

Can any explanation be offered of these differences? I know

of none which covers *all* the facts; but I think that the hypothesis of a Hebrew or Aramaic original (probably the latter) from which were formed two independent or quasi-independent Greek versions, does explain some of the phenomena, and is in itself extremely probable. Our current Greek text and the Greek archetype of ff will thus have stood to one another and to the Aramaic in much the same relative position as two of the Latin versions do to each other and to the original Greek. They will also have suffered just the same chance of mixture and assimilation, so that we are not surprised to find ff sometimes standing quite alone, sometimes agreeing with a single Greek copy or with a larger group of authorities, but almost always having a reading which sets us thinking as to wider probabilities.

The arguments in favour of this hypothesis may be considered under three heads: (A) passages which it helps to explain; (B) probability from parallel cases: (C) probability against St. James' having written in Greek like that before us in the Epistle.

(A) The passages which this hypothesis helps to explain are (1) ii. 7, where *in bono nomine* for the accusative seems to be a Hebraism; cp. 2 Sam. xxiii. 9, and 2 Chron. xxxii. 17, where *charaph* is followed by the preposition. The same construction is found in Syriac with ܒ (Acts xxvi. 11: see Payne Smith, *Lexicon*, I. col. 659).

Perhaps we may class v. 10 oratio *in fide* and v. 15 experimentum *de malis passionibus*, etc., where the Greek has simple genitives, in the same category. Both Hebrew and Syriac, certainly the latter, would use prepositions here.

(2) ii. 25, *exploratores* is, as we have seen, a point of contact with the Syriac version. The gloss *cr XII tribus filiorum Israhel* is a confusion between the two occasions when spies were sent, since Rahab only received two men (Josh. ii. 1). It may be connected with i. 1, ταῖς δώδεκα φυλαῖς.

(3) iii. 6. *Et lingua ignis seculi iniquitatis* has a striking point of contact with the Peshitto Syriac which reads, 'The

tongue is a fire: the world of iniquity is as it were a wood.' The latter is apparently a gloss or expansion of our reading. Certainly the conception, 'The tongue is a fire which lights the world of iniquity,' i.e. the whole mass of iniquity, lying dormant till some evil word sets it in a blaze—is much clearer than that usually attributed to these words. It is said that the 'world of iniquity' is not a Hebrew idea, but that is a difficulty in any case whichever way we interpret it. For the Epistle comes from a man who thought in Hebrew whether he wrote in it or not. It is true that in Prov. xvii. 6, ὅλος κόσμος τῶν χρημάτων in LXX has nothing to correspond to it in the Hebrew. But עולם I presume came to be used very broadly in the later language including not only αἰών (as in Eccles. iii. 11), but κόσμος. Delitzsch, it may be noticed, uses it here, paraphrasing, 'the tongue is a fire, *a world full of iniquity* (עולם מלא עולה).'

We may notice also here that the reading *fornicatores* (instead of *adulterers* or *adulteresses*) is a point of contact with the Peshitto in iv. 4.

(4) iii. 16. *inconstans* (ἀκατάστατον), for ἀκαταστασία is easily explicable if the original of the two types of text was (unpointed) Hebrew or Aramaic. A confusion of פָּתַח and פֶּתַח for instance, or of any one of several other pairs of words in either language, might have been the occasion of the blunder. With this we may plausibly connect *frater* = ἀδελφοί in iv. 11, since 'my brother' and 'my brethren' are written with exactly the same consonants both in Hebrew and Syriac.

(5) v. 2. *res uestrae tiniauerunt*. The confusion of 'things' and 'garments,' which is impossible in Greek, points most probably to the double sense of the Syriac and Chaldee *mân*. It is the word used here and elsewhere for ἱμάτια in the Peshitto, and is also a common word for 'goods,' or 'stuff' of any kind, e.g. it is used in translating τὰ σκεύη (τοῦ ἰσχυροῦ) in the Gospels, Matt. xii. 29; Mark iii. 27, and τὰ σκεύη αὐτοῦ, Luke xvii. 31. For other instances see Payne Smith, *Lexicon*, I. col. 1991, which sufficiently establish the use of the

word in the sense of ornaments, household furniture, baggage, as well as vessels. I had at one time thought of a somewhat similar double sense of the Hebrew כלי; but though a word of broad signification it is not so broad as *mân*.

(6) The subscription *Explicit Epistola Iacobi filii Zebedei* has often been compared with the Syriac note prefixed to the Catholic Epistles in the editio princeps of Widmanstadt (Vienna, 1555), which may probably be translated, 'we here print [1] the three Epistles of James, Peter, and John, who were witnesses to the revelation from our Lord when He was transfigured.'

We cannot indeed see in this note the judgment of the Syrian Church in general, for such a statement does not appear in the oldest MSS. of the Peshi/to known to us [2], which simply ascribe the letter to 'James the Apostle.' It represents, however, almost certainly the judgment of the Syrian ecclesiastics who were associated with Widmanstadt in his edition, and if so is a distinct link of connexion between our MS. and the country of Syria. A similar tradition is hinted at rather than expressed by St. Jerome in his catalogue of ecclesiastical writers [3].

The positive evidence, then, for our hypothesis—of the force of which the reader will judge—is in favour of an Aramaic rather than a Hebrew original for our Epistle.

(B) I will next add a few words as to the *a priori* probability from parallel cases that the Epistle was written in Aramaic—including the evidence which may possibly point to the use of Rabbinical Hebrew.

(1) It seems certain that our Lord spoke in general the

---

[1] This is now generally agreed to be the meaning of the Syriac *ch'tham* (σημειοῦν, τελειοῦν, τυποῦν) in this place. See also Payne Smith's Lexicon, I. col. 1408, where one instance is given of the use of the word for *printing*.

[2] This is frankly acknowledged by Mr. F. T. Bassett in the Introduction to his edition of the Epistle, p. viii. He is, as is well known, strongly in favour of the authorship of the son of Zebedee.

[3] 'Jacobus Zebedaei filius duodecim tribubus quae erant in dispersione omnibus praedicauit Euangelium Domini nostri Jesu Christi.'

vernacular language rather than Greek or Hebrew. Not only have we certain well-known Aramaic words, reported as noteworthy utterances of His when addressing common people, but it would seem that upon the Cross, in speaking from the depths of His soul, He used an Aramaic version of the Psalter rather than the original. He preferred, that is, to say

to the original   אלהי אלהי למה שבקתני
                  אלי אלי למה עזבתני

This was indeed one of the most striking proofs of His condescension, of His wish to be in all things like unto His brethren, and to enforce the lesson of preaching the Gospel to the poor[1].

(2) St. Paul, when addressing his countrymen on the stairs of the Castle, 'spake unto them in the Hebrew tongue,' and so gained a readier hearing (Acts xxi. 40, xxii. 2). This may mean Rabbinical Hebrew, but being a discourse to a mob who had just before nearly torn him in pieces, it is more likely to have been the vernacular dialect[2]. It is of course matter of general knowledge that Ἑβραϊστί covers both languages. In John v. 2, and xix. 13 and 17, *Bethesda* (*Bethzetha*, *Bethsaida*), *Gabbatha*, and *Golgotha* are obviously Aramaic forms, while in the Prologue of Jesus son of Sirach, and Apoc. ix. 11 (Abaddon), Hebrew seems to be intended.

(3) St. Matthew, according to well-known tradition, wrote in 'Hebrew,' and as Papias[3] tells us, 'each one [at first] interpreted as he was able,' i.e. before the single ecclesiastical version at present known to us obtained supremacy. Papias'

---

[1] On the language spoken by our Lord, see a paper by Delitzsch in the Jewish Missionary Magazine, *Saat auf Hoffnung*, Deichert, Erlangen, 1874, and cp. the discussion in Kautzsch's recent Grammar of Biblical Aramaic, pp. 7–12.

[2] See J. H. R. Biesenthal, *Trostschreiben an die Hebräer*, p. 46, Leipzig, 1878, in favour of the view that St. Paul spoke Rabbinical Hebrew on this occasion. This is also the opinion of Delitzsch (*The Hebrew New Testament of the British and Foreign Bible Society*, Leipzig, 1883) and apparently also of Kautzsch, *Gramm. der Bibl. Aram.* pp. 19, 20, Leipzig, 1884.

[3] Papias in Eusebius, *H. E.* iii. 39, Ματθαῖος μὲν οὖν Ἑβραΐδι διαλέκτῳ τὰ λόγια συνεγράψατο (or συνετάξατο), ἡρμήνευσε δ' αὐτὰ ὡς ἦν δυνατὸς ἕκαστος. Observe the aorist ἡρμήνευσε, and see Lightfoot in *Contemporary Review*, August, 1875, vol. 26, p. 397.

pregnant words imply (as Bishop Lightfoot has seen) a time of concurrent rivalry of several versions of St. Matthew, such as we suppose was the case with our Greek versions of St. James, and such as we know to have been the case with the Latin versions before St. Jerome. We need not stop to discuss what is meant here by 'Hebrew,' though for my own part I incline to Aramaic.

(4) St. Peter, the Apostle of the circumcision, according to ancient tradition, needed an 'interpreter.' St. Mark, as all are aware, is named by Papias as 'having *become* (γενόμενος) his interpreter,' that is to say, we may suppose, as having joined himself to St. Peter after having left the service of St. Paul; and Glaucias, who was claimed by the Gnostics as the teacher of Basilides, is named as another 'interpreter' of the same Apostle. By this we understand that when preaching in a synagogue, where Hebraists and Hellenists were both assembled, the Apostle himself used Aramaic, for the benefit of one half of the congregation, while his interpreter translated his discourse into Greek for the benefit of the Hellenists and proselytes. This practice, it may be remarked, obviously accounts for St. Mark's competence as an Evangelist, and for certain peculiarities in his book. Such interpreters would also be used in translating epistles intended for groups of churches, such as the Epistles of St. Peter. Jerome, it will be remembered, takes it for granted that they were not originally written in Greek, and thinks that the difference between them was due to the employment of different men as interpreters[1].

Dr. E. G. King (now Vicar of Madingley) has written a paper on the subject of the relation of the Second Epistle of St. Peter to that of St. Jude which requires mention here[2]. His thesis

---

[1] See Papias, l.c.; Clem. Alex. *Strom.* vii. 17, § 106, p. 898, for Glaucias; Hieron. *Ad Hedibiam*, ep. 120, ch. xii. (tom. i. p. 838, Vallarsi; iv. p. 183, Martianay), 'Denique et duae epistolae quae feruntur Petri stilo inter se et charactere discrepant, structuraque uerborum. Ex quo intelligimus pro necessitate rerum diuersis eum usum interpretibus.' If Glaucias had translated the Second Epistle, this might perhaps have discredite 1 it to some extent in Catholic circles.

[2] *Did St. Peter write in Greek? Thoughts and criticisms tending to prove the*

is that St. Peter wrote this Epistle 'in Hebrew or Aramaic,' and 'that St. Jude read (it) in Hebrew, and wrote his Epistle—probably in Chaldee—as a Targum, or explanatory paraphrase thereon.' This paper was published in 1871, and Dr. King informs me that he still adheres to the theory, but is 'far from satisfied with the mode in which it is propounded,' and thinks that he could now make out a far stronger case for it. We may hope that he will have leisure to restate his position. Whatever may be the value of his arguments in detail (on which I am little qualified to pronounce an opinion) the theory is an attractive one, as offering a plausible solution of a most difficult question. Students of the New Testament need hardly be reminded that the relation of St. James to the first Epistle of St. Peter is in some degree parallel (as to the presence of common and possibly borrowed matter) to the relation between the pair of letters discussed by Dr. King.

(5) The supposition of a Hebrew original for the Epistle to the Hebrews is not unknown to antiquity, and has recently been forcibly maintained by Biesenthal. On this question I do not now wish to express any opinion.

(6) Josephus wrote his book on the *Wars of the Jews* first in his 'national language' and sent it to the 'upper barbarians,' by which he tells us that he means 'the Parthians, Babylonians, the most remote of the Arabians, the Jews beyond the Euphrates, and the Adiabenians.' Their national language would clearly be Aramaic, not Hebrew, which last would not be easily intelligible to the people of those countries. He tells us further that he used the assistance of others in making the translation into Greek, an assistance which he must have employed with great effect, as the style of his book is fairly classical—certainly not so Hebraistic as the Gospel according to St. Matthew or the Epistle of St. James[1]. It will be

---

Aramaic origin of the Second Epistle of St. Peter and the Epistle of St. Jude, by Edward George King, M. A., Tyrwhitt University Scholar, etc. Cambridge, J. Hall and Son, etc., 1871.

[1] See Josephus, *B. J. Prooem.* § 1; *Contra Apion.* i. 9.

noticed that Josephus first addressed himself to the Eastern dispersion, not to the Hellenistic Jews of Syria and Asia Minor, etc.

These parallels, when taken together, and compared with the evidence collected by Dr. Neubauer in another paper contained in this volume, make it very probable, *a priori*, that St. James would have written to 'the twelve tribes of the dispersion' in the language familiar to the Jews of Palestine and the East. In so doing he was following the example of his Master, who thus secured that the Gospel should be preached to the poor; he was acting with St. Matthew and St. Peter, the two other Apostles who specially addressed the 'circumcision;' he was doing what the Apostle of the Gentiles would certainly have commended; he was doing what the renegade Josephus actually did in propagating his views about the great national struggle with Rome. *We* are apt to forget the Jews of the Persian empire, but we may be sure that the Apostles of Palestine did not. 'To the Jew first '— and of Jews they were likely to put ' Parthians, and Medes, and Elamites, and dwellers in Mesopotamia ' in the first rank when their thoughts were turned towards the dispersion (cp. Acts ii. 9). Next to them would probably come the Jews of Antioch and its neighbourhood, who would, notwithstanding the surrounding Hellenism, be more accessible in Aramaic than in Greek.

(C) The negative probability that St. James would not have written such Greek as that in which the Epistle has come down to us is also, I think, very strong. The letter contains some striking Hebraisms and its whole spirit and tone is Jewish, but its vocabulary is distinctly Hellenic.

An analysis of the more striking words of the little book shows that it contains 49 which are not found elsewhere in the New Testament; of these 7 are very rare and scarcely found anywhere else in the whole of Greek literature, except in lexicons and late writers who may have borrowed from St. James; 13 are classical and not found in the LXX; 27 are classical and also found in the LXX; while only 2 are confined to LXX usage. That is to say the ascertained non-biblical element is 20 out of 49, or about two-fifths of the whole number, while as to the remaining three-fifths, which *may* be drawn from the LXX, many of the words have strong classical associations and few of them any distinct Biblical colouring.

Making then all allowances for the proximity of the LXX as a literary source to a Christian author, we are forced to the conclusion that even if it was largely used by the writer of this Epistle, he was also familiar with Greek on his own account, and was a scholar who had rather a wide range of classical reading.

Besides these 48 words peculiar to St. James, there are at least 27 others which occur only in one other New Testament writer, and generally in one single place of his writings[1].

[1] The full lists of these words may be interesting. In making them (as I hope) complete, I am much indebted to my friend, Mr. H. Deane, Fellow of St. John's College, Vicar of St. Giles', Oxford.
  The *seven very rare words* are ἀνίλεος, (ἀνίλεως in Hippolytus, quoting from this place), ἀνεμιζόμενος, ἀπείραστος (for ἀπείρατος), ἀποσκίασμα, δαιμονιώδης, θρῆσκος, χρυσοδακτύλιος. The *thirteen classical non-Septuagint words* are ἀλυκός, ἀμάω, ἀποκυέω (twice), βρύω, δίψυχος, ἐνάλιος, τὰ ἐπιτήδεια, εὐπειθής, ἐφήμερος, κατήφεια, ῥυπαρία, χαλιναγωγέω, χρή. The *twenty-seven Classical and Septuagint words* are ἀδιάκριτος, ἀκατάστατος, ἁπλῶς, βοαί, ἐξελκόμενος, ἐπιλησμονή, ἐπιστήμων, εὐπρέπεια, θανατηφόρος, κακοπάθεια, κατίωται, μαρανθήσεται, μετάγω, μεγαλαυχέω, νομοθέτης, ὀλολύζω, ὄψιμος, παραλλαγή, πρώϊμος, ῥιπιζόμενος, σέσηπε, ταλαιπωρέω, τροπή, τρόχος, τρυφάω, φλογίζω, φρίσσω. The *two* which are confined to LXX are ἀφυστερημένος and σητόβρωτος.
  The *twenty-seven* found only in one other New Testament writer are ἀλαζόνεια (1 John ii. 16), ἀκροατής (Rom. ii. 13), ἀποτελεσθεῖσα (Luke xiii. 32), ἀτμίς (Acts ii. 19 from Joel), δαμάσαι (Mark v. 4), δελεαζόμενος (2 Peter ii. 14, 18), δόσις (Philip. iv. 15), δώρημα (Rom. v. 16), εἰρηνικός (Heb. xii. 11), ἐμπορεύομαι (2 Peter ii. 3), ἔσοπτρον (1 Cor. xiii. 12), ἰός (Rom. iii. 13 from the Psalms), καταδυναστεύω (Acts x. 13), κατακαυχάομαι (Rom. ii. 18), κριτήριον (1 Cor. vi. 2, 4), κύριος Σαβαώθ (Rom. ix. 29), μακαρίζω (Luke i. 48), ὀπή (Heb. xi. 38), ὁρμή (Acts xiv. 5), ὄφελος (1 Cor. xv. 32), πηδάλιον (Acts xxvii. 40), πύρεια (Luke xiii. 22 in rather different sense). πραΰτης (1 Peter iii. 15), ῥυπαρός (Apoc. xxii. 11), σπαταλάω (1 Tim. v. 6), σπιλόω (Jude 23), χαλινός (Apoc. xiv. 20). All of this group of words have some parallel (sometimes only a single one) in the Greek Old Testament or Apocrypha, with the exception of δώρημα and πηδάλιον, for which there is no LXX precedent. To this list we must add χαίρειν in the classical epistolary sense, which would appear strange in St. James, were it not for the formula of the Apostolic letter in Acts xv. 23. Cp. xxiii. 26. It answers to שׁלום in Is. xlviii. 22, lvii. 21 (LXX).

This rich vocabulary is not unlike that which may have been possessed by a professional interpreter, but is very remarkable if we attribute it to an unlearned Jew writing perhaps the earliest book of the New Testament. I have purposely not discussed the question whether James the Just or James the son of Zebedee were the author, though I incline to follow the ordinary opinion which assigns the Epistle to the former. Those who, like Mr. Bassett, assign it to James the son of Zebedee, must of course date it before A.D. 44, in which case the difficulty becomes even greater. But if we suppose the Epistle to have been written (as I incline to do) soon after the καλὸν ὄνομα of 'Christians' had been given to the disciples at Antioch, and before St. Paul had definitely stirred the question of faith and works, we get an early date which hardly allows time for James the Just to have made such an advance in the Greek language as the current text implies.

To sum up in a few words. The hypothesis of an Aramaic original (1) accounts generally for the divergence between the present Greek and that which must have been the parent of our Corbey version, and specially explains some of the more curious phenomena of this divergence.

(2) It is probable from the striking parallel cases of the use of this language by our Lord and His apostles and by Josephus.

(3) It removes the difficulty as to the authenticity of the Epistle, which otherwise might arise from the highly classical and elaborate vocabulary which is employed in the Greek text.

In any case I think it is clear that ff represents a separate class of Greek MSS. (somewhat in the same way that the Codex Bezae does), and is therefore entitled to more consideration than it has hitherto received from editors.

VIII.

AN ACCOUNT OF
A SYRIAC BIBLICAL MANUSCRIPT OF THE FIFTH CENTURY
WITH SPECIAL REFERENCE TO ITS BEARING ON THE TEXT OF THE SYRIAC VERSION OF THE GOSPELS.

[G. H. Gwilliam.]

It is well known to Syriac scholars that the Textus Receptus of the Peshito depends upon very limited manuscript authority. Such is the case with both the Old and the New Testaments in that version: on the present occasion, however, our attention will be directed to the latter alone, and indeed confined to certain points connected with the text of the four Holy Gospels.

The Syriac Textus Receptus is read at the present day either in the pages of the valuable edition of Schaaf, or in some more convenient modern reprint; and these, while presenting some few variations, both among themselves, and from the original type, are substantially only reproductions of the editio princeps of Widmanstadt, published at Vienna, in 1555. Widmanstadt professes to have based his edition on two manuscripts[1]. Subsequent editors have collected a few

---

[1] Widmanstadt, in the course of a long preface, giving an account of the circumstances connected with the publication of his work, says, 'Anno MDXXIX in Divi Caroli Caesaris invictissimi, Sacri diadematis causa Bononiam proficiscentis, comitatu essem, et mihi contubernalibusque meis, Regii Lepidi, a metatoribus hospitium juxta coenobium, ubi Theseus jam senex vitam agebat, forte attributum fuisset . . . qui, ut me de coenobii bibliotheca sciscitari intellexit, e vestigio in conclave introduxit, et arreptis e pluteo Sacrosanctis Evangeliis Syriace scriptis, "Hospes," inquit, "peregrinis his studiis deditus

various readings, and have also corrected the text in certain passages, while Schaaf has brought together all that had been accomplished by his predecessors in these labours up to the publication of his edition at Leyden in 1708. Yet his text is practically that of Widmanstadt. Very little progress has yet been made by any editor in the way of emendation[1].

And in the judgment of some there is but little work for the textual critic in this department of literature. It is thought that the Textus Receptus of the Peshito, although possessing but slender support from external authority, is substantially correct; that the ancient witnesses, to which we now have access, would only demand that we should make a few changes in the text of Widmanstadt, and these chiefly in points of grammar and orthography. This opinion, whether true or false, is derived from conjecture rather than experiment. Until recently no one has attempted to sift the question, although materials for a decision were not wanting. But now manuscripts lie ready to hand at the British Museum, which, in conjunction with other sources of evidence, would enable us to settle permanently what was the text current, as their vernacular version, in the early Syrian Church[2].

sum annis circiter xv,"' etc. And a little further on, 'Quarto post anno in Bibliotheca Lactantii Ptolemaei reperi quatuor Evangelistarum libros.' On these two MSS. his edition was based, so that he says, in the preface to St. Matthew, 'Sanctum hoc Jesu Christi Evangelium, Syriaco sermone, ad duo vetustissima exemplaria exprimi.'

[1] Good work was done by Richard Jones, at the beginning of this century, but he had not then the materials now available. The full title of his book explains his scope and method, and is as follows:—'Textus Sacrorum Evangeliorum Versionis Simplicis Syriacae juxta Editionem Schaafianam collatus cum duobus ejusdem vetustis Codd. MSS. in Bibliotheca Bodleiana repositis, necnon cum Cod. MS. Commentario Gregorii Bar-Hebraei ibidem adservato, a Richardo Jones, A. M., e Coll. Wadham., 1805.' The MSS. of the Peshito which he collated are the Codd. Dawk. iii. and xxvii. Jones was inclined to ascribe to them too high an antiquity. Besides a very careful collation, he proposes a number of emendations. Wichelhaus does not mention his work, and Philip Pusey apparently did not know of it when he made his independent collation of Dawk. iii.

[2] For an account of the critical materials which were available before the Tattam Collection was made public, and the use which had been made of them, see J. Wichelhaus, De Novi Testamenti versione Syriaca antiqua, quam Peshito vocant, Halis, 1850.

When some forty years ago our National Library was enriched with the priceless additions of the Tattam Collection, a few of the MSS. of the Peshito New Testament in that Collection were examined by occasional readers; but it does not appear that any collations were made; certainly no results have been published; and for years the volumes remained unnoticed upon the shelves, until the late Philip Pusey proposed to himself the task of publishing a critical edition of the Peshito New Testament[1]. It is believed that his design was to maintain the value and authority of the Peshito *as it has come down to us;* to demonstrate that it has not been tampered with in later times, but that it presents to us the text of the Holy Scriptures of the New Testament, as they were read in the Syriac-speaking Churches, in the early days of Christianity. In pursuance of this object he collated a number of copies of the Holy Gospels with the Textus Receptus of Widmanstadt; but other studies interfered with this work, and he was suddenly called to his rest before he had published any of the results of his labours. In 1879 the present writer undertook for the Acts and Catholic Epistles what Philip Pusey had commenced for the Holy Gospels, and it was intended at a future time to combine and publish together the results of their labours. After Philip Pusey's death, his Syriac note-books were entrusted to the writer, and Dr. Pusey intimated that he might be willing to publish the revised Syriac text, at his own expense, if completed in his lifetime. His death was a fresh discouragement; but still the work of collating has been continued, though with many interruptions; and now the result has been obtained that, after a little further investigation, it will be possible to produce a text of the Peshito Gospels based, not as in Widmanstadt's edition, on two MSS. of unknown age[2], but on

---

[1] He would seem to have begun his collations about fourteen years ago, for in one of his note-books is an entry to this effect:—'A (i.e. the Cod. Mus. Britan. Add. 14454) finished June 29, 1872. Laus Deo.'

[2] The general character of the codices used by Widmanstadt, that they were Jacobite, and not of great antiquity, is pretty plain from the text, and Church

a number of copies of very great antiquity, and high critical value. The text of the rest of the New Testament could not be published for some time, little having yet been done for it in comparison with the labour bestowed by the two collators on the four Holy Gospels[1].

In the present paper it is proposed to offer a specimen of the kind of authority to which hereafter appeal will be made in settling the text of the Peshito New Testament, by giving an account of one very ancient MS., and indicating some conclusions towards which the study of the text it preserves would seem to tend.

Among the treasures of the Tattam Collection is an ancient book, denominated in the *Catalogue of the Syriac MSS. in the British Museum*, Codex Additionalis 14459, foll. 1-66, and described in the first volume of that work, p. 64. It is not indeed the oldest MS. of the Collection, but is apparently the most ancient of those which contain any part of the Peshito New Testament, and is possibly the oldest book of this kind in the world. Certainly it was written before the majority of those uncial Greek MSS. so highly prized in the emendation of the text of the Greek Testament. It is written on vellum, as are all the more ancient codices of the Tattam Collection, and contains the Gospels of SS. Matthew and Mark, and is bound up with another MS., the Codex Additionalis 14459, foll. 67-169, which is of a later date, in a different hand, and contains the other two Holy Gospels. The first few leaves were lost before the book reached this country, so that the Gospel of St. Matthew is now defective, wanting from i. 1 to vi. 19 inclusive.

The other MS. of a later date, referred to above, has on

Lessons, of the printed edition; but it would be interesting to know more of them. They are probably still in existence, doubtless at Vienna. Jones (Preface) and Wichelhaus (p. 217) refer to Adler as having seen a MS. at Vienna (Cod. Lambecii 258), which was used in Widmanstadt's edition; but as it is 'Mosis Mercdinaei ipsius manu exaratus,' it is probably a copy prepared for the press.

[1] It should be mentioned that the Rev. E. J. Perry, of Worcester College, has most kindly devoted many hours, in the midst of parochial work in London, to assisting the writer in the collation of MSS. of the Gospels.

the last page a note recording the date of transcription, and the circumstances under which it was written. This note is nearly illegible, but the first two lines have been deyphered to the following effect¹:—'This book was finished in the month . . . ;' the name of the month is illegible, and so is the rest of the line; at the beginning of the next line are the words 'eight hundred and forty.' There may be another word expressing a unit figure; but it is clear that the date is anterior to the year 850, i.e. of the Greek era². Reducing this to our own era, we get a date not later than A.D. 540, and which might be that of any year between A.D. 540 and 530, according to the unit assumed after the ܐܘܬܡܢܐ.

But the MS. which is to engage our special attention in this paper is of still older date than that with which it has been bound. Dr. Wright, in the description already quoted, speaks of it as being written in a beautiful Edessene Estrangela, apparently of the fifth century, with the exception of one leaf, which is perhaps of the tenth century, inserted to supply the lost, or defaced, original. Unfortunately there is no note recording the date, at the end, or elsewhere; but the writing, more elegant and flowing, in contrast with the somewhat larger and stiffer characters of the sixth-century MS. with which it is now associated; and the different forms of some of the letters, especially the ܒ, the ؟ and ؟, and the ܠ, points which cannot be fully discussed within the present limits, indicate the work of such an age as Dr. Wright supposes: indeed, we may accept his expressed opinion with much confidence. For it is to be observed that there are peculiar facilities for determining the date of an undated

---

¹ They stand thus in the MS.:—

. . . . ܚܡܫ ܒܗ ܐܕܐ ܕܬܚܡ
. . . . ܐܘܬܡܢܐ ܘܐܬܡܠܝ

N.B.—The characters are Estrangela, as in all ancient Syriac MSS., but throughout this paper the common type has been used for convenience.

² Dates in Syriac MSS. would seem always to be given according to the Greek era, called also the Era of the Seleucidae, and which commenced with the year B.C. 311. Sometimes this era is mentioned by name, as in Cod. Add. 14460; see Catalogue already referred to, vol. i. pp. 52, 53.

Syriac MS. The number of those actually dated is considerable. In the British Museum alone there are eighty-five bearing dates ranging between A.D. 1000 and A.D. 411, the date of the famous Cod. Add. 12150, besides many bearing later dates. These documents afford evidence of the style of handwriting prevalent in particular centuries, and also show that the older writing was very rarely, if ever, imitated in later times. Old MSS. were frequently repaired, particularly (as in the case of the one now under consideration) in the tenth century, but the new leaves substituted were transcribed in the current hand. Rubrics and marginal annotations were frequently added later, but it would seem always in the characters common at the period. So in the case of the codex before us, we may compare its handwriting with that of others known to have been written in the fifth century, and contrast it with the different style which prevailed later, and thus arrive at a date as nearly *proved* as the conditions of the problem will admit. Hereafter, then, it will be assumed that our MS. was written between A.D. 450 and 500, being probably as old as the former date. The question is of paramount importance, because the conclusions to be indicated later on in this paper derive all their value from the supposed early date of the MS. from which they are drawn; yet it is plainly impossible now to do more than indicate the method by which the date may be determined.

Before examining the text of the Cod. Add. 14459, it may be well to give a brief description of the book. It consists of 66 vellum leaves, about 7½ inches × 4⅝. The writing is in a single column, and is divided into paragraphs by the mark [o o] in red, which is sometimes, for want of room, put in the margin. In a very few instances about a quarter of the line is left blank at the conclusion of a paragraph. These divisions are not numbered, nor are the sections and canons indicated, as in some Syriac MSS. There are no rubrics in the text, but many have been noted in the margin by rude and late hands. They are of the ordinary type, but the word ܣܒܪܬܐ often occurs in place of the more common form ܣܒܪܬܐ.

It has already been noticed that the first leaves of St. Matthew are wanting. The MS. begins with the word ܣܝܡܬܐ, 'treasures,' Matt. vi. 20, and thence proceeds, without omission or loss, to the end of St. Mark.

At the end of St. Matthew is the following note:—

ܫܠܡ ܐܘܢܓܠܝܘܢ ܩܕܝܫܐ ܕܡܬܝ ܫܠܝܚܐ ܕܐܟܪܙ ܘܐܟܬܒ ܥܒܪܐܝܬ ܒܐܬܪܐ ܕܦܠܣܛܝܢܐ ܀

'Finished is the Holy Gospel of Matthew the Apostle, which he preached and wrote in the Hebrew tongue, in the region of Palestine.'

The Title of St. Mark is:—

ܐܘܢܓܠܝܘܢ ܩܕܝܫܐ ܟܪܘܙܘܬܐ ܕܡܪܩܘܣ ܀

'The Holy Gospel, the Preaching of Mark.'

And at the end of the same Gospel we read:—

ܫܠܡ ܐܘܢܓܠܝܘܢ ܩܕܝܫܐ ܟܪܘܙܘܬܐ ܕܡܪܩܘܣ ܣܒܪܬܐ ܕܡܠܠܗ ܪܗܘܡܐܝܬ ܒܪܗܘܡܐ ܡܕܝܢܬܐ ܀

'Finished is the Holy Gospel, the Preaching of Mark the Evangelist, which he spake in Roman, in the City of Rome.'

The usual doxology to the Blessed Trinity follows the note at the conclusion of each of the two Gospels.

There is nothing to show whether or not the work originally comprised the two remaining Gospels of SS. Luke and John; or again, whether what is now known as the Cod. Add. 14459, foll. 67-169, was subsequently transcribed to complete the work; or, being an independent copy of the two latter Gospels, was afterwards bound up with the two former. It may be remarked, however, that among the MSS. of the Tattam Collection are copies of single Gospels, also of pairs of Gospels. For example, the Cod. Add. 17115 contains SS. Matthew and John, with the Hebrews, Jude, and the Acts.

I. In considering the text of Cod. Add. 14459[1] in its

---

[1] It is to be observed that throughout the remainder of this paper we are treating only of the *former* part of this volume: what is, strictly speaking, the Cod. Add. 14459, foll. 1-66.

relation to the Textus Receptus of the Peshito, we may turn first to the well-known remarkable addition in the last chapter of St. Matthew, and then to the conclusion of St. Mark. We find:—

(1) That in St. Matt. xxviii. 18, 19 the text stands thus:—

ܐܬܝܗܒ ܠܝ ܟܠ ܫܘܠܛܢ ܒܫܡܝܐ ܘܒܐܪܥܐ. ܘܐܝܟܢܐ ܕܫܕܪܢܝ ܐܒܝ
ܡܫܕܪ ܐܢܐ ܠܟܘܢ. ܙܠܘ ܗܝܟܠ ܬܠܡܕܘ ܟܠܗܘܢ ܥܡܡܐ. κ.τ.λ.

'There is given to me all power in heaven and in earth; and as my Father sent me, I send you. Go therefore, make disciples of all nations.'

Widmanstadt reads ܐܦ ܐܢܐ ܡܫܕܪ ܐܢܐ, 'I also send;' but the omission is confirmed by a number of ancient Syriac codices: the words are no part of the original Syriac text. It will be seen, therefore, that our MS. supports the printed Peshito in this notable addition to the words used by our Blessed Lord in commissioning his Apostles.

(2) The last verses of St. Mark are given in No. 14459, as we read them in Widmanstadt, with a few unimportant variae lectiones. We will give the passage commencing with the middle of verse 8, and thus it will be seen that the scribe copied the words without any mark expressing doubt of their genuineness:—

ܐܚܝܕ ܗܘܐ ܠܗܝܢ ܓܝܪ ܬܗܘܬܐ ܘܪܬܝܬܐ. ܘܠܐܢܫ ܡܕܡ ܠܐ ܐܡܪ̈ܝ ܕܕܚܝܠܢ
ܗܘܝ ܓܝܪ. ○ ◦ ○ ܒܨܦܪܐ ܕܝܢ ܒܚܕ ܒܫܒܐ ܩܡ ܘܐܬܚܙܝ ܠܘܩܕܡ ܠܡܪܝܡ
ܡܓܕܠܝܬܐ. κ.τ.λ.

The mark ○ ◦ ○, in red in the MS., is the usual indication of the conclusion of a paragraph, already mentioned. The variation of ܐܡܪ̈ܝ for ܐܡܪ̈ܝܢ will be noticed: also the substitution of ܬܗܘܬܐ for the synonymous ܬܗܪܐ, which seems to be a reading unsupported by other MSS.

II. We may next examine certain consecutive passages, which will serve as specimens of the general text of the Cod. Add. 14459. It will be desirable, with a view to subsequent considerations, to choose places where we may have the advantage of comparison with the Curetonian; otherwise we can select at random. We will take St. Matt. vi. 20–34, vii,

viii. 1–22, and xv, setting down the text of Widmanstadt first, and the variations afterwards, and noting how far the readings of our MS. are confirmed by other ancient Syriac codices[1].

St. Matt. vi. 21, Widmanstadt ܐܘ ܕܟܣܦܗ | 14459 ܐܘ, and so the other MSS., the Curetonian has also ܐܘ, but the sentence is differently expressed. Ver. 25, ܠܗܘܐ ܠܐ | the MSS. have ܠܐ ܗܘܐ, and so apparently 14459, but the edge of the page is worn. Curetonian different. Ver. 27, ܘܠܡܗ | ܢܘܗ ܚܝ, with the MSS. Curetonian omits. Ver. 29, ܡܚܣܕܗ | ܡܟܣܕܗ, with MSS. and Curetonian. Ver. 32, ܘܟܚܣܐ ܗܘ ܚܣܩܛ | ܚܣܩܐ | omits ܘܚܐܣܐ with MSS., except one. Cur. has ܚܣܐܝ. It will be observed that the omission brings the text into conformity with the Greek. vii. 3, ܠܚܝ | MSS. have ܠܚܝ, but 14459 is doubtful, edge of page being worn. Cur. ܠܚܝ, but the sentence is inverted. Ver. 12, ܘܚܝ ܕܣܕܗܝ | ܐܚܝܗ ܘܚܝ, with the MSS. and Cur. Ver. 13, ܠܡܘܐܗ ܠܡܘܐܗ, with most MSS., but not the Curetonian. ܐܕܐܚܝ ܘܐܚܝ | omits ܠܚܝ with MSS., except two, and Cur. ܣܗܚ | ܗܚ, with the MSS. and Cur. This reading would perhaps represent εἰς αὐτὴν rather than δι' αὐτῆς, but there is no var. lect. in the Greek. Ver. 15, ܟܚܣܩܐ | here the Curetonian and several MSS. omit ribui, but 14459 agrees with Widmanstadt. Ver. 21, ܚܣܝ | our MS. and four others have the form ܠܚܣܝ, but not the Curetonian. Ver. 23, ܘܚܣܕܗܘܢ | ܘܚܣܕܗܘܢ, which appears to be the usual form in the ancient MSS.; so the Curetonian. Vers. 25, 27, ܘܚܣܕܗ | ܘܚܣܕ, and so the Curetonian. In this form of the verb all the ancient MSS. omit ܘ paragogic and ribui. viii. 1, ܠܣܟ | ܣܟ | ܣܟ, with the MSS. Cur. omits ܟܝ. Ver. 4, ܘܡܘܕܡܗ | ܘܡܘܕܡܗ, with several MSS., perhaps reading τὸ δῶρόν σου. Curetonian agrees with Widmanstadt. Ver. 8, ܚܝܝܟ | ܚܝܝܗ, with the MSS. and Cur. Ver. 9, ܐܚܝ | here 14459 agrees with Widmanstadt, while many MSS. and the Curetonian have ܐܚܝ, singular. Ver. 10, ܚܣܕܡܗ | ܚܐܡܗܝܗ, but Cur. has the form more common in

[1] These are for the most part of the Tattam Collection, but include two at Florence, and one in the Bodleian.

the ancient MSS., ܚܒܐܠ. Ver. 15, ܐܒܐ | ܐܒܐ, one of
the var. lect. apparently peculiar to 14459, as though it read
ὁ πρῶτος αὐτῆς. ܠܗܘܢ here our MS. agrees with Widmanstadt and with the Curetonian; but the other MSS. give ܠܗ,
which must be accepted as the correct reading of the Peshito;
i.e. the Peshito supports αὐτῷ, not αὐτοῖς. Ver. 20, ܕܒܗ | ܒܗ,
with four others, but not Cur. ܙܒܢ | all ancient MSS. and
Cur. spell this word ܙܒ. Ver. 22, from end of this verse the
Curetonian is defective to x. 32. xv. 1, ܡܕܝܢ̈ܐ | ܡܕܝܢ̈ܐ, with
many others, but not Curetonian. Ver. 5, ܡܕܝܢ | ܡܕܝܢ,
with two others, but not Cur. This reading is nearer to the
Greek, which has δῶρον alone, the Peshito apparently reading
δῶρον μου. Ver. 6, ܡܠܐܟ̈ܐ | ܘܠܟܠ | ܡܠܐܟ̈ܐ, with
the rest, but Cur. has ܘܒܩܘܡܗܘܢ. Ver. 7, ܗܢܐ
ܟܠܐ | omits ܟܠܐ, with the rest, but Cur. has it. It is a gloss
in Widmanstadt, and thus the true text of the Peshito agrees
with the Greek. Ver. 14, for ܢܚܙܐ, ܚܙܐ: and for ܐܢ,
ܟܝ: apparently without support in other MSS., or the Curetonian. The former variation suggests the reading ὄψες, but
the latter not necessarily γαρ, for ܟܝ is occasionally used in
the Peshito for δε, e.g. Luke ii. 44. Ver. 24, ܢܣܝܘܢܐ | here
ܐܢܫܐ, with several MSS., but Cur. ܐܢܝܫܐ, with two
others: cf. viii. 10. The spelling of this word varies in MSS.
Ver. 26, omits ܣܘܢ, with most MSS., thus bringing text
of Peshito into harmony with the Greek; cf. ver. 7 above.
The Curetonian is quite different. Ver. 27, ܐܘ | ܐܘ, with
two others. The words ܒܩܘܡ̈ܬܐ ܥܡ ܘܒܥܕܡ are written over
the line in 14459, being apparently omitted *prima manu* by
homœoteleuton. Ver. 31, ܡܣܝܘܢܐ | ܐܢܝܫܐ, with others;
but Cur. has here ܐܢܝܫܐ, and does not mark a paragraph
here, as do the other MSS. Ver. 34, ܐܠܐ ܐܚܕ | omit ܐܠܐ
with the other MSS., but Cur. has ܐܠܐ ܐܚܕܡ. Ver. 36,
ܠܗܘܢ | here 14459 and three others agree with Widman-
stadt, but the best supported reading is ܠܗܡ. Cur. omits
the word. Ver. 39, the Curetonian and two MSS. begin the
new section at this verse, but not 14459.

The results obtained by the above collation with the text of Widmanstadt may be summarized as follows. In 105 verses there are 30 variations from the received Syriac text, exclusive of the case of chap. vii. 3, which may be omitted as doubtful, though the probability is great that the codex would agree with the mass of MSS. Of these variations, only nine find any support in the Curetonian, and it cannot be affirmed of even these few that all agree with Curetonian readings. There are also four readings—viz. the ܡܘܕܝܢ, with ribui, vii. 15; the ܐܬܝܢ, plural, viii. 9; the ܠܗܘܢ, viii. 15; the ܠܗܘܢ, xv. 36—where 14459 sides with Widmanstadt, while the best supported text is different; and in one of these cases only, viz. viii. 15, is the reading in harmony with the Curetonian text. It will be seen, however, that while the very ancient text of our codex is seldom in agreement with Cureton's, it is commonly supported by the mass of ancient codices of the Peshito. It will be also noticed that the majority of the variations are of a trivial character, being only differences of spelling, or of the order of words, so that in the 34 readings collected above, there are only eight—viz. those in vi. 32; vii. 13; viii. 4, 15; xv. 5, 7, 14, 26—which have any bearing on the Greek from which the Syriac was translated. But yet the real value of the collation consists in the barrenness of the results. The verses examined in this paper afford a very fair specimen of conclusions fully admitted by those few who have devoted some years to the study of the text of the Peshito, and who are therefore alone qualified to express an opinion about it. Without anticipating what can only be fully set forth when (if ever) the revised text of the Peshito New Testament shall be published, it may be here affirmed, however, that the collation of ancient Syriac MSS. tends to confirm, in all important respects, the traditional text. A certain number of corrections will be made, but these, for the most part, will be in comparatively unimportant points of grammar and orthography.

III. The passages already considered will serve as specimens of the general text of the codex 14459: and as they occasionally present some modification of the printed Syriac text, it will be well next to examine the readings of the MS. at certain selected places, where such modification, if found, might have a value in the criticism of the Greek text. The following twelve passages may be chosen, where variations of considerable importance occur in the authorities on which the Greek text is based, and where, in consequence, the evidence of the Peshito has been adduced on one side or the other.

(1) St. Matt. x. 3. The Greek Textus Receptus is $\Lambda\epsilon\beta\beta a \iota o s$ ὁ ἐπικληθεὶς Θαδδαῖος, but there are several variations in the authorities, and in consequence some editors omit the first three words, others the last three; but the Peshito has ܠܒܝ ܘܐܕܝ ܐܚܘܗܝ, and 14459 confirms the longer reading.

(2) xvii. 21. Tischendorf (8th edition), with ℵ* and B, omits this verse, but the Peshito, confirmed by our MS., has it.

(3) xix. 17. The traditional reading of the Peshito, ܡܢܐ ܩܪܐ ܐܢܬ ܠܝ ܛܒܐ: ܠܝܬ ܛܒܐ ܐܠܐ ܐܢ ܚܕ ܐܠܗܐ, is confirmed by 14459.

(4) The remarkable addition after xx. 28 in D, the Curetonian, and others, is entirely unknown to 14459, as to every other MS. of the Peshito.

(5) xxiv. 36. Text. Rec. οὐδὲ οἱ ἄγγελοι τῶν οὐρανῶν εἰ μὴ ὁ πατήρ μου μόνος. Lachmann and Tischendorf add οὐδὲ ὁ υἱὸς after οὐρανῶν, but the Peshito, confirmed by 14459, omits. This is an instance of a rigid adherence in the Syriac MSS. to what was deemed the true text, against the temptation to borrow from parallel passages, as here from St. Mark xiii. 32, where the addition occurs. While admitting that the Peshito text is often fuller than that of ℵ and B, it has yet to be proved that its scribes indulged in careless amplification.

(6) xxvii. 35. Text. Rec. ἵνα πληρωθῇ τὸ ῥηθὲν ὑπὸ τοῦ προφήτου· Διεμερίσαντο τὰ ἱμάτιά μου ἑαυτοῖς, καὶ ἐπὶ τὸν ἱματισμόν μου ἔβαλον κλῆρον. Tischendorf, who omits the passage, quotes indeed in its favour 'some editions of the

Peshito.' He refers to the editions of Tremellius[1], and of others who follow him; for the editio princeps of Widmanstadt knows nothing of the words. With the help of Cod. Add. 14459. and other ancient MSS., we are now able to determine that they form no part of the Peshito. This case may be compared with the preceding; the text of St. Matthew is preserved without addition from St. John xix. 24.

(7) St. Mark vi. 11. MSS. ℵ and B omit the words ἀμην λεγω ὑμιν, ἀνεκτοτερον ἐσται Σοδομοις ἢ Γομορροις ἐν ἡμερᾳ κρισεως, ἢ τῃ πολει ἐκεινῃ, but they were in the Bible of the ancient Syrian Church. The text of Widmanstadt is assured by the testimony of No. 14459 and all the MSS.

(8) ix. 44, 46. Our MS. shows that the Peshito read these verses, although they are omitted by codices ℵ and B.

(9) xi. 3. The Text. Rec. has και εὐθεως αὐτον ἀποστελει ὡδε, but ℵ, B, and others read ἀποστελλει παλιν ὡδε. Our MS. confirms the reading of Widmanstadt, ܡܥܕܪ ܠܟ ܠܗܠ, showing that the παλιν was unknown to the Peshito in the earliest times: also that it read ἀποστελλει and not ἀποστελει.

(10) xi. 8, the words και ἐστρωννυον εἰς την ὁδον: (11) xiii. 14, the parenthetical clause το ῥηθεν ὑπο Δανιηλ του προφητου: (12) xv. 28, the whole verse;—are omitted by ℵ, B, and other authorities; but Cod. Add. 14459, with other ancient Syriac MSS., confirms the text of Widmanstadt. The several passages were all included in the Peshito of earliest days.

It will be seen that in these twelve important passages the traditional readings of the Peshito are confirmed by the venerable codex now under examination. It shows that the Syriac New Testament was not tampered with in the middle ages, but was read substantially by the ancient Syrian Church as Widmanstadt printed it. What, however, may be the precise value of the testimony of the Syrian Church, when in opposition to the old Greek MSS., is a question for further consideration: but it must be admitted that the researches

---

[1] Tremellius' Edition was published at Heidelberg in 1568. According to Wichelhaus he used a MS. which was subsequently removed to Rome.

among the Tattam MSS. have established for certain the nature of that testimony.

IV. It has already been noticed (II. above) that the text of our MS., where it differs from that of Widmanstadt, is usually supported by other ancient Syriac MSS. Yet the Cod. Add. 14459 has also a number of independent readings. Future collations may discover support for some of them, but the majority must be idiosyncrasies: a few, however, are found in the Curetonian. The following is a list of them:—

St. Matt. viii. 15. Widmanstadt ܐܠܗܐ | ܐܠܗܐ. Ver. 29. ܚܕܐ ܕܝܘܢܐ, Curetonian defective. x. 2, ܡܫܡܗܘܢ ܬܚܘܝܢ, Cur. defective. xi. 7, ܡܢ ܐܡ ܕܡ ܐܠܟ ܡܢ ܐܡ ܕܡ ܐܠܟ ܡܢ ܐܡ ܕܡ, Cur. ܡܢ ܟܕܡ. xii. 13. ܚܝܓܬܐ | ܗܐ | ܗܘܐ ܚܓܡܬܐ, and so the Curetonian. xiii. 53. ܡܠܐ | ܟܕ ܡܠܐ, so Cur. Ver. 54. omits ܗܘܐ; Cur. has it. xiv. 19. ܗܘܗ ܡܢ | ܗܘܐ. Ver. 23. ܣܥܘܬܗ | ܣܥܘܬܗ, a mistake probably; but in Cod. Dawk. iii. in St. Matt. xv. 19, there is a similar reduplication of letters in the form ܡܚܣܒܣܒܬܐ for ܡܚܣܒܬܐ. xv. 14, ܡܚܐ | ܡܚܘܐ; ܘܢܦܠܝܢ ܡܢ ܩܕܡܘܗܝ ܣܢܣܠܐ ܐܡ. Ver. 27, the words ܐܝܣܝܐ ܡܢ ܩܕܡܘܗܝ were omitted prima manu, perhaps by homœoteleuton, and are now written over the line. xvii. 12, omits ܘܡܚܕ ܠܗ. xviii. 6, ܠܘܗܕ ܐܡ | ܚܕܡܫܗ ܚܕܡܩܕܫܘ. Ver. 19. ܐܡܐ ܐܘ ܐܒܐ ܠܐ | ܠܐ ܐܚܕ ܐܡ. Ver. 33. ܐܡܣܝ | ܐܣܝ. xx. 3, ܘܚܙܝܢܚܡ | ܘܚܙܝܢܚܡ. Ver. 8, ܚܒܠܐ | ܚܒܠܐ ܕܒܝ | ܚܒܠܐ, and so the Curetonian. xxi. 25. ܓܒܠܐ | ܓܒܠܐ; Cur. ܚܒܠܐܘ, but the sentence is different. Ver. 32, ܕܣܬܐܠ, with ribui. xxii. 1, ܢܥܡܐ ܠܐܘ | ܠܐܘ ܢܥܡܐ. Ver. 7, ܐܘܕ, and ܐܘܕܐ | ܐܘܕܐ, and ܐܘܕܐ, the latter with the support of two other MSS. Ver. 14, ܩܓܝܠܐ | ܠܗܝܠܡ. Ver. 26, ܘܗܘܐ ܘܗܘܐ; also ܚܒܪܐ | ܚܒܪܐ, and so Cur., but the resemblance is accidental, as the context is differently expressed. Ver. 72, ܐܘ | ܘܐܘ. xxiii. 25, from this place the Curetonian is defective to St. Mark xvi. 17. xxvi. 38, omits ܠܗ. Ver. 42, ܘܗܙܕܟ | ܕܗܙܕܟ. Ver. 43, ܐܡܚ | ܘܐܡܚ; also ܚܣܝ | ܐܡ. xxvii. 41, ܐܘ | ܘܐܘ, but the ܘ apparently added later. Ver. 42. omits ܗܘܐ. Ver. 55, ܘܗܘܐ ܐܡ | ܐܚܓ ܘܐܘ ܗܘܐ ܐܡ | ܘܗܘܐ ܐܡ. Ver. 63, ܚܕ.

St. Mark i. 3, ܐܡܪ | ܐܡܪ. Ver. 10, ܘܚܙܐ | ܘܚܙܐ, but it is a

correction. ii. 3, ܘܠܡܐ | ܘܠܐ. Ver. 12, ܘܠܐ ܣܚܡܕܘ | ܘܠܐ ܣܚܡܕܘܢ.
iii. 20, ܚܢܥܐ ܘܐܚܕܘܗܝ | ܘܐܚܕܘܗܝ ܚܢܥܐ. iv. 2, omits second
ܗܘܐ. Ver. 6, ܗܕܡܐ | ܗܕܡܐ, mistake. Ver. 25, ܚܡ | ܚܡ.
v. 9, ܚܡܝ | ܚܡܡ. Ver. 14, ܗܠܘ | ܗܠ. Ver. 30, ܚܢܥܐ | ܚܢܥܐ,
with ribui. Ver. 34, ܘܐܚܘܗܝ | ܘܐܚܘܗܝ. vi. 31, ܘܐܚܠܠܘ |
ܘܐܚܠܠܘ. Ver. 34, ܘܣܪܐ | ܣܪܘܐ. Ver. 41, ܚܝܝ | ܚܝܝ. viii. 3,
ܐܠܐܡ | ܐܠܐܡ. ix. 1, ܘܠܠܐ | ܘܠܠܐ, now, by correction. x. 29,
omits ܐܘ ܐܘ. Ver. 46, ܠܐܝܣܘ | ܠܐܝܣܘ, but in the second place
where the word occurs it is spelled as in the received text.
This is an instance of the fluctuations which occur in the
MSS., and even in the same codex, in the spelling of proper
names, and of some other words. Also ܣܠܝ | ܣܠܝ. Ver. 31,
ܘܐ | ܐܘ. Ver. 32, ܒܐܚܕ ܚܕ | ܒܐܚܕ. xii. 18, ܚܕܡܐ |
ܚܕܡܐ ܘܪܘܡܬܐ. xiv. 3, omits ܗܘ. Ver. 4, ܐܚܬܡܐ | ܐܚܬܡܐ.
Ver. 29, ܒܐܚܡܕܘ | ܒܐܚܡܕܘ, a mistake, no doubt, as there is
no change of the word in ver. 27. Ver. 39, omits ܠܗ. xv. 1,
ܚܡ ܣܗܪܐ | ܚܡ ܣܗܪܐ ܘܚܡ ܣܗܪܐ. Ver. 29, ܗܠܘ | ܗܠ,
Ver. 36, ܚܠܠܗ | ܚܠܠ. Ver. 41, ܘܡܕܡܩܡ | ܘܡܕܡܩܡ. xvi.
8, ܠܐܗ | ܠܗ.

Among the passages now examined where readings peculiar
to Codd. Add. 14459 occur, there are twenty-two in which
comparison may be made with the Curetonian, that version
being defective in the other places. Among these twenty-two
it will be observed that there are only *three* (St. Matt. xii. 13;
xiii. 53; xx. 8) where the readings of our very ancient text
approximate more nearly than does the common text of
Widmanstadt to the version considered by many to be the
earliest Syriac translation.

These peculiarities of our codex are not only of some
interest in themselves, but they are evidence of the individual
and independent character of the several MSS. of the Tattam
Collection. It has been already observed (p. 161) that where
the ancient text of Codd. Add. 14459 differs from the printed
text of Widmanstadt, such variations are usually supported
by the concurrent testimony of a number of other ancient
codices. But it is not to be supposed that these witnesses

are mere echoes of the same evidence, servile copies of a prototype, and only representing the tradition of some one school or monastery. Their character may be well illustrated by the case of the cursive manuscripts of the Greek Testament. These have indeed all a resemblance, more or less marked, to the type of text preserved in the Codex Alexandrinus. But (to quote the words of a competent judge), 'No one who has paid adequate attention to them can fail to be struck with the *individual character* impressed upon nearly all[1].' And these words apply with equal force to the MSS. of the Peshito in the Tattam Collection. All, as well as the Cod. Add. 14459, have their peculiar readings, and in reference to that particular MS. it will be noticed that in three instances (St. Matt. xxvii. 41; St. Mark i. 10 and ix. 1) the peculiarities are due to correction leading the text further from the type preserved in the mass of MSS., and conforming it to some ancient model, which has now perished. It is unfortunate that the Curetonian is not extant in these places, to allow of comparison. Further evidence of the independence of these MSS. appears in the different arrangement of the paragraphs of the sacred text in the different copies. In some the paragraphs are numerous; in others few, and differently placed. For example, in St. Matt. x. the Cod. 14459 makes a break in our Lord's discourse at the end of verse 10, and seems to stand alone in so doing. In c. xi. it makes its division at the end of verse 1, thus not so distinctly connecting the message of the Baptist with the preaching of Christ recorded in verse 1, as do other authorities. And similarly in other MSS. divisions are constantly made, more or less arbitrarily, according to the fashion of some scribe or school. The MSS. also show their mutual independence in their manner of dealing with the orthography of proper names and some other words. Thus, amid a remarkable agreement which greatly assists the critic in reconstructing

---

[1] Scrivener, *Plain Introduction to the Criticism of the New Testament*, First Edition, 1861, p. 407.

the ancient text, there is yet such independence as gives weight to the testimony of each individual codex.

Having now described the Cod. Add. 14459, and given a sufficient account of its contents, it remains to point out some conclusions which seem to follow from the facts thus brought to light.

I. The text of our codex reproduces that of the version read in the Syrian Church at a period anterior to the two historical revisions of the Peshito. Had we only possessed MSS. written subsequently to the labours of Philoxenus, and of Thomas of Harkel, it might justly have been doubted if what professed to be the original Peshito had not been to some extent modified through the influence of the two later revisions. The well-known date of Thomas of Harkel's work is A.D. 616; but his revision of the Syriac Vulgate would seem to have been based on the translation made by the Chorepiscopus Polycarp for, and perhaps with the aid of Philoxenus, who was Bishop of Mabug from A.D. 488–518. The date assigned to this work is A.D. 508: we have already concluded, on evidence which almost amounts to a demonstration, that the Cod. Add. 14459 was written before the year A.D. 500, and is probably as old as 450. At the latest date assignable to it, it must have been written some years before Philoxenus' work, and may well be half a century older. It therefore cannot have been affected by those two subsequent revisions; and it is found that its text is substantially the same which Widmanstadt printed as the text received in the Syrian Churches. And the remarkable agreement between MSS. of the Peshito from the sixth century downwards is thus seen to have arisen, not from an enforced harmony produced by a new translation or critical revision, but rather because the text had so existed from earliest times, and was jealously transmitted intact. Cod. Add. 14459 assures us that we possess in the received Peshito text the same version, in all important particulars, which was read in the Church of Edessa in the middle of the fifth century.

It may indeed be objected that it is assuming too much to assert of the translation of the New Testament, as a whole, that which is true *prima facie* of only two Gospels. But the remarkable agreement found between the ancient MSS. of the Peshito will convince an unprejudiced critic that from other ancient codices, which are found to agree with this codex, he could reproduce what is lacking therein. Hence we may be assured that the scribe who in the middle, or the latter half, of the fifth century copied out SS. Matthew and Mark in the form preserved in No. 14459, would have produced a New Testament, if he had continued his work, of the same type of text as these two Gospels. From the nature of the case this cannot be demonstrated, but study of documentary evidence produces conviction that so it must be.

II. But every MS. preserves a text older, often far older, than itself, except it be the very autograph of the author. The text of Cod. Add. 14459 carries us back in our inquiries concerning the origin of the Peshito to a period far anterior to the middle of the fifth century; for what reason is there to doubt that the two Gospels which it preserves for us are a part of that Syriac New Testament which St. Ephraem quotes so frequently, and which Aphraates cites in almost every sentence of his Homilies[1]? And if those Gospels, in the form preserved in our codex, are a part of their New Testament, we are assured by the considerations already suggested that the complete Testament in use among the early Syrian Fathers must have been substantially the same as that known for centuries as the Peshito. This point can only be satisfactorily settled by an exhaustive examination of the quotations in the early Syriac writers. It is usually assumed that the quotations in St. Ephraem are made from the Peshito, but the question deserves full investigation, which should extend to all the early Syriac literature. It might be found

---

[1] St. Ephraem flourished about a century before Cod. Add. 14459 was written, his period being A.D. 299-378. The period of Aphraates is not yet precisely determined, but many of his Homilies are dated for different years between A.D. 337 and 345.

that those writers employed, as their vernacular New Testament, some other version which has now perished, being succeeded by the Peshito, in the early years of the fifth century, but that has yet to be proved[1].

III. The importance of these facts and inferences in their bearing upon the criticism of the Greek Testament is obvious. It has hitherto been an easy task to disparage the testimony of the Peshito by the retort that we can only quote it in evidence as it has come down to us: we do not know what it read in the third and fourth centuries. Recent investigations, of which a specimen is given in this paper, enable us to trace back the text of the Peshito to the very verge of St. Ephraem's days, and we think we can follow the stream much further yet. And as far as we follow it, we find it the same: and we know what the great Church of Edessa received as the text of the New Testament in the fifth century, if not indeed in the fourth, and even earlier. That is to say (not to *overstate* the case) at the period when the celebrated uncial Greek MSS. of the New Testament were written, we find the Syrian Church accepting a text which is not altogether in accordance with them, but which rather inclines to that type of text which most modern critics have rejected in favour of one based on those uncial MSS., and in particular on two of them, codices ℵ and B[2]. It is not within the scope of this paper to weigh the evidence of those great codices against that of the venerable version accepted in the Churches of the East. It may be (no opinion is now offered on the point) that the early Syrian Church was so unfortunate as to possess a very corrupt Vulgate. But it is to be observed that we *must commit ourselves to that view* if we resolve to base our text on the evidence of a few early Greek MSS. alone, and

---

[1] It would seem that G. L. Spohn had examined the quotations in St. Ephraem in his *Collatio Versionis Syriacae cum S. Ephraemi Commentario*, Lipsiae, 1785, but the book is very scarce, being neither in the Bodleian nor the British Museum. See also Note, p. 173.

[2] Referring to the twelve passages examined in pp. 162–3 f., and omitting (4) as being of a different character from the others, we find that except in (6) the Peshito disagrees with ℵ, B, and other uncials.

always to reject the witness of the Peshito where it disagrees with them.

IV. The comparison which has been made between some of the readings of the Cod. Add. 14459 and Cureton's Syriac suggests in conclusion a further inquiry as to the relation of the one to the other. It would seem that the two codices were written about the same time. There is no indication of a date in the Curetonian; but as we assign the Cod. Add. 14459, from the character of the handwriting, to the middle or latter half of the fifth century, so did Dr. Cureton assign his manuscript to about the same age, for the same reason. Dr. Wright, in the British Museum Catalogue, vol. i. p. 73, assents to this opinion, and it appears to be held on very good grounds.

It is well known that the illustrious discoverer of the Curetonian Syriac, and after him others, have held that it represents the oldest form of the Syriac New Testament, and that it was succeeded by the more polished, if not more accurate, Peshito; being ultimately so completely supplanted by the latter that it was no longer copied, and has survived to our day, as far as we know, in only one MS. If this were the true account of the relation to one another of the two versions, we should expect to find, in the most ancient text of the Peshito, many traces of the readings of the older version which it had supplanted. These might not be very numerous in the printed text of Widmanstadt, for it has been ascertained that the later MSS. of the Peshito underwent some revision, though this extended for the most part only to grammatical forms and orthography; but the most ancient MSS., and notably that now under particular examination, would surely contain at least some of them. Whether this be so or not can only be determined by an exhaustive comparison of the ancient text of the Peshito with the Curetonian text, but even the passages examined in this paper will afford grounds for an opinion. Among the 34 variations noted in the careful collation of texts made in pp. 159, 160, it was observed that only nine readings of Cod. Add. 14459 found any support in the Curetonian, and the resemblance of some of even that small number was doubtful. But a much more significant fact remains to be noted. In eleven passages, where the text of our ancient codex has a different reading from the text of Widmanstadt, sometimes with, sometimes without, the support of other Syriac codices, the Curetonian text, instead of agreeing with the ancient Peshito, approximates to, or even agrees with, the text of Widmanstadt. The passages shall be set down, that the reader may judge for himself.

(1) St. Matt. vii. 21, Widmanstadt, ܡܢ ܕܥܒܕ ܨܒܝܢܗ ܕܐܒܝ.
Curetonian, ܗܘ ܕܥܒܕ ܨܒܝܢܗ ܕܐܒܝ.
14459 and others, ܡܢ ܕܥܒܕ ܨܒܝܢܐ ܕܐܒܝ.

(2) „ viii. 4, Widmanstadt, ܘܩܪܒ ܩܘܪܒܢܐ.
Curetonian, ܘܩܪܒ ܩܘܪܒܢܐ.
14459 and others, ܘܩܪܒ ܩܘܪܒܢܟ.

(3) and (4) „ 15, Widmanstadt, ܘܫܒܩܬܗ ܐܫܬܐ ܘܩܡܬ ܘܡܫܡܫܐ ܗܘܬ ܠܗܘܢ.
Curetonian, [ܘܩܪܒ ܒܐܝܕܗ] ܘܫܒܩܬܗ ܐܫܬܐ ܘܩܡܬ ܘܡܫܡܫܐ ܗܘܬ ܠܗܘܢ.
14459 alone, ܘܫܒܩܬܗ ܐܫܬܗ ܘܩܡܬ ܘܡܫܡܫܐ ܗܘܬ ܠܗ.

(5) „ „ 20, Widmanstadt, ܠܒܪܗ ܕܝܢ ܕܐܢܫܐ.
Curetonian, ܠܒܪܗ ܕܝܢ ܕܐܢܫܐ.
14459 and four others, ܒܪܗ ܕܝܢ ܕܐܢܫܐ.

(6) „ xv. 5, Widmanstadt and Curetonian, ܩܘܪܒܢܝ.
14459 with two others, ܩܘܪܒܢ.

(7) „ „ 7, Widmanstadt and Curetonian, ܐܫܥܝܐ ܢܒܝܐ.
14459 and other ancient MSS. omit ܢܒܝܐ.

(8) and (9) „ 14, Widmanstadt, ܫܒܘܩܘ ܠܗܘܢ . . . . . ܣܡܝܐ ܕܝܢ ܠܣܡܝܐ ܐܢ ܢܕܒܪ.
Curetonian, ܫܒܘܩܘ ܠܗܘܢ . . . . . ܣܡܝܐ ܕܝܢ ܕܠܣܡܝܐ ܡܕܒܪ.
14459 alone, ܫܒܘܩ ܠܗܘܢ . . . . . ܣܡܝܐ ܓܝܪ ܠܣܡܝܐ ܐܢ ܢܕܒܪ.

(10) „ „ 27, Widmanstadt, ܐܦ ܟܠܒܐ ܐܟܠܝܢ.
Curetonian, ܐܦ ܟܠܒܐ ܓܝܪ ܐܟܠܝܢ.

14,459 and two others, ܘܐܦ ܚܕܬܐ ܐܚܪܝܢ.
(11) St. Matt. xv. 34, Widmanstadt, ܟܡܐ ܠܚܡܝܢ ܐܝܬ ܠܟܘܢ.
Curetonian, ܟܡܐ ܠܚܡܝܢ ܐܝܬ ܠܟܘܢ.
14,459 and all MSS., ܟܡܐ ܠܚܡܝܢ ܠܟܘܢ.

It may be remarked in the above examples that not only does the Curetonian approximate to the historically later text of Widmanstadt, but several of the readings are of a more modern character. Thus (2) may be suspected of having been conformed to the Greek; (3) is apparently an epexegesis; and (7) is evidently a gloss, while (1), (5), (10), and (11) look like linguistic corrections. In fine, there is nothing in results derived from our present investigations to warrant the belief that the true text of the Peshito would more nearly resemble the Curetonian type of text, than does the current Syriac text with which scholars are familiar in the pages of Widmanstadt. The bearing of this position upon the question of the age of the Curetonian is obvious, but it is not within the scope of this paper to pursue the subject further than to remark, that, if it should hereafter be proved that the Curetonian, rather than the Peshito text, can be traced in the writings of the earliest Syrian Fathers, it will by no means follow that the Peshito was derived from the Curetonian *as we have it*, although it is possible that both are derived from still earlier versions made in the very first days of Syrian Christianity. But no conjectures are offered. We insist, however, on the evidence which has been adduced of the great age of the text of the Peshito, and we affirm that while it has thus the unimpeachable credentials of immense antiquity, and the authority of universal acceptance in the Syrian Church, the Curetonian presents itself as a solitary, an unique, and an unsupported work.

It may be convenient to summarize the results arrived at in this paper under four heads:—

1. That we possess, in the hitherto almost unexplored treasures of the Tattam Collection in the British Museum, manuscripts of the Peshito of such value and antiquity (one

of the most important being described in these pages) that by their aid, and in conjunction with other materials, we can restore the text of the Peshito at least as it existed in the fifth century of the Christian era.

2. That this restoration involves very little alteration of the received text of Widmanstadt.

3. That these alterations are moreover of such a character that they affect but very slightly the relation of the Syriac Version to the original Greek Text.

4. That the ancient text thus restored does not, on the whole, approximate to the Curetonian type of text, but shows as great an independence of it as does the received text of Widmanstadt.

Note referred to on page 169.

THE Rev. F. H. Woods, of St. John's College, Oxford, who has lately collated all the New Testament quotations in the *Opera Omnia S. Ephraemi Syri, Romae*, MDCCXXXVII, with the Syriac text of Widmanstadt, and also those made by the same Father from the portions of the Gospels extant in the *Curetonian Fragments* with the published edition of that version, has kindly supplied me with the following results of his investigations:—

1. The text of the Syriac version employed by St. Ephraem was one resembling very closely that published by Widmanstadt.

2. The differences, which are certainly very considerable in number, are mainly such as naturally arise from a careless or free quotation, it being the habit of the writer generally to interweave passages of Scripture into his argument instead of quoting directly.

3. Some few of these differences are true variants, and correspond to similar variations in the Greek text or other versions. Thus, in quoting Acts v. 41 (vol. iv, p. 371) St. Ephraem has ܕܝܫܘܥ, corresponding to τοῦ ὀνόματος αὐτοῦ, the reading of some cursive manuscripts, the Aethiopic version, and Origen, instead of ܫܡܐ, τοῦ ὀνόματος, the reading of ℵABCD, etc.

4. In some cases his quotation agrees with the Greek text as against the Peshito. Thus, again in Acts v. 41 he has ܩܕܡ ܟܢܫܐ, πρόσωπον τοῦ συνεδρίου, while the Peshito has only ܟܢܫܐ. In

quoting St. Luke i. 75 (vol. i. p. 438 c) he adds ‍ܘܙܕܝܩܘܬܐ, καὶ δικαιοσυνη, as in the Greek [1].

5. In those quotations where comparison can be made with the Curetonian version, St. Ephraem's words agree rather with the Peshito. There is only one exception (vol. iv. p. 18 E), where, quoting St. John i. 3, St. Ephraem has ܠܐ ܡܕܡ ܗܘܐ, with the Curetonian, whereas the Peshito has ܠܐ ܚܕܐ ܗܘܐ. The passage is too short to prove anything. On the other hand, there are at least ten passages where the quotation either agrees entirely with the Peshito, and differs from the Curetonian, or agrees more closely with the former than with the latter. In many other passages the quotation differs verbally from both, especially where they agree with each other; but this is to be accounted for by the obviously loose manner in which St. Ephraem quotes. In vol. vi. p. 585 D, St. Ephraem, quoting St. Matt. xv. 27, has ܩܨܝܐ for ܦܬܘܪܐ, a word which occurs neither in the Peshito nor the Curetonian, but is found in the Harkleian version.

On the whole, Mr. Woods concludes that it is obvious that St. Ephraem did not use the Curetonian version.

---

[1] Though Widmanstadt did not print the ܘܙܕܝܩܘܬܐ, the evidence of ancient MSS. requires its restoration to the text of the Peshito.—G. H. G.

IX.

THE DATE OF S. POLYCARP'S MARTYRDOM.

[T. RANDELL.]

A. = Aristides' *Sacred Discourses*. These ἱεροὶ λόγοι are contained in Vol i. of Dindorf's *Aristides*, published at Leipzig in 1829; and to that volume the pages given in the following notes refer.

M. = *Joannis Massoni Collectanea Historica ad Aristidis Vitam*, as reprinted in Vol. iii. of Dindorf's *Aristides* (see above).

P. = Vol. ii. of Pearson's *Minor Theological Works*, edited by Churton.

W. = W. H. Waddington's Memoir on the Chronology of the Life of Aristides, as printed in the first part of Tome xxvi. of the *Mémoires de l'Institut Impérial de France: Académie des Inscriptions et Belles Lettres* (Paris, 1867).

Wo. = Bp. Chr. Wordsworth's *Church History to the Council of Nicaea* (3rd ed. Rivingtons, 1883).

A LONDON bookseller of the seventeenth century, Featherstone by name, speculated in a bold way by a transaction that may fairly rank with the greatest exploits of Mr. Quaritch. He bought what seems to have been the bulk of the manuscript portion of the library of a Venetian gentleman, and brought it to England for sale. The fact was of course made known to the literary men of the time, as well as to the wealthy patrons of literature; and fortunately the valuable collection was not seriously broken up or scattered. There was an English nobleman who saw what a rare opportunity was offered him to testify his esteem for literature and to benefit future generations of students. Moreover, he had been well 'bred'—to use his own expression—by the University of Oxford, which had also lately honoured him by electing him to the high dignity of Chancellor; and he would fain show gratitude for both the past privilege and the recent compliment. Accordingly, he entered into negotiations with Mr. Featherstone before many volumes of the Venetian gentleman's collection had been sold, and the result of the negotiations was that he purchased and presented to this University the 242 valuable manuscripts now known as the Barocci Collection in the Bodleian Library. The name given to the collection is that of the Venetian gentleman, Giacomo Barocci, to whom the manuscripts had formerly belonged. The munificent donor of them to Oxford was William Herbert, Earl of Pembroke, whose name is over the inner entrance of the passage that leads out of the old 'Schools' quadrangle, on the south side towards the Camera Radcliviana. The price he paid for the manuscripts was £700, a sum which (Mr. Thorold Rogers kindly informs me) may fairly be considered as equivalent to at least £2000 at the present day. The benefaction was made in the year 1629[1].

The Barocci MS. No. 238, assigned by the late Mr. Coxe to the eleventh century, contains, among other things, the original Greek text of the 'Martyrium Polycarpi;' and from it Archbishop Ussher published the *editio princeps* of that work in 1647. Even now no other manuscript in England is known to contain it, although there are three others in continental libraries[2].

A Latin version of the Martyrium was apparently made at a very early date, and the extant manuscripts of this are more numerous than those of the Greek original, at least seven having been used by editors. The translation is, however, so very free that it is of but little service for the criticism of the Greek text.

More help is obtained from Eusebius, who has quoted *verbatim* a great part of the Martyrium in his 'Historia Ecclesiastica,' iv. 15. Some portions are also transcribed *verbatim* in the tenth-century manuscript of the 'Chronicon Paschale,'

---

[1] Macray's *Annals of the Bodleian Library*, pp. 53, 54. At p. 55 Mr. Macray tells us that 'a further portion of the collection (consisting of twenty-two Greek MSS. and two Russian), which had been retained by the Earl, was subsequently purchased by Oliver Cromwell, and given by him to the Library in 1654.'

[2] One at Paris (No. 1452), formerly at Florence; one at Vienna (*Hist. Grace. Eccles.* No. 3); and one at Moscow (No. 159).

a work otherwise known as the 'Fasti Siculi' and as the 'Alexandrian Chronicle.'

There are thus seven authorities practically available for the establishment of the Greek text of the Martyrium, viz. the four Greek manuscripts, Eusebius, the Latin version, and the Paschal Chronicle.

The Martyrium is the only original account of the death of S. Polycarp. So far as I am aware, the event is not elsewhere mentioned with anything like a date until we find it in the writings of Eusebius; and, seeing that he used the Martyrium as apparently his only authority or source of information on the subject, we may well suppose that all later writers have depended solely on the same account.

From internal evidence it is fairly inferred that the Martyrium was written within a year of the event which it describes, and although some modern critics have suspected parts of it to be interpolations, or the whole of it to be untrustworthy, yet most scholars have accepted it as genuine and authentic.

When, at the suggestion of Professor Wordsworth, I undertook to prepare a paper on the date of S. Polycarp's Martyrdom, I naturally began by making a careful investigation of this document. I have used the recent edition of the 'Patres Apostolici' by Funk. The Barocci MS.—the only original material within my reach—I collated with Funk's text: although that may perhaps seem to have been a work of supererogation, and has certainly furnished no additional information as to the date.

The Martyrium appears at first sight to afford abundant materials for fixing the date. Not only does it mention the names of several persons, some of whom held important public offices in Smyrna, but it states the hour, the day of the week, the day of the month—and that according to two reckonings—as well as the name of the proconsul who was holding office when the martyrdom took place. And as the proconsulate was an annual office, naming the proconsul may be considered equivalent to stating the year. Hence it would seem that no chronological question could well be found easier to answer than that which asks the date of S. Polycarp's martyrdom. Yet, as a matter of fact, hardly any question of the kind has been answered in so many ways. This may be seen from the foot-note [1], in which are shown some of the dates that have been actually assigned to S. Polycarp's death by various scholars, all of whom have some claim on our attention.

These dates will be seen to range over nearly thirty years, viz. from A.D. 147 to A.D. 175; and to belong to the reigns of two Roman Emperors, viz. Antoninus Pius, who died in March, 161, and his successor, Marcus Aurelius. Some writers, who do not assign the martyrdom to any particular year, place it in the reign of the latter emperor, and so far favour one of the later dates.

Of all the clues to the date which are found in the Martyrium by far the most important is the name of the proconsul under whom S. Polycarp suffered; and the investigation of the time during which the person bearing that name held office will occupy most of our attention. The genitive of the name is given in the Barocci MS. as Στρατίου Κοράτο[υ], but editors have all agreed to correct this (in conformity with the Latin version) into Στατίου Κουαδράτου [2]. The name, therefore, in its Latin form is Statius Quadratus.

---

[1] The martyrdom of S. Polycarp has been assigned to the year—
   147 by Pearson; Dodwell; Gallandi.
   155 by Waddington; Zahn; Renan; Hilgenfeld; Lightfoot; Letronne; Borghesi; de Rossi.
   156 by Lipsius.
   158 by Pagi (with some hesitation).
   161 by Baratier; Idatius.
   163 by the Paschal Chronicle.
   164 by Greswell.
   166 by Clinton; Noris; Tillemont; Masson; Wieseler; Uhlhorn.
   167 by Valesius.
   168 by Eusebius and S. Jerome (as some think).
   169 by Baronius; Mosheim; Ussher.
   175 by Petit.

[2] Or Κοδράτου, according to the orthography found in the editions of

From the 'Fasti Romani' we learn that a person of this name was *consul* in the year A.D. 142: he would thus have been eligible for the *proconsulate* in any of the years assigned to S. Polycarp's martyrdom. Doubtless, therefore, the consul of 142 and the proconsul who conducted S. Polycarp's trial are one and the same person. This Quadratus is frequently mentioned in the extant works of Ælius Aristides, the rhetorician, who was not only a contemporary of S. Polycarp, but lived much in the same city. From the data furnished by Aristides modern scholars have attempted to fix the year of the proconsulate of Quadratus, and I will now proceed to show the method by which (as I believe) they have obtained a correct result.

As a basis for calculating the date of Quadratus from the writings of Aristides, it may be best to investigate the date of another proconsul of Asia, whose name was Julianus; and we shall be able to fix the date of Julianus with remarkable precision. Two contemporary inscriptions enable us to do this.

The first is an inscription[1] from the ruins of the Odeum of Ephesus; it was discovered in March, 1864, by Mr. J. T. Wood, the English architect, and is now in the British Museum. It is mutilated, but its purport and dates are clear and certain. It is the transcript of a letter from Antoninus Pius to the magistrates of Ephesus, dated in his eighth possession of tribunician power, which is definitely known to have been the year 145; and at the end it mentions 'Julianus, the most excellent proconsul.'

The second is an inscription[2] on a medal, also from Ephesus, now in the National Library at Paris. On one side it exhibits

---

Aristides (o.g. Dindorf's ed. vol. i. p. 521, lines 3 and 15): this would only imply the omission of one letter (δ) in the Barocci MS.

[1] Appendix A, Inscription No. 3. The other inscription (No. 4) given in Appendix A suggests or confirms many of the conjectural readings in the lost portions of No. 3, and the comparison of the two is very interesting.

[2] W., p. 211. Also Mionnet's *Description de Médailles antiques*, tome iii. Ionie, No. 321 (p. 103). The British Museum possesses a sulphur cast of this medal, a full description of which has been kindly sent me by B. V. Head, Esq.

the heads and names[1] of Verus Cæsar and Faustina; on the other side the legend[2] informs us that the medal was struck when Julianus was governing the people of Ephesus. Beyond doubt, therefore, Julianus was proconsul at the time of the marriage of Verus Cæsar and Faustina, which this medal commemorates. And we know, from quite independent historical testimony, that this marriage took place early in 146, the Verus Cæsar being the person better known to us under his subsequent imperial title of Marcus Aurelius, and his bride being his cousin Annia Faustina, daughter of the reigning emperor, Antoninus Pius.

The year of the proconsulate in the province of Asia was not reckoned from January to January, but from May to May. So that these two inscriptions, fixing the proconsulate of Julianus to the years 145 and 146 respectively, are not discordant with each other. On the contrary, the two in combination give us the date of Julianus' proconsulate with greater precision than could be attained from either of them separately; and we may consider it absolutely certain that Julianus was proconsul of Asia in 145-6, from May 145 to May 146.

It also appears that he was proconsul during the second year of the long malady of Aristides, of which that author gives so many and such curious details in his 'Sacred Discourses.'

This, however, by no means appears on the surface, and I have to endeavour to explain how it is arrived at.

Towards the end of the fourth Sacred Discourse, Aristides recounts several transactions that had happened between himself and different proconsuls: 'the first of all which transactions was,' he says[3], 'a service rendered him by Julianus:' and we learn that this happened:—

(1) Not long after the series of travels that had kept Aristides many years from home;

[1] ΟΥΗΡΟC · ΚΑΙCΑΡ · [Φ]ΑΥCΤΕΙ[Ν]Α · CE.
[2] ΕΠΙ · ΦΑ · ΙΟΥΛΙΑΝΟΥ · ΕΦΕCΙΩΝ.
[3] A., p. 532 esp. line 10, τὸ πρῶτον ἁπάντων τούτων.

(2) When Aristides was residing at Pergamos ; and
(3) While he was ill, and (in particular) suffering from difficulty of breathing—εἶχον μὲν οὕτως τὸ σῶμα ὥστε ἀναπνεῖν μόλις¹.

Now we know that his series of travels immediately preceded his long malady, or rather that the malady began just before the travels ended. He also tells us that at the end of a year and some months after the commencement of his malady, having made a short stay at Smyrna, he went to reside at Pergamos—καὶ παρελθόντος ἐνιαυτοῦ καὶ μηνῶν ἐπὶ τὴν ἐν Περγάμῳ καθέδραν ἤλθομεν².

Again, in the Second Discourse, he mentions that after his return from Italy he had been troubled by some asthmatic complaint, and he describes it in precisely the same words as he uses in the Fourth Discourse about his suffering at Pergamos—Χαλεπώτατον δ' ἁπάντων ὅτι τοῦ πνεύματος ἀπεκεκλείμην, καὶ μετὰ πολλῆς τῆς πραγματείας καὶ ἀπιστίας μόλις ἄν ποτε ἀνέπνευσα βιαίως καὶ ἀγαπητῶς³.

It seems quite certain, therefore, that about the middle of the second year of his malady Aristides was residing at Pergamos, and suffering from great difficulty of breathing ; precisely as was the case when the transaction took place between him and Julianus the proconsul. But after he had stayed some little time at Pergamos, he was able to resume his professional occupation, and once more to deliver his rhetorical discourses in public. We may reasonably infer that the resumption of public speaking did not take place until the difficulty of breathing had passed off : and this justifies us in fixing the proconsulate of Julianus to the second year of Aristides' malady.

As this synchronism is of the utmost importance, I should like to say that I quite recognise the element of uncertainty in it. It is, in my opinion, absolutely certain that Julianus was proconsul in 145-6 ; also that Aristides was at Pergamos

¹ A., p. 532, lines 23-4.   ² A., p. 483, lines 32-3.
³ A, p. 466, lines 17-20.

at the same time; also that the date of his transaction with Julianus was not *earlier* than the second year of his malady. I do not think it is quite certain that it may not have been *later* than the second year of the malady. Nevertheless, the indications that I have mentioned as being furnished by his condition of health, and the references to his recent travels, point to the very earliest stage of his residence in Pergamos, and render the hypothesis that Julianus was proconsul in any later year of the malady highly improbable; and the later the year the more improbable the hypothesis. I therefore consider the synchronism between Julianus' proconsulate and the second year of Aristides' malady to be only slightly removed from positive certainty; and the element of uncertainty is made still less important by the discovery that other data fit in conveniently when we adopt this synchronism as a working hypothesis.

From this starting-point let us now advance a step. Not yet, however, to the proconsulate of Quadratus, but to that of a certain Severus. This step gives us very little trouble. For, in his 'Sacred Discourses,' Aristides definitely states[1] that Severus was proconsul in the tenth year of his malady. As we have fixed the second year of this sickness at 145-6, we must, of course, fix the tenth year by adding on eight, making the date of the proconsulate of Severus to be 153-4[2].

[1] A., p. 502 ab init., and p. 505, lines 5 and 6. Cf. M., p. cxx. bottom.
[2] Here, however, I must point out the possibility of making a mistake of a year.

Aristides' malady began in the autumn, so that, if he reckoned the years of the malady strictly, every one of those years would begin at autumn-time, say October 1. But the proconsular years began (as I have already said) in the early summer, about May 1. Hence any given year of Aristides' malady would be contemporaneous, roughly speaking, with the second half of one proconsulate and the former half of the next.

It follows that unless we know at what part of the year of the malady (whether early or late) any particular event happened, we may assign it to the wrong proconsulate. In the present case our argument really proves only that Severus was proconsul either in 153-4 or in 154-5: it cannot decide between the two.

But as we have supposed an event of the second year of the malady to have happened in the proconsular year 145-6, we now suppose an event of the tenth

One step more will bring us to Quadratus. But to take it requires what some may deem a venture of faith rather than an exercise of reason. It can only be done by interpreting in a definite manner a sentence of Aristides' which some may deem too indefinite to bear such an interpretation.

In a certain place[1] Aristides says that he thinks Severus was proconsul the year before his friend, without naming the friend—'Ο Σεβῆρος ὁ τῆς 'Ασίας ἡγεμὼν ἦρξεν, οἶμαι, ἐνιαυτῷ πρότερον τοῦ ἡμετέρου ἑταίρου. In order to take the final step in fixing the date of proconsulate of Quadratus we have to suppose—

    (1) That Aristides' οἶμαι is equivalent to an οἶδα: in other words, that we may trust the accuracy of his memory as regards such a matter.

    (2) That Aristides' unnamed friend was none other than Quadratus.

As regards the force of οἶμαι, I will only say that I have found it elsewhere in the writings of Aristides in passages where it could scarcely have implied any serious doubt, and that I therefore look upon it as practically of no more weight to disparage a statement than our own oft-heard expression 'if I remember rightly.' It is also just to remark that if Aristides had made a mistake on this point, in the rough draft of his book, he would surely have afterwards discovered and corrected a statement which could so easily have been tested.

As to the identification of Aristides' unnamed friend with Quadratus, I do not think doubt would be felt on the point by anyone who had read the context in which the above-quoted passage occurs. Quadratus was a rhetorician by profession, as was Aristides; and when they met, Quadratus treated Aristides with many marked expressions of courtesy and honour. Aristides, who is fond of flattery if of anything, has

---

year to fall in 153-4. Such reasoning is fair; but it must be allowed to involve the unexpressed condition that both the events happened in the same half (in this case it would be the earlier half) of the year. Cf. Appendix G.

[1] A., p. 523, lines 3-5.

been delighted to recount all this, and at the end of the recital says: 'Severus, if I remember rightly, was proconsul the year before my friend.' Surely the friend was Quadratus.

I may add that, after reading carefully through the whole of the Sacred Discourses, I have found in them no person named or alluded to who is so likely to have been the friend here referred to as Quadratus is. Further, if we accept the common identification of the proconsul Quadratus with the 'Quadration' who is mentioned by Philostratus in his *Lives of the Sophists*[1], we have there additional evidence that Aristides and Quadratus were men of similar tastes and pursuits.

Assuming, therefore, that Quadratus was the immediate successor of Severus in the proconsulate of Asia, it follows that, as we have fixed the date of Severus' period of office at 153-4, we must fix the year of office of Quadratus at 154-5, that is, from May 154 to May 155. Thus we have at length reached our goal.

It further follows that since, on any interpretation of the month and day of the event, S. Polycarp's martyrdom happened in the spring of the year, before the month of May, it must have taken place in the latter part of the proconsulate of Quadratus, that is, in the year 155.

Assuming that the Martyrium is correct in assigning the death of the Saint to the early part of the year and to the proconsulate of Quadratus, and that the foregoing calculation of the period of this proconsulate is correct, we therefore conclude that *S. Polycarp was put to death in the spring of* A.D. 155.

But when we come to compare our conclusion with the date assigned to the same event by Eusebius, S. Jerome, and the largest number of historians, we find that our conclusion by no means agrees with their date. True, it is not easy to say precisely what their date is. Eusebius and S. Jerome seem to differ from one another, and their modern interpreters are not

[1] ii. 6.

of one mind as to what date either Eusebius or S. Jerome
meant to give for S. Polycarp's death. But decidedly it was
not 155, nor, indeed, in that decade at all. Decidedly it was
in the next decade, whether 166[1], 167[2], 168[3], 169[4], or some
earlier year. Decidedly, Eusebius' date falls within the reign
of Marcus Aurelius; whereas our date is, quite as decidedly,
within the reign of Antoninus Pius. How then are we to
choose between the two?

The learned Bishop of Lincoln, in his recent 'Church History,'
states[5] that he does 'not feel justified in abandoning' the later
date; and he opposes a series of objections to the earlier date,
which, out of respect to such a writer, I propose now to
consider.

OBJECTION 1.—Quadratus was proconsul in the *sixth* year of
the malady of Aristides[6], and not in the *eleventh*, as the
advocates of the earlier date wrongly maintain.

ANSWER.—That Quadratus was proconsul in the sixth year of
the malady was indeed the opinion of Masson, who, with great
industry, endeavoured to construct a chronological account of
the life of Aristides from the many scattered notices in his
writings. But, even on Masson's own interpretations of some
of Aristides' statements, it becomes impossible that Quadratus
could have been proconsul in the sixth year of the malady; and
Masson could only defend his theory by attributing looseness
and inaccuracy of statement to Aristides.

As a matter of fact, Aristides distinguishes between different
stages of his malady, two of the chief of which stages he
describes as τὸ τοῦ ἤτρου and τὸ τοῦ φύματος, characterized
respectively by abdominal pains and by a troublesome tumour.
The proconsulate of Quadratus synchronised with the abdominal
pains. But this stage of the malady was preceded, many years
before—πολλοῖς ἔτεσιν πρότερον—by the appearance of the

---

[1] As Bp. Wordsworth.
[2] As von Gutschmid.
[3] As Waddington.
[4] As Schoene.
[5] Wo., p. 164, lines 32-35 of note.
[6] Wo., p. 162, lines 18-20 of note.

tumour, which itself followed after the asthmatic complaint of the second year of the malady. Clearly, therefore, Masson's date must be wrong, and thus this objection falls.

OBJECTION 2.—The emperor was in Syria during the proconsulate of Quadratus, and therefore cannot have been Antoninus Pius, who never left Rome[1].

ANSWER.—Merivale[2] certainly states that Antoninus Pius resided constantly at Rome; but he gives no authority for the statement. This is rather remarkable, for when he has occasion to repeat the assertion, he refers the reader for proof of it to his own previous mention of it.

The extant original records of the age of the Antonines are very meagre; and Merivale seems to have supposed that, because he found in his authorities no mention of any journey from Rome undertaken by Antoninus Pius, he was at liberty to conclude that no such journey had ever been made. But such an inference is quite unwarrantable. And students have since had their attention drawn to a passage in a Byzantine historian, which, if Merivale had known it, would pretty certainly have prevented him from making the rash statement that has apparently been accepted by the Bishop of Lincoln.

The passage is in Malalas, p. 280 of the Bonn edition, and is to the following effect—conclusively proving that Antoninus Pius visited Syria. Malalas was himself a Syrian, a native of Antioch, and therefore may claim some credit for his contributions to the history of his native land: he lived probably in the sixth century, though some have assigned him to the ninth.

He sketches the reign of Antoninus Pius[3], and devotes quite half the sketch to that emperor's doings in the East at Heliopolis in Phœnicia, at Laodicea in Syria, at Alexandria and elsewhere in Egypt, at Antioch in Syria, at Cæsarea in

---

[1] Wo., p. 162, lines 21 and 27 of note.
[2] Vol. vii. pages 500 and 512, referred to by Bp. Wordsworth.
[3] The sketch is given in full in Appendix B.

Palestine, at Nicomedia in Bithynia, and at Ephesus. The emperor's presence in person at some, at least, of these places is necessarily implied in the language, and at the end of this list of Eastern places visited we have the words: καὶ ἀνελθὼν ἐπὶ Ῥώμην, he did so and so.

OBJECTION 3.—In the proconsulate of Quadratus, Aristides refers to an interview between the elder emperor and Vologesus, king of Parthia, to a Parthian war, and to the prospect of peace between Rome and Parthia: all of which tallies with the reign of Marcus Aurelius, and not with that of Antoninus Pius[1].

ANSWER.—This reference does not tally in one important point with the reign of Marcus Aurelius, for it alludes to the emperor who was in the East as the *elder* emperor, whereas in the reign of Marcus Aurelius it was not the elder emperor that was engaged against the Parthians, but the *younger*, viz. Verus. On the other hand, if we compare it with the reign of Antoninus Pius, then (as we have just learnt from Malalas) the *elder* emperor *was* himself in Syria. Again: although Capitolinus[2] may be literally correct in saying that there was no Parthian war in the reign of Antoninus Pius, he may only have meant that there were no actual passages of arms, no battles, no great slaughters, as there were afterwards in the days of Marcus Aurelius. For there certainly were military preparations so far carried out as to be popularly spoken of as a Parthian War, in the reign of Antoninus Pius.

Capitolinus probably had this in mind when he wrote[3] that Antoninus Pius stopped the attacks of the Parthians by his mere letters. The letters would certainly have carried more weight if they were known to be seconded and supported by military preparations.

But the fact is placed beyond doubt by an inscription[4] still

---

[1] Wo., p. 162, lines 22–37 of note.
[2] In M. Aurel., c. 8 (referred to by Bp. Wordsworth).
[3] In Anton. Pi., c. 9.   [4] Appendix C.

to be seen over the public fountain at Sepino[1]. There we are informed that, at least four years before the death of Antoninus Pius, a certain Neratius was entrusted with some of the preparations for the Parthian war: 'Missus ab imperatore Augusto Pio ad deducendas vexillationes in Syriam ob bellum Parthicum.'

Moreover, Aristides makes no reference to any actual conflicts: so that the mere imminence of a war, and preparations for it, would quite satisfy all the requirements of the case.

OBJECTION 4.—An ἀτέλεια, or immunity from official service, was confirmed to Aristides in the proconsulate of Severus (having been granted to him by Pollio, the previous proconsul); and yet we find that, in the proconsulate of Quadratus, Aristides was elected to an onerous public office, and did not plead his ἀτέλεια. Therefore it is unlikely that Quadratus succeeded Severus[2].

ANSWER.—We are not sure that Aristides did not plead his ἀτέλεια. All he tells us on this point is that, at the public meeting which had by acclamation elected him to this honourable dignity, he obtained permission to speak, and succeeded in persuading his hearers to desist from their request: λόγον δὲ αἰτήσας, οὕτως ἔπεισα ὥστε ὁ δῆμος ταύτης μὲν ἀπέστη τῆς ἀξιώσεως[3].

I do not find that he tells us what arguments he used. Of course it may have been the case that 'he prayed the people to excuse him, in order that he might be relieved from so burdensome and expensive an office,' as the Bishop of Lincoln thinks; but his fondness for popularity, his delight in receiving flattering distinctions, and his high estimate of his own powers of persuasion by oratory, may well have combined to make him refrain from pleading his ἀτέλεια. Such a plea

---

[1] The ancient Sepinum, a Samnite town, half-way in a direct line between the mouth of the Tiber and the seaport of Bari.
[2] Wo., p. 162, lines 37-42 of note; and p. 163, lines 14-28 of note.
[3] A., p. 531, lines 17-18.

would in all likelihood have been far from popular with his audience.

In connexion with this objection the Bishop of Lincoln says[1] that Aristides 'goes back' to Quadratus 'in a retrograde course as by a ladder upward to Pollio' (Severus' predecessor): but, after carefully reading the page of Aristides to which reference is made in support of it, I am inclined to think that there must be some misprint or mistake in this statement.

OBJECTION 5.—In the proconsulate of Severus, Aristides received letters 'from the emperor, καὶ τοῦ παιδός, i.e. and from his son.' This accords better with Marcus Aurelius and Commodus than it does with Antoninus Pius[2].

ANSWER.—Those who hold to the later or Masson's chronology fix Severus' proconsulate in or about the year 169; whereas those who advocate the earlier (or Waddington's) chronology fix it in 153-4 or thereabouts. Let us consider each date separately.

Even in 169 there are difficulties in the way of understanding the expression 'the emperor and his son,' of Marcus Aurelius and Commodus. For firstly, *Verus* did not die till the end of the year; and as he was during his lifetime co-emperor with Marcus Aurelius, all imperial decrees being issued by the '*Augusti fratres*,' it is surprising (even though he may have been absent from Italy) that his name is not mentioned. And as to Commodus, he was born in 161, and so could not have been more than eight years old—hardly old enough to send letters to anyone. And if it is argued on the one side that he had been made Cæsar in 166, it is also alleged on the other side that he was not associated in the actual government of the empire until 176.

But in 153-4 we can explain the expression much more easily. True, that then the emperor Antoninus Pius had *two* adopted sons; yet one, Verus, was too young to be likely

---

[1] Wo., p. 163, lines 22-23.
[2] Wo., p. 162, line 41 of note; p. 163, line 8 of note.

either to ratify an ἀτέλεια or to write a letter to Aristides, whereas the other, afterwards Marcus Aurelius, had already made Aristides' acquaintance.

The use of the word παῖς instead of υἱός does not seem to present any insuperable difficulty to the adoption of this view. And there is a very strong argument in favour of it, to which the Bishop of Lincoln has made no allusion.

The same messenger who delivered to Aristides the gratifying communications sent by his imperial correspondents, whoever they were, brought him other letters also from another correspondent of distinction, viz. Heliodorus, the prefect of Egypt[1]. Aristides had made his acquaintance during his travels in Egypt, before the commencement of his malady. These Egyptian tours had occupied some time, for in the course of them Aristides had (as he himself tells us[2]) gone the whole length of the land, up to the cataracts, four times. He had also acquired so much fame in that country that at least one statue was erected with an inscription[3] to his honour[4]. And Heliodorus had now not only written to him, but had written also to the proconsul Severus, highly eulogising Aristides.

It so happens that we possess an item of very definite information respecting the date of Heliodorus' prefecture in Egypt. In an inscription[5] over the door of a temple at Kasr-Zayan, in the oasis of Thebes, he is mentioned as prefect of the country: and the inscription is dated the eighteenth of the month Mesori, in the third year of Antoninus Pius, i.e. August 12, 140.

Of course it is *possible* that a man who was prefect of Egypt in 140 may still have been prefect of Egypt in 168 or thereabouts, but it is not very *probable*, especially as there are reasons for supposing that he had been appointed to the office some years prior to 140. The passage of Malalas previously referred to increases the probability to a very high degree: for

---

[1] A., p. 524, lines 8–10.
[2] Aristides, ed. Dindorf, ii. p. 437, line 7.   [3] Appendix D.
[4] Letronne: *Recherches pour servir à l'Histoire de l'Égypte*, p. 294.
[5] Appendix E.

it mentions another prefect of Egypt, whose name was Deinarchus, as holding office in the reign of Antoninus Pius, and as having been slain by Egyptian insurgents. Nay more, it informs us that Antoninus Pius conducted a campaign in Egypt for the purpose of quelling the insurrection, that he was successful in this campaign, and at the end of it went to Alexandria and beautified that city with new gates and a race-course. Since Antoninus Pius was upwards of seventy when he died, it is hardly likely that this journey of his was undertaken towards the close of his reign: so that in all probability Deinarchus had succeeded (whether immediately or not) to Heliodorus some years before the death of Antoninus Pius.

This harmonises well with the earlier date, 153-4, assigned to Severus' proconsulate in Asia; but it is almost irreconcilable with the later date of 168.

In fact, it was the difficulty of harmonising the Kasr-Zayan inscription with the commonly-received date of Severus' proconsulate that led Letronne[1] to re-examine the data furnished by the writings of Aristides, and to point out other hindrances in the way of accepting Masson's chronology. To Letronne is due the credit of having shown how much more in harmony with other records the writings of Aristides would become if an earlier chronology were applied to them, and of detecting the two cardinal errors into which Masson had fallen. These were the following:—

(1) Of two dates for Aristides' birth, 117 and 129 A.D., which equally fulfilled the conditions required by the astronomical data furnished in his writings, Masson chose the later[2].

(2) Masson accepted without hesitation Eusebius' date for S. Polycarp's martyrdom, as he understood it,

---

[1] *Recherches pour servir à l'Histoire de l'Égypte pendant la domination des Grecs et des Romains*, pp. 253-259 [published at Paris in 1823]. These pages are reprinted almost *verbatim*, in the same author's *Recueil des Inscriptions grecques et latines de l'Égypte*, tome i. pp. 131-135 [published at Paris in 1842].

[2] M., p. xxiii. paragraph 3.

viz. 166; and made all the other dates of Aristides'
narrative square with that as nearly as he could[1].

But Letronne's hints, after having been taken up and strengthened by Bartolomeo Borghesi, 'the celebrated epigraphist of San Marino,' were much more fully worked out in 1866 by Mons. W. H. Waddington, who is at present the French Ambassador to our English Government; and his name has therefore become inseparably connected with the theory of the earlier dates.

We may the more readily acquiesce in giving him the credit for it when we remember that—Frenchman though he chooses to consider himself—he has an English name, comes of an English family, was brought up at the English public school of Rugby, and was educated at the English University of Cambridge.

But we must return to the Bishop of Lincoln's objections.

OBJECTION 6.—Aristides says that Severus was proconsul soon after the great plague, which was presumably the same that raged in Italy in 167[2].

ANSWER.—The advocates of the earlier date for Severus' proconsulate quite recognise the mention of this great plague: but they find that it raged in Asia Minor, not *before* the proconsulate of Severus, but *several years after*[3] that time. Aristides was himself attacked by it; so were all his servants: his physician was obliged to do servant's work for him in consequence, he tells us[4]. But all this was after the termination of his long malady, which was itself not cured until seven years or so after the proconsulate of Severus. The epidemic may therefore be easily identified with the great plague that raged in Italy in 167, especially as it is well known that that particular pestilence (like so many later ones) gradually travelled westward from Asia across Europe.

[1] M., p. lxxxix, paragraph 7; W., p. 207.
[2] Wo., p. 163, line 39 of note; p. 164, line 3 of note.
[3] A., pp. 475 and 504.
[4] A., p. 475.

OBJECTION 7.—The martyrdom of Polycarp does not seem to be in harmony with the times of Antoninus Pius, but agrees very well with those of Marcus Aurelius [1].

ANSWER.—I do not know what Archdeacon Farrar might say on being told that a martyrdom such as that of S. Polycarp 'agrees' 'very well' with the times of Marcus Aurelius. For myself, I will only venture very respectfully to remark that, considered as an act of intolerant cruelty, it ill accords with the character of either of these excellent emperors; but, considered as the result of mistaken state-policy, it may be reconciled with the rule of the one as easily as with that of the other [2]. It was (I would fain believe) not so much the persecution of a Christian as the execution of one who was deemed a disaffected subject. The Martyrium tells us that Polycarp was the twelfth Christian who suffered death at that time in the two cities of Philadelphia and Smyrna, and that his own death *ended the persecution*. And although his death was certainly preceded by all the forms of a regular judicial process, yet his offence was not so much his being a Christian as his refusing to obey imperial orders—his stubborn denial when urged to acknowledge imperial authority in the usual way.

Melito's statement that 'Antoninus Pius wrote to certain cities that they should not raise tumults or commit outrages against the Christians,' seems to imply the occurrence in his reign of some such events as the martyrdom of S. Polycarp, to which the proconsul was incited by the clamours of the populace: and the decrees put forth by Marcus Aurelius, of which Melito complains, may have been new ones, without implying the previous non-occurrence of such events as attended S. Polycarp's death.

These are all the objections which the Bishop of Lincoln makes against the earlier date, unless we add to the list two others which he expresses in a less pronounced manner.

---

[1] Wo., p. 164, lines 4-6 of note.

It may be noted that Valesius (according to Pearson, *Minor Works*, ed. Churton, ii. 526) thought Justin was martyred in the reign of Antoninus Pius.

OBJECTION 8.—Eusebius, S. Jerome, and others, give the later date; and their testimony is important. Eusebius particularly is usually correct in events relating to the East[1].

ANSWER.—S. Jerome and the rest all follow Eusebius, and therefore add nothing to his authority. And a plausible explanation can be given of his mistake—supposing it to be a mistake—about this date. Another Quadratus was *consul* in the year 167. If we may conjecture that Eusebius, who did so much literary work that he must have done some of it hurriedly, mistook the *consul* Quadratus of 167 for the *pro*-consul Quadratus of the Martyrium, the difficulty is at once satisfactorily solved.

OBJECTION 9.—Irenaeus tells us that Polycarp visited Rome during the bishopric of Anicetus, which has generally been dated between 157 and 168[2].

ANSWER.—But, as Bishop Wordsworth acknowledges[3], reasons have recently been given for placing the pontificate of Anicetus at an earlier date than that to which it has hitherto usually been assigned. Lipsius, who has probably studied the chronology of the early Roman bishops more carefully than any one else of our own time, quite recognises the possibility of harmonising the date of Anicetus with the early date of S. Polycarp's martyrdom; although he prefers so far to take advantage of the one uncertain link, which I pointed out[4] in the chain of evidence for the earlier date, as to assign the martyrdom to 156 instead of 155.

All the objections of the Bishop of Lincoln have now been fairly stated, and should, of course, be allowed their due weight. But I do not think any one of them or any combination of them is unanswerable, or sufficient to justify the retention of the later date.

Let me more briefly state a series of objections of another

---

[1] Wo., p. 161, lines 1-8 of note. [2] Wo., p. 161, lines 9-15 of note.
[3] Wo., p. 161, line 25 of note—p. 162, line 3 of note. [4] See p. 182.

kind, made by another learned English prelate, whose name will similarly command profound respect for every word he says. I refer to John Pearson, Bishop of Chester.

Pearson minutely studied the chronology of the early bishops of Rome, and his researches for ascertaining the date of Anicetus caused him to investigate that of the martyrdom of S. Polycarp. So far from feeling the interview which Anicetus had with Polycarp to be in harmony with the later date of the latter's death, which was in his days universally accepted, he felt so strongly the difficulty of reconciling that date with several historical considerations, that he boldly asserted—without any knowledge of the inscriptions I have mentioned—without any Letronne or Borghesi or Waddington to guide or support him—he boldly asserted that the later date must be given up as hopelessly devoid of historical probability. At great labour and pains he set himself to find a truer date, more in harmony with known history than was the date given by Eusebius; and he persuaded himself that he had found it in the year 147. I will presently explain [1] how he arrived at this conclusion, and it will easily be seen why we cannot accept it. At this point I will only say that I sincerely believe, if Bishop Pearson had possessed the data which Waddington possessed, he would have arrived at Waddington's conclusion.

I have now to state his objections to the later date.

1. An anonymous manuscript Chronicle of ancient date, lent to Pearson by Isaac Vossius, puts the martyrdom of S. Polycarp in the reign of Antoninus Pius [2].

2. Irenaeus, contra Haer. iii. 3, in a passage which was written certainly not later than 185, speaks of οἱ μέχρι νῦν διαδεγμένοι τὸν Πολύκαρπον [3]: therefore we may fairly suppose that he knew of several men who had, one after the other, succeeded to Polycarp's office in the interval between that saint's martyrdom and the writing of this passage. This

---

[1] See p. 197 N.B.   [2] P., p. 526.
[3] A various reading for Πολύκαρπον is τοῦ Πολυκάρπου θρόνον.

suggests that the interval was greater than twenty years, whereas the later date for Polycarp's martyrdom would reduce the interval to less than twenty years[1].

3. Irenaeus, in the same chapter, also says that Polycarp was a disciple of apostles, had conversed with many who had seen the Christ, and had been appointed bishop for Asia in Smyrna by apostles. Therefore he is scarcely likely to have lived until 166 or later: for few who had seen Christ, and certainly no apostle, survived the year 100; nor is it probable that Polycarp was appointed bishop for Asia sixty-six years or more before his martyrdom.

4. Irenaeus further says that he himself had seen Polycarp and listened to him: but deems it necessary to remove the inherent improbability of this assertion by stating two things in explanation, viz.—

    (1) That Polycarp had lived to old age before suffering martyrdom; and

    (2) That at the time of seeing and hearing Polycarp, he (Irenaeus) was himself very young.

Would he have felt any necessity for making these statements, particularly the latter, if Polycarp had suffered martyrdom less than twenty years before the time at which he was writing?

5. In the celebrated passage of Irenaeus' Epistle to Florinus, preserved in Eus., H. E., v. 20, the writer describes his vivid recollection of his juvenile visits to Polycarp, thanks God that the details thereof were so well impressed upon his memory, and observes—'I remember those things better than others which have happened recently.' Such remarks are scarcely harmonious with the theory that Polycarp had been dead less than twenty years; in which case S. Irenaeus might have listened to him year after year as an adult, and a vivid recollection of his person and teaching would have been in no way remarkable.

6. The Martyrium represents S. Polycarp as having said to

[1] P., p. 527.

the proconsul:—'Ογδοήκοντα καὶ ἓξ ἔτη ἔχω δουλεύων τῷ Χριστῷ. All the ancients, both Greeks and Latins, understood this to mean that Polycarp was eighty-six years of age at the time of his martyrdom. Halloix, in 1633, was the first to suggest that the eighty-six years referred (not to Polycarp's age, but) to the period during which he had professed Christianity. Very soon Blondel went further, and asserted that Polycarp had been in the Christian *ministry* eighty-six years! Such theories, however, have no internal probability or external support. Believing therefore that S. Polycarp was martyred at the age of eighty-six, and that he had associated with apostles (even if he were not made bishop by them), it is incredible that the date of his death was so late as 166 A.D. or any time in the reign of Marcus Aurelius.

7. Nicetas, father of the Irenarch, mentioned in the Martyrium as a very old man, is perhaps to be identified with Nicetas the Smyrnaean, mentioned by Philostratus[1] as flourishing under Nerva (who died in 98). This identification would be rendered absurdly improbable if the later date for the martyrdom be taken.

8. The Quadratus of the Martyrium was consul in 142. It is in the highest degree unlikely that there was an interval of more than twenty years[2] between his consulate and his proconsulate.

N.B.—Pearson knew that the ordinary interval between a consulate and a proconsulate was five years, and hence he arrived at the conclusion that Quadratus was proconsul in 147, five years after his consulship in 142.

9. There certainly were early errors, even in good authors, about the date: for example, Socrates actually placed it in the reign of Gordian (238-244 A.D.). Hence we need not feel

---

[1] *Vitae Sophistarum*, i. 19.
[2] Wo., p. 162, lines 14–16 of note, remarks that 'Marquardt quotes several instances of a seventeen years' interval, and one of nineteen, between the consulship and proconsulate.' But this does not justify us in assuming an interval of *twenty-four* years, which the date 166 would involve.

obliged to accept the date given by Eusebius, if it is shown to be intrinsically improbable.

On a review of the whole question, therefore, I feel constrained to adopt the earlier date for S. Polycarp's martyrdom. I find that almost all continental writers have adopted it, except—

(1) Keim[1], who throws discredit on the whole of the Martyrium in its present form;

(2) Wieseler[2], who refuses to accept the identification of Aristides' friend with Quadratus; and

(3) J. Reville[3], a young French savant, who concludes an essay on the subject with the philosophic sentence,—'*nihil prodest affirmare ubi dubitare tutius est.*'

The Bishop of Durham has also expressed his acceptance of the earlier date[4].

As to the day on which S. Polycarp suffered, similar certainty cannot be felt. As I have already observed, the Martyrium appears to fix it very precisely; but, owing partly to variations in the text and partly to our ignorance of the meaning of some of the chronological terms, each of the items of information given is shrouded in uncertainty.

Twice in the Martyrium we are told that the event happened on a 'great Sabbath.' But we are not sure what a 'great Sabbath' was. It has been variously supposed that it was—

(1) The Saturday before Easter,
(2) The 15th Nisan,
(3) The 16th Nisan, and
(4) An ordinary Saturday made great either by
    (i) Some civil and local festivity, or by
    (ii) The martyrdom of S. Polycarp itself.

---

[1] *Aus dem Urchristenthum*, Band i. pp. 90-170 (published at Zürich in 1878).

[2] *Die Christenverfolgungen der Cäsaren* (1878), pp. 34 et seqq.

[3] *De Anno Dieque quibus Polycarpus Smyrnae Martyrium tulit* (Geneva, Schuchardt, 1880).

[4] *Contemporary Review* for May, 1875, vol. xxv. pp. 828 and 838.

In giving the day according to the Roman Kalendar, our witnesses agree in the formula 'VII. Kal.' but differ in the month, which is diversely designated as 'Feb.,' 'Mart.,' 'Apr.,' and 'Mai.'

By the Eastern reckoning we are told that the day was the second of Xanthicus; but the name Xanthicus was given to almost every month in the year by some or other of the inhabitants of the sea-board of the Levant[1].

Although Pearson and others take the 26th of March as the most likely day, I am inclined (without now going into the tedious details of my reasons) to agree with the majority in preferring to think that the day meant is the 23rd of February.

A few moderns have given up what they term the 'Appendix,' i.e. the paragraph of the Martyrium which contains the date of the event, as spurious or at least incorrect.

But this so-called 'Appendix,' and indeed the whole Martyrium, have been signally corroborated by the discovery (on Dec. 30th, 1879) of the last inscription[2] I wish to lay before you, my knowledge of which I owe to the kindness of Professor Sanday. It will be seen that this also strongly favours the earlier date for the martyrdom.

The inscription informs us that Philip the Trallian was Asiarch in A.D. 149. It so happens that Philip the Trallian is mentioned in one passage of the Martyrium and Philip the Asiarch in another: now we are sure that the two are identical, which previously we could only conjecture. And since the passage where Philip is denominated 'the Trallian' forms part of the so-called 'Appendix' we see that the author of that 'Appendix' is in undesigned harmony with the author of the rest of the Martyrium (if not, as is most probable, the same person), and may be trusted as giving genuine items of information. Again, the Asiarch was presi-

---

[1] Ideler, *Handbuch der mathematischen und technischen Chronologie*, Band i. pp. 393-476.
[2] Appendix F.

dent of the provincial council, and chief priest of the cultus of the emperor connected therewith: the sittings of this council were held in rotation at the great cities of the province: and hence we have an explanation of the otherwise strange circumstances that both proconsul and Asiarch were present in *Smyrna* in connexion with the celebration of public games. And with regard to the date, it is far more likely that a man who was Asiarch in 149 was again (or still) Asiarch in 155 than that he was so in 166.

It will have long since become quite evident that I cannot, in the face of so many contrary facts and real difficulties, consider the later date of S. Polycarp's martyrdom to be any longer tenable: it rests solely on the authority of Eusebius, and is opposed to all probability.

On the other hand, I think it almost absolutely certain that 155 is the true date of the event. I do not believe it possible that this date is more than two years in error: it is just possible that it may vary one year from the truth. On the strength of this bare possibility the high authority of Lipsius favours the choice of 156: but while I admit that as a possibility, I feel that it does not amount to a probability. I do not therefore shrink from avowing my own conviction that S. Polycarp was martyred in the year 155 A.D.

Every student of early Christian literature and antiquities will recognise the importance of settling this point: and most of my hearers (I have reason to hope) will consider that its bearing upon questions touching the Fourth Gospel is of itself a sufficient justification for having detained them so long over the discussion of 'a mere date.'

Appendix A.

INSCRIPTIONS FOUND AT EPHESUS IN THE RUINS OF THE ODEUM.

By Mr. J. T. Wood.

3. [Αὐτοκράτω]ρ Καῖ[σα]ρ, θ[εοῦ Ἀδριανο]ῦ
   υἱός, θεοῦ Τραϊ]αν̣ο[ῦ Παρθ]ικο[ῦ υἱω]νός,
   [θεοῦ Νερούα ἔ]κγον[ος Τίτος] Αἴλιο[ς Ἀδρι]ανὸς
   [Ἀντωνεῖνος Σεβ]αστύ[ς, ἀρχιερεὺς μέγιστος, δημαρ-]
5 [-χικῆς ἐξουσίας τ]ὸ η̄, α[ὐτοκράτωρ τ]ὸ β̄, ὕπατος [τὸ δ̄]
   [π]ατὴρ π[ατρίδος, Ἐφεσί]ων τοῖ[ς ἄ]ρχουσι κ[αὶ τῇ] βουλῇ καὶ [τῷ]
   [δήμῳ χ]αίρε[ιν.] Τὴν φιλοτιμίαν ἣ[ν] φιλοτιμ[εῖται]
   [πρὸς ὑμ]ᾶς Ο[ὐήδιος] Ἀντωνεῖνος ἔμαθον οὐχ οὕτω[ς ἐ]κ
   τῶν ὑμετέρω[ν γραμ]μάτων ὡς ἐκ τῶν [ἐκ]είνου· βουλόμε-
10 -νος γὰρ παρ' ἐμοῦ τυχεῖν βοηθείας [εἰς τὸ]ν κόσμον τῶν
   ἔργων ὧν ὑμεῖν ἐπηγγείλατο ἐδήλ[ωσεν ὅσα κα]ὶ ἡλίκα οἰ-
   -κοδομήματα προστίθησιν τῇ πόλ[ει, ἀλλ' ὑμ]εῖς ο[ὐκ] ὀρ-
   -θῶς ἀποδέχεσθε αὐτόν· κἀγὼ καὶ συ[νωμολόγησα] . . .
   ἃ ᾐτήσατ[ο] καὶ ἀπεδεξάμην ὅτι . . . . [συ]υπο-
15 -λειτευομένων τρόπον οἱ του . . . . ειν χά-
   [-ρ]ιν εἰς θέας καὶ διανομὰς καὶ τὰ τῶ[ν] . . . . ω
   [τὴ]ν φιλ[οτιμ]ίαν, ἀλλὰ δι' οὗ πρὸς τὸ . . . . εμνο
   . . σειν τὴν πόλιν προῄρ[ηται. *Τὰ γράμματα ἔπεμψεν]
   . . [Ἰο]υλιανὸς ὁ κράτιστος ἀνθ[ύπατος. Εὐτυχεῖτε.]

4. Αὐτοκράτω[ρ Καῖσαρ, θεοῦ]
   Ἀδριανοῦ υἱός, θεοῦ Τ[ραϊανοῦ]
   Παρθικοῦ υἱωνός, θεοῦ [Νερ-]
   -ούα ἔκγονος, Τ[ίτος Αἴλιος Ἀ]δριανὸς
5 Ἀντωνεῖνος Σεβασ[τός, ἀ]ρχιερεὺς
   μέγιστ[ος, δ]ημαρχικῆ[ς ἐξ]ουσίας τὸ
   ῑγ̄, αὐτοκράτω[ρ τὸ β̄, ὕπατο]ς τὸ δ̄,
   πατὴρ πατρ[ίδος, Ἐφεσίων τοῖς]
   ἄρχουσι καὶ τῇ β[ουλῇ καὶ] τῷ δήμῳ
10   χαί[ρειν.]
   Εἰδότι μοι δηλο[ῦτε τὴν φιλ[οτι]μίαν
   ἣν Οὐήδιος Ἀντ[ωνεῖνος] φιλοτιμεῖ-
   ται πρὸς ὑμᾶς ο . . . . . παρ' ἐμοῦ
   χάριτας εἰς τὸν [εὐεργέτην] τῆς πό-
15   -λεως.
   [τὸ ψή]φ[ισμα ἔπεμψεν] . . . .
   . . . .
   ἀνθύπατος. Εὐτυχεῖτε.

   * Τὸ ψήφισμα (?)

Appendix B.

Account of Antoninus Pius and his Reign

as given by Joannes Malalas.

Pages 280-1 of the Bonn edition of 1831 in the 'Byzantine Historians.'

Μετὰ δὲ τὴν βασιλείαν Ἀδριανοῦ ἐβασίλευσεν Ἤλιος Ἀντωνῖνος Πίος εὐσεβὴς ἔτη κγ΄. ἦν δὲ εὐήλιξ, εὔστολος, λευκός, πολιὸς καὶ τὴν κάραν καὶ τὸ γένειον, εὔρινος, πλατόψις, οἰνοπαὴς τοὺς ὀφθαλμούς, πυρράκης, ὑπογελῶν ἀεί, μεγαλόψυχος πάνυ. Ὅστις ἔκτισεν ἐν Ἡλιουπόλει τῆς Φοινίκης τοῦ Λιβάνου ναὸν τῷ Διὶ μέγαν, ἕνα καὶ αὐτὸν ὄντα τῶν θεαμάτων. ἔκτισε δὲ καὶ ἐν Λαοδικείᾳ τῆς Συρίας τὸν φόρον, μέγα θέαμα, καὶ τὸ Ἀντωνινιανὸν δημόσιον λουτρόν. Ἐπεστράτευσε δὲ κατὰ Αἰγυπτίων τυραννησάντων καὶ φονευσάντων τὸν αὐγουστάλιον Δείναρχον· καὶ μετὰ τὴν ἐκδίκησιν καὶ τὴν νίκην ἔκτισεν ἐν Ἀλεξανδρείᾳ τῇ μεγάλῃ κατελθὼν τὴν Ἡλιακὴν πύλην καὶ τὴν Σεληνιακὴν καὶ τὸν δρόμον. Ἐλθὼν δὲ καὶ ἐν Ἀντιοχείᾳ τῇ μεγάλῃ ἐποίησε τὴν πλάκωσιν τῆς πλατείας τῶν μεγάλων ἐμβόλων τῶν ὑπὸ Τιβερίου κτισθέντων καὶ πάσης δὲ τῆς πόλεως, στρώσας τὴν διὰ μυλίτου λίθου, ἐκ τῶν ἰδίων ἀγαθῶν λίθους ἀπὸ Θηβαΐδος καὶ τὰ δὲ λοιπὰ ἀναλώματα ἐκ τῶν ἰδίων φιλοτιμησάμενος, καθὼς καὶ ἐν λιθίνῃ πλακὶ γράψας ταύτην τὴν φιλοτιμίαν ἔστησεν αὐτὴν ἐν τῇ πύλῃ τῇ λεγομένῃ τῶν Χερουβίμ· ἐκεῖθεν γὰρ ἤρξατο. ἥτις στήλη ἐστὶν ἕως τῆς νῦν ἐκεῖ, ὡς μεγάλης οὔσης τῆς φιλοτιμίας. Ἔκτισε δὲ καὶ ἐν Καισαρείᾳ τῆς Παλαιστίνης λουτρόν, καὶ ἐν Νικομηδείᾳ τῆς Βιθυνίας, καὶ ἐν Ἐφέσῳ τῆς Ἀσίας· ἅπερ δημόσια λουτρὰ εἰς τὸ ἴδιον ἐπεκάλεσεν ὄνομα. Καὶ ἀνελθὼν ἐπὶ Ῥώμην ἔκτισεν ἐν τῇ Ῥώμῃ ἀγωγὸν μέγαν· καὶ ἔκαυσε τοὺς χάρτας τοῦ ταμιείου, ἐφ᾽ οἷς ἡ σύγκλητος ἐγγράφως ὡμολόγησεν ἐπὶ τοῦ Καίσαρος Ἰουλίου Γαΐου, παρ᾽ αὐτοῦ κελευσθέντες, μὴ ἐξεῖναι συγκλητικὸν διαθήκην ποιεῖν εἰς τοὺς ἰδίους, εἰ μὴ τὸ ἥμισυ μέρος τῆς αὐτοῦ περιουσίας διατίθεται εἰς τὸν κατὰ καιρὸν βασιλέα, εἰρηκὼς ὁ αὐτὸς εὐσεβέστατος Ἀντωνῖνος διὰ θείου αὐτοῦ τύπου ἕκαστον ἀπολαύειν τῶν ἰδίων καὶ βουλεύεσθαι ὡς θέλει. Ὁ δὲ αὐτὸς Ἀντωνῖνος, ὡς ἐστὶν ἐν Λωρίῳ, νοσήσας ἡμέρας ὀλίγας ἀπέθανεν, ὢν ἐνιαυτῶν οζ΄.

Appendix C.

INSCRIPTION AT SEPINO, S. ITALY.

<small>Borghesi: Œuvres, v. 373, &c.</small>

        L . Neratio . C . F .
        Vol . Proculo .
   X . Vir . Stlitibus . Iudican .
    Trib . Militum . Legion .
5   VII . Gemin . Felic . et . Leg .
    VIII . Aug . Quaest . Ædil .
    Pleb . Cerial . Praet . Leg .
    Leg . XVI . Flaviae . Fidel .
    Item . Misso . Ab . Imp .
10 Antonino . Aug . Pio . ad . Deducen
   das . Vexillationes . in . Syriam . ob .
   Bell . Parthicum . Praef . Ærari .
        Militaris .
          Cos .
15   Municipes . Saepinat.

Appendix D.

INSCRIPTION IN HONOUR OF ARISTIDES

FOUND IN EGYPT AND NOW AT VERONA.

[See *Museum Veronense*, pp. xli-ii.]

Ἡ πόλις ἡ τῶν Ἀλεξαν-
-δρέων, καὶ Ἑρμούπο-
-λις ἡ μεγάλη, καὶ ἡ βου-
-λὴ ἡ Ἀντινοέων νέ-
-ων Ἑλλήνων, καὶ οἱ
ἐν τῷ Δέλτα τῆς Αἰ-
-γύπτου καὶ οἱ τὸν Θη-
-βαϊκὸν νομὸν οἰκοῦν-
-τες Ἕλληνες, ἐτίμη-
σαν Πόπλιον Αἴλιον
Ἀριστείδην Θεόδωρον,
ἐπὶ ἀνδραγαθίᾳ καὶ
λόγοις.

Note.—The above inscription was first edited in Giuseppe Bartoli's *Due Dissertazioni, etc.*, published at Verona in 1745: the second of his dissertations is entirely devoted to the elucidation of it.

Appendix E.

INSCRIPTION AT KASR-ZAYAN

IN THE OASIS OF THEBES.

Letronne, *Recueil des Inscriptions de l'Égypte*, i. 123.

Ἀμενήβι θεῷ μεγίστῳ Τχονεμύρεως καὶ τοῖς
συννάοις θεοῖς, ὑπὲρ τῆς εἰς αἰῶνα διαμονῆς Ἀντωνείνου
Καίσαρος τοῦ κυρίου καὶ τοῦ σύνπαντος αὐτοῦ οἴκου, ὁ σηκὸς τοῦ ἱεροῦ καὶ τὸ
πρόναον ἐκ καινῆς κατεσκευάσθη, ἐπὶ Ἀουιδίου Ἡλιοδώρου ἐπάρχου Αἰγύπτου,
Σεπτιμίου Μάκρωνος ἐπιστρατήγου, στρατηγοῦντος Παινίου Καιπίωνος·
ἔτους τρίτου αὐτοκράτορος Καίσαρος Τίτου Αἰλίου Ἀδριανοῦ Ἀντωνείνου,
Σεβαστοῦ, Εὐσεβοῦς, μεσορὴ ὀκτωκαιδεκάτῃ.

Appendix F.

INSCRIPTION DISCOVERED DEC. 30, 1879, AT OLYMPIA.

Described by Dittenberger in *Archäolog. Zeitung* for 1880, pp. 61-2.

ἡ Ὀλυμπι[κὴ]

βουλὴ Γ. Ἰούλιο[ν]

Φίλιππον Τραλ-

-λιανὸν τὸν ἀσι-

-άρχην ἤθῶν ἕνε-

-κα Ὀλυμπιάδι

σ̄λ̄β

APPENDIX G.

CHRONOLOGY OF THE MALADY OF ARISTIDES.

PROCONSULS OF ASIA. Year of Office commencing May 1st (approximately).		Years of Christian Era, commencing Jan. 1st.	Years of the Malady of Aristides, commencing Oct. 1st (approximately).		Events.
Less probable name	More probable name.		More probable year.	Less probable year.	
	JULIANUS	143			
		144		I	
		145	I	II	—Ephesine inscription mentions Julianus as proconsul 145.
		146	II	III	{ Julianus rendered a service to Aristides at Pergamos. { Marriage of Verus (Marc. Aurel.) and Faustina, early in 146.
		147	III	IV	
		148	IV	V	
		149	V	VI	—Olympian inscription names Philip of Tralles as Asiarch.
		150	VI	VII	
		151	VII	VIII	
	POLLIO	152	VIII	IX	
POLLIO	SEVERUS	153	IX	X	[Emperor's son (Marc. Aurel.); 3. Heliodorus, praef. of Egypt.
SEVERUS	QUADRATUS	154	X	XI	—Aristides receives letters from 1. The Emperor (Antoninus Pius); 2. The
QUADRATUS		155	XI	XII	—The elder Emperor is in Syria, treating for peace with Vologesus III. —Martyrdom of S. Polycarp, February 23, 155.
		156	XII	XIII	
		157	XIII	XIV	
		158	XIV	XV	
		159	XV	XVI	
		160	XVI	XVII	
		161	XVII		—Death of Antoninus Pius and accession of Marcus Aurelius.

X.

ON SOME NEWLY-DISCOVERED TEMANITE AND NABATAEAN INSCRIPTIONS.

[AD. NEUBAUER.]

UNEXPECTED discoveries have been made during the past year relating to Aramaic epigraphy and philology. Three travellers of various nationalities have lately visited that part of Arabia which borders on the Hedjâz, viz. Mr. Charles Doughty, an Englishman; Dr. Euting, of Strasbourg; and M. Huber, an Alsatian, sent out by the French Academy. Alas! a violent death has overtaken him, though fortunately his materials have been recovered[1]. Dr. Euting happily escaped the fate of his fellow-traveller, and has secured a large number of inscriptions[2], Nabataean, Himyaritic, and four Aramaic from the land of Tema. Tema is mentioned in the Bible as an Ishmaelitic land and tribe in the neighbourhood of the land and tribe of Dedan[3], through which a caravan-road passed in the time of Job[4], just as it passes now. The Tema of the Bible is undoubtedly identical with the Arabic Taïma[5], and the Θέμμη of Ptolemy[6]. Teman[7], in the land of Edom, is identified by Gesenius with Tema; it is indeed mentioned, like Tema, in connexion with Dedan[8]. According to Eusebius, however, Taïman[9] was a Roman city

---

[1] See *Nouvelles Inscriptions nabatéennes de Medaïn Salih*, par Philippe Berger (*Comptes rendus de l'Académie des Inscr. et Belles Lettres*, Paris, 1884, p. 377 seqq.). See below, p. 231.

[2] See David Heinrich Müller in the *Anzeiger der philos.-histor. Classe*, 17 Dec., Wien, 1884, No. xxviii.

[3] Isaiah xxi. 14, 15; Jeremiah xxv. 23.   [4] Job vi. 19.

[5] تَيْمَاء, Jacut's *Geographisches Wörterbuch*, ed. Wüstenfeld, a. v.

[6] Ptolemy, V. xix. 6.

[7] Jer. xlix. 7, 20; Amos i. 12; Obadiah 9; Hab. iii. 3.

[8] Ezekiel xxv. 13.   [9] Onom. Θαιμάν.

five miles (Jerome says fifteen) from Petra or the Hebrew
סֶלַע. The inhabitants of Teman, together with the Edomites,
had a reputation in antiquity for wisdom. Jeremiah[1] writes,
'Thus saith the Lord of hosts: Is wisdom no more in
Teman?' And Obadiah[2], 'Shall I not in that day, saith the
Lord, even destroy the wise men out of Edom, and understanding out of the mount of Esau? And thy mighty men,
O Teman, shall be dismayed.' Here Edom and Teman are
mentioned together. The most eloquent speaker in the book
of Job is Eliphaz the Temanite[3]. We read in the apocryphal
book of Baruch: 'It hath not been heard of in Canaan,
neither hath it been seen in Theman. The Agarenes that seek
wisdom upon earth, the merchants of Meran[4] and of Theman,
the authors of fables, and searchers out of understanding[5].'
Of the inscriptions brought, as I said, by Dr. Euting from
Tema, four have been published and explained, first by Prof.
Nöldeke[6], and afterwards by M. Joseph Halévy[7]. Prof. D. H.
Müller, of Vienna[8], and M. Clermont-Ganneau[9] have contributed valuable notes elucidating particular passages. I shall
give first the text and the translation of the three short ones:—

(1)   מ[יתבא זי קר
       ב מענן בר עמ
       רן לצלם אלה
       א לחיי נפשה

'A seat which Ma'anan, son of Amran, offered to the god
Zelem[10] for the life of his soul (or, for his own life).'

---

[1] xlix. 7.   [2] Verses 8 and 9.   [3] Job ii. 11; iv. 1.
[4] Medan (?), Gen. xxv. 2.   [5] Baruch iii. 22, 23.
[6] *Sitzungsberichte der ... Akademie zu Berlin* (July 10, 1884), xxxiv, xxxv,
p. 813 seqq.
[7] *Revue des Études juives*, t. ix, p. 2 sqq.
[8] *Oesterreichische Monatsschrift für den Orient*, 1884, p. 208 seqq.
[9] *Revue critique d'Histoire et de Littérature*, 1884, pp. 265 and 442 seqq.
See below, p. 230.
[10] According to M. Clermont-Ganneau, l.c., p. 442. See below, p. 231.
Others translate: 'to the statue of "Allah."'

We observe that the name אלהא is in use among heathen as early as 3–4 century B.C., for upon palaeographical grounds the inscriptions of Tema cannot be later than the time of Alexander the Great[1], and they may even be earlier.

(2)   נפש עלן ² ברת שבען

'Monument of 'Alân, daughter of Shabân.'

Âu being merely a determinative syllable, it is plain that ברת שבען ³ is analogous to the well-known name of Bath Sheba, wife of Uriah the Hittite, of course a Semitic Hittite.

(3)   מיתב זי רמננתן בר ...

'Seat of Rimmonnathan, son of ...'

Here we have a name compounded with that of the Syrian god Rimmon[4] or the Assyrian Raman (compare the names Tabrimmon[5] and Hadad-rimmon[6]) and the verb *nathan*, 'to give,' exactly resembling Jehonathan and Nethan-el.

(4) An inscription of twenty-four lines, of which the first ten lines and the last two are so badly injured as to be undecypherable. In addition to the inscription, there is also a representation of Zelem-Shezeb[7] the priest. In point of style, the workmanship shows the influence of Assyro-Babylonian art. The inscription runs as follows[8]:—

No. 4.

10   .... הגם להן אלהי
11   תימא יט[ר]ו (?) לצלמשוב בר פטסרי
12   ולורעה בבית צלם זי הגם ו[גב]ר

---

[1] See p. 213.   [2] M. Clermont-Ganneau, *l.c.*, p. 444.
[3] *Revue,* p. 7. Prof. Nöldeke translates 'seventy years old.'
[4] בית רמון, 2 Kings v. 18.
[5] 1 Kings xv. 18. Compare טבאל (Tab-el), Isaiah vii. 6, and טוביה (Tobiah).
[6] Zechariah xii. 11.
[7] Zelem saves. Compare אלישע and אלימור. See below, p. 230. For שוב, see Daniel vi. 28.
[8] The words and letters in brackets are according to M. Halévy's suggestions, *Revue,* pp. 2 and 3. See below, p. 232.

13 זי יחבל סות[א] ז[א] אלהי תימא
14 ינסחוהי וזרעה [ו]שמה מן אנפי
15 תימא והאנא צדקתא זי(יהב?)
16 צלם זי מחר ושנגלא ואשי[מ]א
17 אלהי תימא לצלם [זי] הגם כ(דין?)
18 מן חקלא דקלן %||| ומן שימתא
19 זי מלכא דקלן [||||||] כל דקלן
20 %|[||||||] ש[נה בשנה ואלהן ואנש
21 לא יהנ[פק ל]צלמשזב בר פטסרי
22 מן ב[י]תא ז[א] ולז[ר]עה ושמה

10 '....... Hagam. Therefore may the gods
11 of Tema protect (?) Zelem-Shezeb, son of Petosiri,
12 as well as his descendants in the house of Zelem of Hagam. And [the man]
13 He who shall injure this monument (?), may the gods of Tema
14 extirpate him, and his seed, and his name from the surface
15 of Tema. And this is the contribution which [gives]
16 Zelem of Mahar (?), and Shangala, and Ashi[m]â (?),
17 gods of Tema, to Zelem of Hagam [as follows]:
18 From the [public] land, twenty-three palm trees, and from the possession
19 of the king, six palm trees; in all, twenty-nine palm trees
20 y[ear] by year. No princes[1] or men
21 shall remove Zelem-Shezeb, son of Petosiri,
22 out of this house, or his descendants, or his name.'

In Petosiri we have an Egyptian name, for it is only natural that the caravan route from Egypt to Mesopotamia should be marked by traces of Egyptian civilization. The

---

[1] אלהן in the sense of divine persons, i.e. royal family. Compare אלהא אלהדרין in a Palmyrene inscription De Vogüé, *La Syrie Centrale*, pp. 17-18), corresponding to the expression Θεοὶ Ἀλεξάνδρου Halévy, *Revue*, p. 4).

expression 'From the face of Tema' reminds us of similar biblical expressions[1]. Gods of Tema in the original is *Elâhê Tema*, a plural like *Elohim*. Of the four divinities Maḥar, Shangâla, Ashi[m]â(?), and Hagam very little is known. The מ in Ashimâ is doubtful; though if the reading be correct, we should have here the Hamathite god mentioned in the Old Testament[2].

These inscriptions, and more especially the long one, are written in archaic Aramaic characters; some letters are, however, of a more modern type. When I first saw them, it struck me that the ה in אלהי was archaic, whilst in other words it is of a later type. I therefore put the question in the *Academy* whether this mode of writing might not be a kind of *scriptio sacra* for the name of אלהים? But the ה and the מ, as I now see, have the same variations in writing, so that the inscription must, I think, be assigned to the period of Alexander or the Ptolemies, after which a more cursive style of character was introduced in Aramaic writing[3]. Dr. Euting assigns them at the latest to the sixth century B.C. I wish I could agree with him, for in that case we should have evident proofs of an advanced civilization in Tema at least as early as the eighth century B.C. For, if I am not mistaken, it may be assumed that a people does not begin its history with inscriptions of twenty-four lines; and when we find such a long document as either this or (to take another example) the inscription of Mesha, the nation which produced them must have been accustomed to literary work for at least two centuries previously. Of course the influence of Assyria may be reasonably inferred when we know from the annals of Tiglath-pileser II that this king received tribute from Arabian towns called Tema, Saba, Hayapa,

---

[1] 1 Kings ix. 7 'Then will I cut off Israel from the face of (A. V. out of) the land which I have given them.' Cf. Deut. xxviii. 63 (with נשׁל).
[2] 2 Kings xvii. 30.
[3] Halévy, *Revue*, p. 5. Clermont-Ganneau, l.c., p. 266.

Hatea, Badana, and the tribe of Idibíli[1]. Tema is the country where our inscription was found: Saba is the biblical Seba; Hayapâ, as we shall see later on, is identified with the biblical Epha[2]; the Hatea is at present unknown (not the Hittites); Badana is perhaps a name like Bedan[3]; and the Idibíli are perhaps the descendants of Adbeel[4], a son of Ishmael.

The language of these inscriptions, although on the whole old Aramaic, is not Assyrian. Aramaic inscriptions were known up to the present time only in Babylonia, Egypt, and Cilicia. It is worth observing that the termination *ân* in the names of the second inscription '*Alân, daughter of Shabân*,' has a similarity to the Horite names[5], 'And these are the children of Dishon: Hemdân and Eshbân, and Ithrân, and Cherân[6].' The Horites, as all know, inhabited this district before the Edomites. Proper names are very useful for philology, for they undergo the least alterations possible. How interesting it would therefore be if indeed we could find out a Horite vocabulary! That, however, must be a work for the future.

Let us now leave the Horites and pass to the Nabataeans, who are the authors of the inscriptions found by Mr. Doughty and M. Huber[7] at Medain Salih. I shall give a few passages quoted (*verbatim*) from this courageous traveller's note-book, printed in English at the head of the volume of Inscriptions, published by the Academy of Inscriptions and Belles-Lettres in Paris, under M. Renan's editorship[8] :—

'In the spring of the year 1875, I came upward with Beduins from Sinai to *Maan* upon the Haj road in Edom, and

---

[1] Halévy, *Revue*, p. 6.
[2] עיפה, Gen. xxv. 4; Isaiah lx. 6.
[3] בדן (for בדד?), 1 Chron. vii. 17.
[4] אדבאל, Gen. xxv. 13. Schrader, *Die Keilinschriften und das alte Testament*, 2nd ed., 1883, p. 148.
[5] Gen. xxxvi. 26.   [6] Halévy, *Revue*, p. 7.
[7] See above, p. 209, note 1, and below, p. 232.
[8] *Documents épigraphiques recueillis dans le nord de l'Arabie* par M. Charles Doughty, Paris, Imprimerie Nationale, 1884.

went on to visit the chambered rocks of Petra, where the villagers of *Elgy*, in Wady Mousa, seeing one arrive, as it were an *hajjy* from the southward, asked me if I had not already visited *Medain Salih* upon the derb el-Haj, and where, they said, lie seven cities hewn in as many mountains, and the monuments there like these before our eyes, as they might be the work of one craftsmaster. Such also said the secretary of the small road garrison at Maan, who, a well-lettered man, spoke to me further of inscriptions sculptured in some strange characters, which, he said, to be commonly upon those Medain Salih frontispieces, and the *effigies* of a bird with his wings displayed. In former years he had very often passed the place, riding with the guard in every pilgrimage to the *Haramcya*. Such birds are not seen sculptured upon the Petra frontispieces or most rarely; nor in all the Wady Mousa monuments had I found more than one inscription, and that is very large and several lines, of some well-sculptured Semitic characters upon a simple frontispiece in the western valley side with three pilasters, which, with their parietes, are broken through below[1].'

I shall pass over Mr. Doughty's narrative describing the caravans and the perils of his life, and give the passage relating to Medain Salih:—

'The twentieth morrow of our marches we descended by the passage *Mábrak e' Náka*, a place of cursing (so called by the devout pilgrims after their doctors' mythology as where the miraculous she-camel fell down wounded to death, but by the country Beduins, ignorant of these forged vanities, *el-Mezham*), to the valley plain of *Medain Salih*, a name which is of the same Mohammedan mythology, but the site is only named by the country Beduins *El-Hejr* (*El-Hijr* of the Koran, Ἔγρα in Ptol., *Hejra* of Plin.)[2].'

Medain Salih, it will be seen, is no ancient place: it is merely a collection of caves belonging to some rich families

[1] *Ibidem*, beginning of the preface.   [2] *Ibidem*, p. 11.

from a neighbouring town[1]. Its name Salih is derived from a passage of the Qorân[2], in which Mohammed says, 'And unto the tribe of Tamud we sent their brother Saleh. He said, O my people! worship Allah; ye have no Allah besides him. Now hath a manifest proof come unto you from your lord. This she-camel of God is a sign unto you; therefore dismiss her freely, that she may feed in God's earth; and do her no hurt, lest a painful punishment seize you. And call to mind how he hath appointed you successors unto the tribe of 'Ad, and has given you a habitation on earth; ye build yourself castles on the plains thereof, and cut out the mountains into houses.' In another chapter we read[3], 'And the inhabitants of al Hejr .... hewed houses out of the mountains to secure themselves.' Finally, Mohammed says[4], 'The tribe of Tamud also charged the messenger of God with falsehood. When their brother Saleh said unto them, Will ye not fear God? Verily I am a faithful messenger unto you: wherefore fear God, and obey me. I demand no reward of you for my preaching unto you; I expect my reward from no other than the Lord of all creatures. Shall ye be left for ever secure in the possession of the things which are here; among gardens, and fountains, and corn, and palm-trees, whose branches sheathe their flowers? And will you continue to cut habitations for yourselves out of the mountains, showing art and ingenuity in your work?' Elsewhere the ancient dwellings of the Tamud are considered by Mohammed as the houses of giants, punished by God for their crimes[5]. The Tamud had ceased to exist in the time of Mohammed; a part of them had been transported by Sargon with other tribes to Samaria, as the following Assyrian inscriptions

---

[1] Possibly the ancient caves of the Horites, who, as the word חֹרִי indicated, were dwellers in caves or Troglodytes.

[2] Qorân, Surah vii. 71 seqq. (according to Sale's translation).

[3] Surah xv. 81.

[4] Surah xxvi. 114 seqq.

[5] See M. Renan's preface to the Inscriptions, p. 4.

show[1]: 'The Tamudi, the Ibadidi, the Marsimani, the Hayapâ, of remote countries in Arabia, inhabitants of the desert who know no master and no .... (?), who never paid any tribute to my father, I have crushed them by the arms of the god Assur, the remainder of them I have transported and established in the town of Samaria.' And in another place Sargon is called[2] 'the conqueror of the Tamudi, of the Marsimani, of the Hayapâ, the survivors of whom were transported and established by him in the land of Beth-Humria (Beth Omri, land of Israel).' Now the Tamudi and the Marsimani are mentioned by the classical geographers. The Hayapâ have been identified by Prof. Friedrich Delitzsch[3] with the Midjanitic tribe Ephah; the Ibididi, M. Halévy proposes to explain as 'the servants of Dad[4].' To this part of the world belong probably the Arabian tribes Bazu and Hazu, conquered by Esarhaddon, names which correspond to the biblical Buz[5] and Hazo[6], both sons of Nahor. The Nabatacans occupied subsequently the Arabian districts which have been mentioned, as may be seen from the first book of the Maccabees[7], where Judah and Jonathan find them on the other side of the Jordan, after having travelled for three days in the desert; and in another place of the same book they are alluded to as neighbours of the land of Gilead[8]. According to Josephus[9] and Ammianus[10], their dominion extended from the Euphrates to the Red Sea. They were rich, and having their home upon a road frequented by caravans, they were naturally merchants, as Apuleius[11] calls them 'Nabathaei mercatores.' They were governed by kings, one of whom, Aretas,

---

[1] Schrader, *op. cit.* (see p. 214, note 5), p. 277; Halévy, *Revue*, p. 11.
[2] Halévy, *ibidem*, p. 12.   [3] Halévy, *ibidem*.
[4] Halévy, *ibidem*.
[5] Gen. xxii. 21; Jeremiah xxv. 23 (in connexion with Tema); Job xxxii. 2, 6 'Barachel the Buzite.'
[6] Gen. xxii. 22.   [7] 1 Macc. v. 24; ix. 39.
[8] *Ibidem*, 26 seqq.   [9] *Antiquities*, I. xii. 4.
[10] Ammianus Marc., xiv. 18.
[11] Apul. flor. i. 6. See *Bibl. Realwörterbuch*, etc., von G. B. Winer (1848), ii. p. 129 (art. Nabatäer).

is mentioned in the New Testament[1]. Most of the Doughty inscriptions date from the reign of this king; and we learn from the third and the fourteenth inscriptions that his reign lasted forty-eight years (till 40 A.D.) He was followed, according to the first inscription, by king Malku, who reigned eleven years, and was succeeded by Dabel, to whose fourth year No. 19 belongs.

The inscriptions are sepulchral, and contain imprecations against those who should bury in the tombs other than members of the family to whom they were appropriated, except by a written permission. Here are the text and translation of the two which are best preserved[2]:—

No. 2.

1 דנה כפרא די עבדו כמכם בר חואלת בר תהרם
2 וכליבת ברתה לנפשהם ואחרהם בירח טבת שנת
3 תשע לחרתת מלך נבטו רחם עמה וילן דושרא
4 ומרהבה ואלת מן עמנד וכנותו וקישה מן יובן
5 כפרא דנה או מן יובן או ירהן או יתן יתה או ינפק
6 מנה גת או שלף או מן יקבר בה עיר כמכם וברתה
7 ואחרהם ומן די לא יעבד די עלא כתיב ואיתי עמה
8 לדושרא והבלו ולמנותו שמרין יעלא וכל אקנם
9 בסלעין אלף חרתי בלעד מן די ינפק בידה כתב מן יד
10 כמכם או כליבת ברתה בכפרא הנאך ימרתא הו
    והבאלהי בר עבדעבדת עבד

1 'This is the cave which Camcam, son of Ḥaw-allath, son of
    Taḥaram, made,
2 and Coleibat, his daughter, for themselves and their
    posterity, in the month of Tebeth, the year

[1] 2 Corinthians xi. 32.
[2] See the Supplementary Notes, pp. 231 and 232.

3 ninth of Ḥartat (Aretas), king of Nabataea, lover of his
   people. May Dusara
4 and Marḥaba and Allat of .... (?) and Menutu and Kaïsa
   curse him who sells
5 this cave, or him who buys it, or who pledges it, or who
   gives it as a present, or who removes
6 from it a corpse, or exchanges it (?) or who buries in it
   others than Cameam, and his daughter
7 and their posterity. And whoso shall not do according to
   what is here written, shall be answerable
8 to Dusara and Hobalu and Menutu, the guardians of ....
   shall pay a fine
9 of 1000 new *Selain*, except he produce a written permission
   from the hand
10 of Cameam, or his daughter Colcibat [saying], "So and so
   may be admitted to this cave."

(Then follows the name of the sculptor): 'Wahbelahi, son
of Abdobodat, has made this.'

No. 10.

1 דנה כפרא די להינת ברת עבדעבדת לנפשה
2 וילדה ואחרה ולמן די ינפק בידה מן יד הינת
3 דא כתבא התקבראָ יתקבר בכפרא הוא
4 כפרא דנה הוה לעבדעבדת אבד הוה למכתב
5 למו֯ש֯ ֯כת בר קנה להינתו או עבדעבדת בר
6 מליכת אם שמי בנה אם עבדעבדת אם הינתו אם
7 כלהם די עבד[ום?] כפרא דנה אנדתיבאן איכתבא
8 דא יתקבר בכפרא בכפרא דה אצדקת עבדעבדת
9 ולא יהוא אנוש רשו די יובן כפרא דנה או [ירהן]
10 יתה או יתאלף בכפרא דנה לכתב כלה ומן יעבד
11 כעיר די עלא די איתי ינדהה חציאה

12 לדושרא ומנותו כסף סלעין אלף חד חדתי
13 ולמראנא דבאל מלך נבטו בירח איר שנת
14 תרתין לדבאל מלך נבטו

1 'This is the cave of Hoïnat, daughter of 'Abdobodat, for herself
2 and her son and her posterity, and for whoever produces from the hand of Hoïnat
3 this written form [saying], "Such and such a one may be buried in this cave."
4 This cave belongs to 'Abdobodat ....
5 .... to Hoïnat or 'Abdobodat, son
6 of Malikat, or .... (?) or 'Abdobodat, or Hoïnat, or
7 all those who made (?) this cave .... this document:
8 "Let him be buried in this cave by the side (?) of 'Abdobodat."
9 And no man shall have authority to sell this cave, or [to pledge]
10 it, or .... (?) on this cave anything .... And whoso shall do
11 otherwise than it is above [prescribed] .... shall be liable for a fine
12 to Dusara and Menutu of a thousand new *Selaia* in silver?
13 As also to our lord Dabâl, king of Nabataea. In the month of Iyyâr, year
14 the second of Dabâl, king of Nabataea.'

Only No. 1 contains an inscription of a different kind. This reads:—

No. 1.

1 דנה מסגדא די עבד
2 שרוחו בר תובא לאיערא
3 די בבצרא אלה רבא לירח
4 ניסן שנת חדה למלכו מלכא

1 'This is the *Mesgeda* (a kind of shrine[1]) which

---

[1] See De Vogüé, *La Syrie Centrale* (Paris, 1868), pp. 106, 119, 120, where it is used to denote a sacred stone or column.

2 Seruḥu, son of Tuca, has made for Aera (or, Aeda)
3 of Bosra, the great god. In the month
4 of Nisan, the first year of the reign of king Malku.'

Altogether these inscriptions date from between 3 B.C. to 79 A.D. Two (Nos. 3 and 14) naming the 48th year of Aretas.

To judge from the length of their inscriptions, the Nabataeans, like the Temanites, must have enjoyed an ancient civilization. In fact, they are mentioned in the Assyrian inscriptions of Assurbanipal[1], by the side of the Kidrai, just as in the Bible, Nebaioth and Kedar, sons of Ishmael, are associated together[2]. It is indeed generally allowed that Nebaioth represents the father of the Nabataeans[3], although the spelling is slightly different[4]. Isaiah[5] says, 'All the flocks of Kedar shall be gathered together unto thee, the rams of Nebaioth shall minister unto thee.' Possibly Jeroboam, son of Nebat, was of Nabataean descent; *ben*, 'son,' having the sense of the Arabic *ibn*[6]. Jeroboam was in the service of Solomon, just as Uriah the Hittite served David. Naboth also, put to death by Ahab[7], may have been of Nabataean origin. In the later books of the Old Testament, such as Ezekiel and Chronicles, the Nabataeans are in all probability comprehended under the common designation of *Arabians*. Gashmu[8] the Arabian, to judge by the Nabataean and Sinaitic inscriptions, in which the termination ו (û) is so frequent[9], must have been a Nabataean. Perhaps at a certain period the word נבטו acquired an ethnic sense like *Arabian*, since

---

[1] Schrader, *op. cit.* (see p. 214, note 3), p. 147.
[2] Gen. xxv. 13. [3] See Dillmann on Gen. xxv. 13 (1882).
[4] נבט and נביות. In Talmudic writings we find the following forms for Nabataeans: נבטי; נוטבי; נווטה; נויהאה; and נבטי. See Levy's *Hebr. und Chald. Wörterbuch*, etc., a.v. נבט.
[5] Isaiah lx. 7. [6] *Athenaeum*, No. 2985 (Jan. 10, 1885), p. 46.
[7] 1 Kings xxi. 1 seqq.
[8] Neh. vi. 6. Compare גשם, Neh. ii. 19; iv. 1, 2.
[9] In addition to *Malku* and the other names mentioned already, we have *Matiu*, *Vaalu*, *Gothomu*, *Anamu*, etc., and *Nabtu* itself (Nabataea); the same termination also occurs constantly in the Palmyrene and Nabataean inscriptions, edited by De Vogüé (*La Syrie Centrale*).

in the cuneiform inscriptions the Nabataeans in Arabia are distinguished from others in Babylonia.

That the Edomites and the Nabataeans were, if not of the same race, at all events closely related, cannot be doubted. Esau married Mahalath, a sister of Nebaioth [1], and the form עֵשָׂו itself has the Nabataean termination -w. Among the sons of Esau we find the name Reu-el [2], and a grandson bears the name of Zepho [3]. An Edomite town is called Paoo [4]. We shall claim the Midianite Jethro [5] or Reu-el as a kinsman of the Nabataeans [6]. Allusion has been made above to the tradition of the Wisdom of Teman and Edom [7]; the Nabataeans have the same reputation amongst the Arabs. The historians and geographers of this nation regularly represent the Nabataeans as a nation learned in astronomy, agriculture, medicine, and, above all, in magic; sometimes even they are described as the inventors of all sciences, and the civilizers of the human race. There exists a book by one Kuthami, translated into Arabic in 904 A.D. by Ibn Waḥshiyah, and entitled the 'Nabataean Agriculture.' This remarkable work contains history of various kinds, chapters on agriculture, on medicine, botany, physics, and astrology; together with special treatises on mysteries, and on symbolic painting, likewise one on the history of the deity Tammuz, and on many other subjects, attributed to different patriarchs of the Old Testament, Adam, Noah, etc. Libraries are mentioned in it; and, in a word, it implies a very considerable development of all branches of religious and profane literature.

---

[1] Gen. xxviii. 9.   [2] Gen. xxxvi. 4.
[3] Gen. xxxvi. 11, 15.   [4] Gen. xxxvi. 39.

[5] Compare the other forms of this name יתר; יתרא (like עברא; Renan, *Des noms Théophores*, etc. in the *Revue des Études juives*, v. p. 166); יתרי like עברי, שמעי, Renan, *Ibidem*); יתרן (a Horite name'; and יתרעם (where עם represents an Ammonite divinity; see p. 224. He is the son of Eglah, certainly a Moabite or an Ammonite woman).

[6] We mention for curiosity's sake the names of בתואל, נמואל, המואל, to which many others could be added.

[7] See p. 210.

It is not our object here to discuss the age to which the composition of this great Nabataean encyclopedia may be assigned. E. M. Quatremère refers it to the time of Nebuchadnezzar, and Prof. Chwolson places it at an earlier period still. More moderate critics, such as M. Renan and Prof. Gutschmid, assign it to the beginning of the Christian era[1]. To be sure, this work is believed by some critics to have originated among the Nabataeans in Irâk or Babylonia, since in Greek writings Chaldean wisdom is always described as coming from that country[2]. But the Sabaeans, who are also Arabian, were famed for their wisdom; and the apocryphal tradition may equally well allude to those Nabataeans who were the neighbours, and ultimately the successors, of Edom and Tema, both of whom in the Bible already appear with the same character. In point of fact, the inscriptions discovered by Mr. Doughty confirm this tradition. That the Nabataeans had intercourse with the Hebrews we have already seen[3]. The language of the inscriptions is Aramaic mixed with Arabic words, but with forms such as we find them in the Aramaic sections of Daniel and Ezra. Thus for the pronoun, in lieu of הן they use דהם[4]. Instead of *Ethpaal*, we find in them the form *Hithpaal*[5]. Words and expressions used in the Mishnah[6] and the Talmud[7] are also met with. Possibly even Hebrew forms occur, such as אנוש (No. 2) and תמונה (Nos. 3, 4) for שפונה (*right*). The word *Marânâ* (No. 10) throws light upon St. Paul's *Maranatha*[8].

As to the mythology of these inscriptions, we find in the

---

[1] Renan, *Histoire générale des Langues sémitiques* (1863), p. 246.
[2] Renan, *ibidem*, p. 243.   [3] See p. 221.
[4] משדהם: and אהרהם (in No. 2, see p. 218, line 2); ביזהב (No. 7); בלהב (No. 9). Halévy, *Revue*, p. 9. See also קים (No. 29, l. 3) and Dan. vi. 9.
[5] התקברא. See above, p. 219, line 3.
[6] הרהן (No. 2, p. 221, line 5), 'to pledge.' קים (κῆνσος). The coin סלע (p. 218, line 9).
[7] כסל דמי (No. 6), 'double value.' לא יהוא אנש רשו (No. 10, above, p. 219, line 9) is the Talmudic אין אדם רשאי. ינסק בידה (No. 2, line 9, and No. 29, line 2, pp. 218 and 231) is the usual juridic expression in the Talmud.
[8] See above, p. 73.

first instance, the gods Manutu, Kishah, Hablu, and Marhabah, which (with slight variations) are mentioned as having been worshipped by the pre-Islamite Arabs. The name Dusara has been found before[1] in Nabataean texts, and is mentioned in classical authors as that of a divinity (Δουσαρής) worshipped throughout Arabia, especially at Petra, Adran, and Bosra. It has been thought to mean *lord of Shera*[2],—Shera being a mountain of Arabia (cf. בעל לבנן, etc.). Other names of deities are compounded with the root הר = הוה, 'to announce.' Thus הואלת, 'announcement of Allath,' and הושוח, 'announcement of Shuah,' probably the god of Shuah, son of Abraham and Keturah, father of the tribe of the same name[3], the country from which Bildad the Shuhite came[4]. The Shuhites are mentioned, as Prof. Sayce kindly informs me, in the cuneiform inscriptions. In them the god Nergal is also called Sergal, a name which may be identical with the Sangala mentioned in the inscription of Tema[5].

The root הר occurs also in the Phœnician הומלך, 'Malik announces[6].' We have seen in the Tema inscriptions Rimmonnathan. Here we find the name קסנתן (No. 7), which M. Renan transliterates Xanten (scarcely probable), but which is read by M. Halévy[7] Kosnathan, a compound of Kos, the Idumean god Kos, or, as Josephus calls him, Koze[8], and *nathan*, 'to give,' analogous to יונתן and נתנאל. This happy suggestion is confirmed by the name Κοσνάταρος, found in a Greek inscription of Memphis, and by Kosmalchos,

---

[1] De Vogüé, *La Syrie Centrale*, p. 120.

[2] ذو الشرى, as it is written by Arabic authors.

[3] Gen. xxv. 2.

[4] Job ii. 11 and elsewhere.

[5] It is, however, possible that Sangala (or Sengala) means the deity of the moon, from *Sen*, the moon, and Gala. Perhaps *ner* in Nergal may be connected with *ner* in Abner and in Neriah. The word *gal* may be contained in the names Goliath and Abigail.

[6] See, however, M. Renan, *Revue*, v. p. 175, who takes הו from the root היה (היה), 'to live.' The inscription, which is an interesting one, will be found at length in the *Corp. Inscr. Sem.* (Paris, 1881). No. 1.

[7] *Revue*, p. 16.   [8] Κοζέ. *Antiquities*, XV. vii. 9.

'Kos has reigned' (in cuneiform, Kaushmalak): Kosgeros, 'Kos is friend;' Kosanedos, 'Kos binds;' and in cuneiform, Ka-ush-gab-ri, 'Kos has vanquished.'

Χουζᾶς[1], the name of Herod's[2] steward, who may fairly be inferred to have been of Edomite extraction, may be another derivative; this seems at least more probable than to suppose it is connected with the Rabbinical כוזא, 'a little pitcher,' which is Dr. Edersheim's opinion[3]. It may appear a rash suggestion to make that the name *Kos* is derived from the Arabic قوس, *a bow*, in Syriac קשתא, in Hebrew קשת[4]. The fact is, however, that Ishmael and Esau were both great hunters with the bow. We know how the ideas of mythology pass from one tribe to another. In these inscriptions we find the Syrian god Rimmon[5], four Arabic gods[6], a god from the tribe of Shuah, an Edomite deity, and the doubtful *Zelem*[7]. The same fact may be substantiated from biblical names. Ammi, to judge from the name Amminadab in a cuneiform inscription, seems to represent an Ammonite local deity[8]; this fact at once explains the words[9] *Ben Ammi* in Genesis (A. V.), 'Son of my kindred[10].' The name of this deity occurs in the compounds Ammiel, Ammihud (analogous to Kemoshnadab), Ammishaddai. In my opinion the names of Rehoboam and Jeroboam are compounded with Amm, the Ammonite god. As to the first, we know that Rehoboam's mother was an Ammonitess[11]; as

---

[1] Luke viii. 3.

[2] I may be allowed to add that the name of Herod seems to me to be possibly identical with Irad in Genesis, the ע being pronounced as a guttural resembling ה. The use of the word עיר in proper names is not rare in the Bible. We find names of persons, Ira, Iru, and Iri, all with ע. Iram is an Edomite name, which may even be compared with the Phœnician חירם. See however, Renan, *Revue des Études juives*, v. p. 169.

[3] *Life and Times of Jesus the Messiah*, vol. i. p. 572.

[4] See Halévy, *Revue*, p. 16.   [5] See above, p. 224.

[6] See above, p. 211.   [7] Pages 211, 212, and 230.

[8] An Assyrian tablet states that among the Shuhites the name of Nergal was נרגל.

[9] Gen. xix. 38.   [10] J. Derenbourg, *Revue des Études juives*, t. ii. p. 123.

[11] We see from the examples of Tamar, Hannah and others, that mothers had the privilege of naming their children.

to the second, it can only be analogous with Jerubbaal. We find Rehabyah as well as Rehab-am, Yeqamyah and Yeqam-am. Perhaps לא עם opposed to לא אל in the song of Moses may have some reference to the god Amm. In the Authorised Version, 'They have moved me to jealousy with that which is not God... And I will move them to jealousy with those which are not a people.' Compare יתריעם, p. 222. Balaam (Bil'am) also, I venture to think, is a compound of Bel (Baal) and Am[1], analogous to the names Elijah, El-jahu; and Joel, Jeho-el.

Analogous are two names compounded with that of the Syrian god Dad[2] (הדד and אדד), viz. that of Bildad the Shuhite, which means Bel-dad, and Eldad which is = El-dad. If the latter is rightly rendered in the dictionaries by 'God loves (him),' the former cannot be anything else but a compound of Bel and Dad. It is possible that Dad was pronounced in the Canaanitish dialects Dod, in which form we may be allowed to recognise it in the name of the town Ashdod (analogous to the personal names Ashbel and Ashbaal), and in the personal names Dodo, Dodi, Dodaï, possibly even in David. Conjectural as this explanation of some of the names compounded with divine titles may appear to be, it is certain that the principle will prove ultimately of great importance to ethnology and mythology, and probably also to philology as well.

Mention has been made of the termination *oa* in Horite names[3], and *o* in Nabateo-Midianic names; we may compare Yeriho and perhaps Slomoh (Solomon). The termination *on* seems to be more general amongst the Canaanitish tribes. Ephron, Hebron among the Hittites; Ekron, Dagon amongst the Philistines; Mahlon, Chilyon in Moab; and often in Hebrew names. Specially Aramaic, perhaps, are the names formed with a yod at the beginning, such as Yatlet, Yamlek,

---

[1] Mr. W. Wright regards it as a Hittite name. Of course no derivation is given, since the Hittite vocabulary, so far as appears, consists at present of two words!

[2] Schrader, *op. cit.* (on p. 214, note 5), p. 454.   [3] See p. 214.

Yiçhar, Yishaq, Jacob, Yiskah, Yishbak, etc. The ending *aï* as in Saraï, Yishaï, Radaï or Dadaï, Shaddaï, as well as *î* as in Abi, Aḥi, may also be Aramaic. Lastly, I may mention the termination *ath*, not in feminine words, but in names like Goliath, Genubath, Ahuzzath, special, perhaps, to the Philistine dialect[1].

From these facts it is evident what a mixture of tribes must have peopled the country known generally in the Old Testament under the name of "*Arab*" (ערב), and in the cuneiform inscription as Arabu or Arabia. The name עֲרָב itself may even be derived from the root ערב, 'to mix.' If we are right in supposing that the tribes of Tema and the countries around spoke Aramaic dialects at the time of the Assyrian conquest, we shall have to place Uz, Hul, Gether, and Mash, sons of Aram, in the Arabian desert, in the neighbourhood of Edom and the Hedjâz, and not in Mesopotamia, as has commonly been done. In fact M. Halévy[2] expressed this opinion some years ago, and no reason has yet appeared for abandoning it. It may be observed that towns of these countries are mentioned on Egyptian monuments, dating from a period before the immigration of the Israelites to Canaan, with the Nabataean termination -*u*[3]. So again there is the locality Ono[4] in Benjamin, which is probably derived from the Egyptian On, *sun*, the native name of the city called in Greek Heliopolis. This latter place is meant by the *Aven* of Ezekiel[5], which should rather be read *On* (*Aven* being meant by the punctuators to have the sense of *idolatry*). In Jeremiah[6] it is represented by its Hebrew equivalent Beth Shemesh. Possibly the name *Ben Oni*[7], for Benjamin, contains an allusion to the sun or the south; for it corresponds to Jamin or Yemen. The use of Beth-Aven for Beth-El[8] may

---

[1] Compare Prof. Driver's *Hebrew Tenses*, ed. 2 (1881), p. 261.
[2] *Revue*, p. 15.
[3] See O. Blau in Merx's *Archiv*, 1869, p. 352 f.
[4] Ezra ii. 33.   [5] Ezekiel xxx. 17.   [6] Jer. xliii. 13.
[7] Gen. xxxv. 18.   [8] Hosea iv. 16.

have been facilitated by the recollection that Beth-el was once called Beth-On. Perhaps the name of Onan¹, the son of Judah, is derived also from On, with the addition of the syllable -*ân*². We may therefore, with M. Halévy³, group the Semitic languages as follows:—Towards the east the Assyrio-Babylonians; to the south the Yoqtanido-Cushites; to the west the Phœnicians; and to the north the Hittites. In the central parts, Syria and the Arabian desert, the Aramaic-speaking races. The Israelites, Moabites, and perhaps also the Ammonites (all of whom inhabited Canaan-itish countries) spoke the language of the Canaanites with some slight Aramaisms, as may be seen from the inscription of Mesha (the 'Moabite stone'), and from various passages in the Old Testament. The question arises now, what language did the Israelites, or the descendants of Abraham, originally speak, Hebrew or Aramaic? There can be no doubt as to the answer. Abraham came from Ḥaran, which certainly was an Aramaic-speaking district. Abram, if we may understand אב, like the Arabic *Abu*, in the sense of 'ancestor,' may be explained as a compound of Ab and Aram (אב ארם), i.e. the father of Aram or Aramean. Saraï is an Aramaic form. In Canaan his name was changed to Abraham, which may perhaps signify 'the beloved father' (אב רחם), as the Arabs call him *Khalîl Allah*, 'the beloved of God.' Saraï is changed to a Canaanitish form Sarah⁴. When Isaac is of an age to be married, Abraham sends to his own family in Aram Naharaim, Aram of the two rivers, to the town of Nahor. Jacob also, when fleeing from Esau, takes refuge in the same country, and seeks a wife in the house of his relative Laban

---

¹ Gen. xxxviii. 4.

² Perhaps the word און (Aven) in Isaiah lxvi. 3 ought to be read On. In fact this verse refers to some heathen ceremonies, perhaps in Cyprus, where worship of dogs is mentioned in inscriptions. I translate consequently: killing the ox, beating a man, sacrificing a lamb, breaking the neck of a dog, offering an oblation, lifting (כלב (פ)) for חזיר) a swine, celebrating the moon (לבנה?) for לבנה), blessing On or the Sun.

³ *Revue*, p. 15.

⁴ Compare, for instance, בלי and בליד (Neh. x. 9 and xii. 5).

the Aramean. Jacob is called *Arami* in Deuteronomy[1], 'A wandering Aramean was my father;' (A.V. 'A Syrian ready to perish was my father.') The Canaanitish language may even have been adopted by Abraham, since Jacob gives a Canaanitish name, *Galeed*, to what Laban calls *Yegar Sahadutha*[2] in Aramaic; possibly, however, it was only adopted by the tribes after they had taken possession of the land of Canaan, since it is related that the Israelites in the desert said with regard to the manna, *man hu*[3], 'what is it?' *man* for *mah*, 'what?' In fact, the language spoken in Palestine is called by Isaiah the language of Canaan[4]: 'In that day will five cities in the land of Egypt speak the language of Canaan.' The expressions *Yehudith*[5] and *Ibri* are only used in conversation with foreigners. The 'God of the Ibrim' is used when Moses speaks to Pharaoh[6]; Jonah[7] says to heathen sailors, 'I am an Ibri;' and Rabshakeh is asked to speak *Yehudith*[8]. The Aramaic origin of the Israelites will perhaps explain the Aramaic form of Jehovah or Jahveh, which in Hebrew ought to be Jehovah or Yihyeh, at least in accordance with the derivation given in Exodus[9], 'I am (*ehyeh*), hath sent me unto you.'

I cannot leave out an ingenious conjecture made by M. Halévy[10]. He sees in the word for 'bastard,' *Mamzer*[11], 'And a bastard shall dwell in Ashdod,' an allusion to the Nabataeans. Not only do the Rabbinical legends speak of the excessive promiscuity of the Idumaeans and the people of Seir, but Stephanus of Byzantium also says: Ναβαταῖοι, ἔθνος τῶν εὐδαιμόνων Ἀράβων. Ναβάτης δέ ἐστιν ἀραβιστὶ ὁ ἐκ μοιχείας γενόμενος ... Nabates Arabice significat eum, qui ex adulterio natus est.

That the Nabataeans must have been early in Philistia is

---

[1] Deut. xxvii. 5. [2] Gen. xxxi. 47. [3] Exodus xvi. 15.
[4] Isaiah xix. 18. [5] See above, p. 42. [6] Exodus v. 3.
[7] Jonah i. 9. [8] Isaiah xxxvi. 11.
[9] Exodus iii. 14. See the First Essay in this volume, and Halévy, *Revue*, t. ix. p. 14 and seqq.
[10] *Revue*, p. 10. [11] Zach. ix. 6.

probable from the statement of Herodotus[1] that in his time the Arabs, i.e. the Nabataeans, were masters of the whole coast of Palestine. We know, moreover, that the Assyrians transplanted Aramaic-speaking races to Samaria and to Philistia. If, indeed, the Nabataeans were settled at Ashdod, the *Ashdodith*, the language of Ashdod, which the young generation of the returned exiles spoke, according to Nehemiah, must have been the Nabataean language[2]. With all this, it is easy to understand what a mixture of dialects must have prevailed in Palestine in the time of Ezra: Hebrew, Nabataean, Aramaic from Kutha and Avva or Samaritan; to say nothing of the Babylonian dialect, which many who returned from exile must have brought with them. How far Ezra and Nehemiah succeeded in re-establishing Hebrew amongst the Jews, has been explained in a previous paper[3].

[1] Herod. iii. 5.   [2] See above, p. 42.   [3] See above, pp. 40–74.

Supplementary Notes.

THE following are further particulars of the readings adopted by MM. Berger and Clermont-Ganneau, whose articles arrived too late to be alluded to (pp. 209, 210) in the preceding essay except in the notes.

P. 210, Inscription 1, l. 3, and p. 211, Inscr. 4, ll. 11, 12, 16, 21, I have accepted M. Clermont-Ganneau's ingenious interpretation of צלם as the name of a Deity (see the *Athenaeum*, Feb. 28, 1885 (No. 2992), p. 280, where I have suggested that the word צִלָּם (Numbers xiv. 18), 'their defence or shade,' ought perhaps to be read צַלְמָם, and translate 'Tsclem is departed from them, and Jehovah is with us'). Zalamu in Assyrian is the god of eclipse or darkness (see Prof. Sayce's *Assyrian Grammar*, p. 24). The word צלם, however, usually means in the Bible 'image,' and in this sense we find it also in a Sabaean or Himyaritic inscription (see David

Heinrich Müller in the *Anzeiger der philosophisch-historischen Classe*, Wien, 17 December, 1884, No. xxviii).

P. 211, Inscription 2. M. Clermont-Ganneau's reading נפש, 'a sepulchral monument' (see Levy, *Neuhebr. Wörterbuch*, s. v.), has been adopted.

P. 212, Inscription, l. 13. I have translated כותא, 'monument,' from the root כתת, 'aptare lapides.' Compare שתת, שתם (שתות, Isaiah xix. 10; Ps. xi. 3; and perhaps שת, Numbers xxiv. 17), and אבן שתיה, the foundation-stone in the Temple (*Mishnah*, Yomâ, v. 2). כותא, 'vêtement,' as translated by M. Halévy, does not give a good sense.—Ibidem, l. 15. I read והאנא for M. Halévy's זא והא.— Ibidem. I have supplied יהב for M. Halévy's בית.—Ibidem, l. 17. I have supplied כ[רין] for M. Halévy's כ[מרא].

P. 218, Inscription 2, l. 1. For כפרא we find in M. Huber's facsimiles of similar inscriptions קברא.—ll. 1 and 4. I have accepted M. Halévy's readings חואלת and ומרחבה for M. Renan's ומרחבה.—l. 7. יעבדה יעלא for די לא יעבד די עלא.—l. 8. and חואלת Perhaps שמרין די עלא; probably on p. 219, Inser. 10, l. 11, בעיר די עלא. There are still several passages doubtful in the Nabataean inscriptions of Mr. Doughty, which will no doubt be elucidated by the comparison of the facsimiles taken by the late M. Huber and Dr. Euting. So, for instance, I read חרתי (p. 218, Inser. 2, l. 9, and p. 219, Inser. 10, l. 12), 'new coins' (compare above, p. 84, note 4), for M. Renan's strange word תרתי; the reading חרתי is certain in M. Huber's facsimiles (see M. Philippe Berger's article, p. 379, note 11).

Specimen of the Nabataean Inscriptions copied by M. Huber[1].

1 דנה כפרא די עבד עידו בר כהילו בר
2 סלבסי[2] לנפשה וילדה ואחרה ולמן די ינפק בידה
3 כתב תקף[3] מן יד עידו קים[4] לה ולמן די ינתן דיקבר[5] בה
4 עידו בחיוהי בירח ניסן שנת תשע לחרתת מלך

---

[1] No. 40 of M. Huber's *Catalogue*, No. 29 in the article of M. Ph. Berger.

[2] M. Berger thinks that the name may be Seleucus (?).

[3] Not from the Arabic ثقف, as M. Berger suggests, but the Aramaic הוק = תקף; cf. in the *Mishnah* הזקה, 'right of possession.'

[4] Daniel vi. 8 [7 Engl.], a kind of firman, as M. Berger rightly explains.

[5] In the facsimile rather ויתקבר (M. Berger).

5 נבנו רחם עמה ולענו דושרא ומנותו וקישה
6 כל מן די [יעיר?] כפרא דנה או יזבן או [ירהן?] או יתן או
7 יפגר' או יתאלף עלוהי כתב כלה או יקבר בה או
8 [?] למא די עלא כתיב וכפרא וכתבה די לה חרם²
9 דחליקת חרם נבטו ושלמו לעלם עלמין

1 'This is the cave which made Aïdu, son of Coheilu, son
2 of .... (?), for himself, his children and his posterity, and for whosoever shall produce
3 a written permission from the hand of Aïdu, valid for him; and for any to whom Aïdu shall grant the right of burial there
4 during his lifetime. In the month of Nisan, the ninth year of Aretas king
5 of Nabataea, lover of his people. And may Dusara, Manutu, and Kaïsa curse
6 every one who may make alterations (?) in this cave, or who may sell it, or [pledge it], or give it as a present, or
7 destroy, or .... (?) on it any writing, or bury in it, or
8 alter (?) anything which is written above. And the cave and the writing (inscription?) that is upon it is sacred
9 .... (?), sacred for the Nabataeans and the Shallemites, for ever and ever.'

¹ נגר in the Targum, 'to destroy,' which will remove M. Berger's difficulty.
² The biblical word חרם.

XI.

SOME FURTHER REMARKS ON THE CORBEY ST. JAMES (ff).

[W. SANDAY.]

I HAVE had the advantage of looking over the proofs of the most interesting and valuable paper that was read to us on this subject by Prof. Wordsworth. Everything has now been done that can possibly be done for the description and history of the MS. A number of isolated passages have received skilful and delicate handling (see esp. pp. 137–141): and all the necessary materials have been collected or indicated for forming a judgment on the Latin text. It is on this last point that I propose to offer a few additional remarks, suggested by my own work at other parts of the Version. The brief time at my disposal since Prof. Wordsworth's Essay came into my hands will prevent me from attempting to travel over the whole ground of the Epistle. I shall therefore confine myself merely to what seems to me to be the key to the position, the passages where m (the so-called Speculum of Augustine) is also extant and available for the illustration of ff (the Corbey MS.) on the one hand and of the Vulgate on the other. The three texts, m, ff, and the Vulgate, as given by Cod. Amiatinus, are printed conveniently in parallel columns on pp. 131, 132.

As it will be necessary for me to draw upon materials collected for another though nearly related purpose, it may be well for me to explain at the outset what those materials are, so that it may be seen how far the evidence to which I have access extends and what are its limits. It is unfortunate that I should have to make use of an inquiry which is not so much as half completed; and yet even the small portion that is in any sense finished seems to point so distinctly to certain conclusions that it will not be altogether premature to apply them to the question before us, and it seems best to do so while its interest is still fresh and unexhausted.

It was at the beginning of the last Long Vacation that I began to work systematically at the Old Latin. If I had been alone, as may well be supposed, I should not have advanced very far at present, but I have had the benefit of much help from the first, and now Mr. H. J. White of Christ Church has definitely joined me, and we have been for some little time prosecuting our inquiry together, so that it is in a more forward state than might otherwise have been expected.

My first step was to get indices made to all the earlier Latin Fathers that had not been hitherto indexed, especially Novatian, Hilary, Lucifer of Cagliari, Victorinus Afer, Optatus, Zeno, the Arian fragments published by Mai, and the Speculum of Augustine. These, with the indices already existing to Irenaeus, Tertullian, Cyprian, Ambrose, gave a fairly wide basis to start from.

By comparing them it was not difficult to see in what passages MSS. and Fathers would throw the greatest light upon each other. With the help of Mr. White and of the Rev. Wilmore Hooper, Fellow of Durham, I got a number of these selected passages written out in parallel columns. A simple inspection of the parallels brought out much that was instructive, and I hoped to be able to exhibit this to the eye by the use of different types. At first, however, the number of the different authorities was baffling and bewildering, and I was obliged to give up the idea for the time. I think that we now see our way to return to it by dividing the authorities into groups, and following out the same system of marking in each group. At present the boundaries of the different groups are not yet all settled: some are clear, but others will require further investigation: when that has been made, I hope that this part of our material may be worked up with advantage.

My next step was to take certain passages and reduce the

variations in reading and in rendering to such a form as they would take in an 'apparatus criticus.' It was then possible to express the relations of the different MSS. to each other numerically. This furnished some rough preliminary conclusions which might help to guide our future work. But the process was really too mechanical, and involved an expenditure of labour hardly commensurate with the result.

We then tried the experiment of singling out only what seemed to be more important readings over a wider area; and Mr. White has filled the greater part of a good-sized notebook with the analysis of readings of this kind. But here again the objection was that we were apt to be mistaken as to what was really important and what was not. It is indeed in this as in most other matters of science: nothing is really insignificant, and it is impossible to tell beforehand, or without considerable experience, what phenomena have the greater significance and what the less.

It was at this point that Professor Wordsworth gave me the opportunity of writing that part of his Introduction to the Bobbio MS. (k) which deals with the Latin text. For us the chance was a happy one, because experience has shown that the particular MS. k is of the very first importance for the understanding of the Version; it is indeed, I believe, little less than the key to the whole, and in working at it I seemed to fall naturally into what I conceive to be the right method, and a method which seems likely to yield well founded and satisfactory results. The MSS. must be dealt with singly; they must be collated together point by point; the peculiar element in each must be isolated; and its structure and composition must be thoroughly studied.

It will be remembered that k contains, roughly speaking, about the first half of the Gospel of St. Matthew, and about the second half of the Gospel of St. Mark. This is really the only portion of the Old Latin New Testament that we can claim to have worked at in this thorough-going way. Neither have we treated as completely the chapters in St. Matthew as we have done those in St. Mark: for the method grew under our hands, and it took some little time to bring it into shape. There is the further limitation that we have as yet only paid close attention to the older MSS.: the later texts must stand over for further investigation.

But the analysis that we have been making, partial as it is, does I think bring out certain facts of great importance. They may be subject to modification, and I should only like to affirm them for the limited area that we have examined. I believe that they extend some way beyond this; and the scattered evidence which we had collected previously points all in the same direction; but it is well not to anticipate, and I should prefer to restrict what I say specially to the first two Gospels.

Taking these, I believe that we are able to give a more definite answer than has yet been given to the question as to the origin of the Old Latin version. Was that version, it is asked, originally one, or was it more than one? We reply that there were originally two main versions, two parent stocks from which all the texts that we now have were derived with different degrees of modification. In saying this I naturally exclude cases where the particular writer has translated for himself directly from the Greek, and speak only of texts which circulated over some greater or less extent of ground.

The parent stocks I believe to have been two, and as far as I can see at present, not more. It is perfectly true that MSS. like a in St. Mark, and I may add St. Luke, and d throughout, have a peculiar element—a peculiar element so marked that it must have a separate origin. But in neither case are they independent of the great family to which they belong: the peculiarities are grafts upon the main stock; they do not form a new and distinct stock by themselves.

We cannot do better than keep to the names that have been already given to these two main stocks—the African and the European. To the African belong, at a stage not quite the earliest k (Cod. Bobiensis), at a stage somewhat later e (Cod. Palatinus), and at a later stage still m (Speculum Augustini). To the European belong the great mass of other MSS. Large modifications have taken place in both families, perhaps at least one systematic recension in the European, and in the later members especially there is much mixture and interchange between the two families: but underlying all these vicissitudes the two fundamental types remain distinct from each other; and the differences between these types are no longer, like the later modifications, differences of degree merely but of kind.

The great proof of this is that whereas between different members of the same family the diction varies, especially in some more prominent words, but the general framework and essential cast of the sentences is, with comparatively rare exceptions, the same; on the other hand, between members of the two opposing families, though here and there we may find an agreement in words borrowed from one by the other, yet the framework and essential cast of the sentences are different.

Mr. White and I have catalogued the peculiarities of k which come out upon a collation with the oldest European MSS. a b d f, and the result is such as I have described. Many points that we were at first inclined to pass over as trivial contribute to it. For instance, k repeatedly has 'fui' where the European MSS. have 'eram:' this occurs no less than twenty-four times in the eight chapters of St. Mark, and there is only a single exception where the contrary relation holds good. There are two constructions of which k is very fond: 'cum' with imperf. or pluperf. subj., especially common in St. Matthew, and the construction of two coordinate verbs ('respondit et dixit') especially common in St. Mark. The first of these constructions is found in St. Matthew twenty-three times where the European MSS. have the present participle, and ten times where they have the abl. abs. The second construction occurs in St. Mark no less than forty times where the European MSS. express themselves differently, not counting some twelve instances where the construction is shared by k with some one or two European MSS. against the rest. To set against these fifty-two instances there are only five exceptions. There is one construction which is especially characteristic of k: 'cum serum factum esset' (or 'est') occurs five times, while in b f the regular phrase is 'vespere facto:' in one case b d have 'cum vespere (sic) factum esset,' and in two cases a has an approximation to k, but in each with 'sero' instead of 'serum.' Another marked peculiarity of k is its fondness for compounds of 'eo' where these are avoided in the European text (fourteen instances in St. Matthew, nine in St. Mark, and only two exceptions). In like manner k repeatedly has the preposition 'de' where the others have 'ex' and once 'a:' so five times in St. Matthew, six times in St. Mark, with three exceptions.

But I must not stay to enlarge on these points. I will therefore only give a list of some of the words that are most characteristic of k, and will then pass on to ff of St. James. These are 'adoro,' 'adoratio' (for 'oro,' 'oratio'), 'claritas,' 'clarifico' for 'gloria,' 'magnifico,' 'colligo' for 'congrego,' 'commotus' for 'misertus,' 'continuo' for 'statim' or 'protinus,' 'corripio' for 'comminor' (where 'objurgo' is specially characteristic of a), 'crastinus' without 'dies,' 'demoniacus' for 'daemonium habens,' 'discentes' for 'discipuli' (eight times, but with three exceptions), 'emundo' for 'mundo,' 'excito' for 'suscito' or 'resuscito' (a marked usage), 'excludo' alternating with 'expello' in the phrase 'excludere' or 'expellere daemonia' where the Europeans have 'eicere' (this also is very marked), the little word 'illic' for 'ibi' and 'iste' for 'hic,' 'ita' for 'utique' and 'itaque' for 'ergo' (but not without exception), 'de longinquo,' 'lumen' for 'lux,' 'mortuus' for 'defunctus,' 'natio' for 'gens' and for 'generatio' (two striking usages), 'nequam' for 'malus,' etc., 'nimis' for 'valde,' 'obsecror' or 'obsecro' for 'rogo,' 'palla' for 'sindon,' 'peregrinor' for 'peregre proficiscor,' 'ploratio' for 'fletus,' 'poto' for 'potum do,' 'pressura' for 'tribulatio' (not common in k, but marked in Cyprian and e), 'propterea' for 'ideo,' 'proximum tibi' for 'tuum,' 'quasi' for 'tamquam,' 'qui' for 'quicumque,' 'quoadusque' for 'donec,' quomodo' for 'sicut,' 'salvo' for 'salvum facio,' 'sermo' for 'verbum,' 'similitudo' for 'parabola' (very marked), 'simulo' (sic), the preposition 'super,' 'tego' for 'operio,' 'totus' several times for 'omnis,' 'universus.' These are all instances which occur often enough to justify a real induction. In many cases the induction would be largely strengthened by taking in Cyprian and e; and there is of course much to be said about details.

These examples, selected from a large number where the evidence is less cogent, will be enough to show what a radical divergence there is between the two texts, and what an inner coherence and consistency there are in each. We now have to ask, how far anything of the same kind holds good in regard to the extant texts in St. James. And here I would at once lay down that I do not think there is the slightest *a priori* probability that it would be so. The evidence for the acceptance of the Epistle in the West is so gradual and comparatively late, that we should not at all expect that it would be included in the original translation, even if that translation extended to the Epistles, as at first sight it seems to have done. We must therefore put aside all presumptions before the fact and look strictly at the facts as we have them. Taking the passages where we have three MSS. to compare together, how many original versions do they imply? I answer, though as yet tentatively, two.

We must bear in mind two things: (1) that we are dealing with an altogether later stratum of text than in the case of k: k is an established text by the middle of the third century: the earliest evidence for the text of ff is on the extreme verge of the fourth century (Chromatius), and though the reading so attested is important it does not follow that the whole text is as old even as that: between the date of Chromatius and the MS. there is plenty of time for other readings and groups of readings to be introduced; so that we should expect to find in ff a mixed and composite text at a rather advanced stage of degeneracy: the text of m too, whatever its relation to that of St. Augustine, in any case dates from his period and is not on a level with older texts like those of k and Cyprian. And (2) we must remember that the phraseology of the Epistle of St. James is not like the simple language of the Gospels: it contains a number of unusual expressions which are just of the kind in which the divergence even of nearly allied MSS. would be most apparent. Some allowance should be made on both of these grounds.

In order to show more exactly the relation of the three texts to each other, the most satisfactory plan will be to bring it into relief by the use of different types. In the columns that follow

Ordinary type = points common to all three texts.
Thick type = points common to Vulg. and ff, or Vulg. and m.
Small capitals = points common to m and ff, not found in Vulg.
Italics = peculiarities of the text in which they occur.
(o) = order agreeing with Vulg.
(o') = order differing from Vulg.
(o'') = order of m agreeing with ff against Vulg. (only one instance, IV. 12).

SPECULUM (m).	VULGATE (COD. AM.).	CORBEY MS. (ff).
I. ¹⁹ Sit *uero* omnis homo *citatus* audire, et tardus *loqui*, *piger in* IRACUNDIA:	¹⁹ Sit **autem** omnis homo **uelox ad audiendum**, **tardus autem ad loquendum** *et* **tardus ad** *iram*	¹⁹ Sit **autem** omnis homo **uelox ad audiendum, tardus autem ad loquendum, tardus** *autem* **ad** IRACUNDIAM.
²⁰ IRACUNDIA enim uiri iustitiam Dei non operatur.	²⁰ *Ira* enim uiri iustitiam Dei non operatur	²⁰ IRACUNDIA enim uiri iustitiam Dei non operatur.
²⁶ Si quis putat † *superstitiosum* se(o) esse, non refrenans linguam suam, sed FALLENS cor sum (*sic*), huius uana † religio est (*o*).	²⁶ Si quis **autem** putat † se **religiosum** (o) esse, non **refrenans linguam suam**, sed *seducens* cor **suum**, huius uana † est religio (o).	²⁶ Si quis **autem** putat † se **religiosum** (o) esse non *infrenans* **linguam suam**, sed FALLENS cor **suum**, huius uana est religio (o).
²⁷ *Sanctitas* autem *pura* et	²⁷ **Religio** autem **munda** et	²⁷ **Religio** autem **munda** et

Corbey St. James (ff).

SPECULUM (m).	VULGATE (COD. AM.).	CORBEY MS. (ff).
(o) *incontaminata* haec est aput **Deum patrem**, uisitare ORFANOS et uiduas in *angustia ipsorum* † et inmaculatum se SERUARE (o) A *mundo*.	(o) inmaculata apud deum *et* patrem haec est, uisitare *pupillos* et uiduas in tribulatione eorum, † et inmaculatum se *custodire* (o) *ab hoc* saeculo.	inmaculata apud *Dominum* (c) haec est, uisitare ORFANOS et uiduas in tribulatione eorum ; † SERUARE se *sine* macula (o) A seculo.
II. ¹³ Iudicium enim sine misericordia *his* qui non fecit misericordiam ; *quoniam* misericordia *praefertur* iudicio.	II. ¹³ Iudicium enim sine misericordia *illi* qui non fecerit misericordiam ; super*exaltat* autem misericordia iudicio.	II. ¹³ Iuditium *autem non* misere*bitur ei*, qui non fecit misericordiam. Super *gloriatur* autem misericordia iudicium.
'Quid prode EST, fratres, *si* † fidem quis dicat (o) *in semet ipso manere*, opera autem non habeat ? Numquid potest † fide (sic) sola saluare eum (o) ?	¹⁴ Quid prode*rit*, fratres mei, si † fidem quis dicat se (o) habere, opera autem non habeat ? Numquid poterit † fides saluare eum (o) ?	¹⁴ Quit prodEST, fratres mei, si † quis dicat se fidem (o) habere opera autem non habeat ? Numquit potest † fides eum sola saluare (o) ?
⁵ Si frater aut soror nudi *fuerint* et DEfuerit EIS *cottidianus cibus* (o) ; ¹⁶ dicat autem † eis aliquis *UESTRum* (o) : Ite in pace, *et* calefacimini, et *satiemini, et* non det eis necessaria corporis, quid prode EST *haec dixisse eis* ?	¹⁵ Si *autem* frater aut soror nudi sint et *indigeant* † uictu cotidiano (o), ¹⁶ dicat autem † aliquis *de uobis* illis (o) : Ite in pace, calefic*amini* et satur*amini*, non dederit*is* autem eis *quae* necessaria sunt corporis quid prode*rit* ?	¹⁵ Si*ue* frater si*ue* soror nudi sint et DEsit EIS † uictus cottidianus, (o) ¹⁶ dicat autem † illis *ex* UESTRis aliquis (o) : *Uadite* in pace, cali*di estote* et sat*ulli* : non dederit autem *illis alimentum* corporis ; quid et prodEST ?
⁷ Sic et fides *quae* non habet opera, mortua est *irca* se.	¹⁷ Sic et fides si non habeat opera mortua est *in* semet*ipsa*.	¹⁷ Sic et fides si non habeat opera, mortua est *sola*.
⁶ Sicut enim corpus sine *piritu* mortuum est, SIC et fides sine operibus *mortua* est.	²⁶ Sicut enim corpus sine spiritu mortuum est, *ita* et fides sine operibus mortua est.	²⁶ Sicut *autem* corpus sine spiritu mortuum est, SIC fides sine opera mortua est.
II. ¹ Nolite MULTI*loqui* ESSE, fratres mei ; *quia* maius indicium ACCIPIET*is*: multA enim † omnes	¹ Nolite *plures* magistri *fieri* fratres mei, scientes quoniam maius iudicium sumitis. ² *In* mult*is* enim	¹ Nolite MULTI magistri ESSE fratres mei, scientes quoniam maius iuditium ACCIPIEM*us*. ² Multa autem

R

SPECULUM (m).	VULGATE (Cod. Am.).	CORBEY MS. (ff).
delinquimus (o). Si quis in uerbo non *delinquid* (sic) hic †*perfectus* uir est (o), potest FRAENARE totum corpus *et dirigere*. ³ *Quare ergo* equis frena in ora mittuntur, *nisi in eo* UT *suadeantur a* nobis, et TOTUM corpus circum*ducamus*? ⁴ Ecce et naues quie*TAM* (*i. e.* quae tam) *inmensae* sunt, *sub* uentis *duris* FERUNTUR, *et* circum*ducuntur a* PAR*uissimo* gubernaculo, ubi impetus dirigentis uoluerit. ⁵ Sic et lingua *pars* membri est, sed est *magniloqua*. *Et sicut paruus* ignis magnam siluam incendit. ⁶ *Ita* et lingua ignis est: *et mundus* iniquitatis *per* linguam const*at* in membris nostris, quae maculat totum corpus, et inflammat rotam (otum *m.* 2) *geniturae* ET inflamm*etur a genitura*. ⁷ Omnis enim natura bestiarum et *auium* et serpentium ET *beluarum maritimarum* domatur et †*subiecta* EST *naturAE humanAE*: ⁸ linguam (o) autem †*hominum* domare NEMO (o) potest, *nec retinere a malo, quia* plena est †*mortali* ueneno (o).	†*offendimus* omnes (o). Si quis in uerbo non *offendit*, hic † perfectus est uir (o): potest *etiam circumducere freno* totum corpus. ³ Si autem equis frenos in ora mittimus *ad* consenti*endum* nobis, et *omne* corpus *illorum* circum*ferimus*. ⁴ Ecce et naues *cum* magnae sint, et a uentis ualidis *minentur*, circum*feruntur a modico* gubernaculo ubi impetus dirigentis uoluerit: ⁵ *ita* et lingua *modicum quidem* membrum est, et magna *exaltat*. Ecce *quantus* ignis quam magnam siluam incendit. ⁶ Et lingua ignis est: *universitas* iniquitatis lingua const*ituitur* in membris nostris, quae maculat totum corpus et inflammat rotam natiuitatis *nostrae* inflamm*ata a* gehenna. ⁷ Omnis enim natura bestiarum et *noluerum* et serpentium *ceterorumque* domantur et †*domata sunt a* natura humana: ⁸ linguam (o) autem †*nullus* hominum domare (o) potest. *Inquietum* malum, plena †ueneno mortifero (o).	†*erramus* omnes (o). Si quis in uerbo non *errat*: hic † *erit consummatus* uir (o). Potens est se INFRENARE *et* totum corpus. ³ Si autem *equorum* frenos in ora mittimus UT possint consentire, et TOTUM corpus *ipsorum conuertimus*. ⁴ Ecce et naues TAM magne sunt, et a uentis *tam* ualidis FERUNTUR, *reguntur autem* PAR*uulo* gubernaculo *et ubicumque dirigantur uoluntate eorum qui eas gubernant*. ⁵ SIC et lingua *paruulum* membrum est, et magna *gloriantur*. Ecce *pusillum* ignis, *in* quam *magna* silua incen*dum facit*. ⁶ Et lingua ignis *seculi* iniquitatis. Lingua *posita* est in membris nostris, que maculat totum corpus et inflammat rotam natiuitatis ET *incenditur a* gehenna. ⁷ *Omnis* enim natura bestiarum *siue* uola*tilium*, repentium ET *natantium* domATUR † domita EST. NATURE autem humane ⁸ linguam (o) NEMO hominum domare (o) potest. *Inconstans* malum, plena † ueneno mortifero (o).

SPECULUM (m).	VULGATE (COD. AM.).	CORBEY MS. (ff).
¹³ Quis *prudens* et *sciens* uestrum MONSTRET DE bona conuersatione opera sua in †mansuetudine et *prudentia* (o).	¹³ Quis sapiens et disciplinatus *inter* uos ? *Ostendat ex* bona conuersatione *operationem* suam iu †mansuetudinem sapientiae (o).	¹³ Quis sapiens et disciplinosus *in uobis ? demonstrat* DE bona conuersatione opera sua in sapientie *clementiam* (o).
IV. ¹ Unde bella ? UNDE RIXAE IN UOBIS ? nonne de UOLUNTATIBUS uestris quae militant in membris uestris, *et sunt uobis suauissima* ?	¹ Unde bella et *lites inter uos ?* Nonne ex *concupiscentiis* uestris quae militant iu membris uestris ?	¹ Unde *pugne* et UNDE RIXE IN UOBIS ? Nonne *hinc ?* ex UOLUpTATIBUS uestris que militant in membris uestris ?
⁷ *Humiliate uos* Deo, et resistite diabulo, et a uobis , ⁸ *proximate* Deo et †*proximauit* uobis (o). ¹⁰ Humiliamini ANTE conspectum Domini et exaltabit uos.	⁷ *Subditi igitur* estote Deo, resistite autem diabolo, et fugiet a uobis (o), ⁸ *Adpropinquate* Deo et †*adpropinquauit* uobis (o). ¹⁰ Humiliamini *in* conspectu Domini et exaltauit uos.	⁷ Subditi estote Deo resistite autem *zabolo*, et fugiet a uobis (o). ⁸ *Accedite ad Dominum* et ipse †*ad uos accedit* (o). ¹⁰ Humiliate *uos* ANTE Dominum et exaltabit uos.
¹¹ †Fratres nolite uos [uobis *Flor.*] detrahere (o). Qui *enim* [autem *Flor.*] *uituperat* †fratrem suum ET iudicat (o) †*legem uituperat* et iudicat (o). Si †legem iudicas (o), iam † non factor legis sed iudex es (o). ¹² Unus est enim legUM *dator* et iudex, qui potest †SALUARE et perdere (o). Tu autem quis es qui iudicas proximum ?	¹¹ †Nolite detrahere alterutrum fratres *mei* (o). Qui *detrahit* fratri *aut qui* †iudica fratrem suum (o) † *detrahit* legi et iudicat legem (o). Si autem †iudicas legem (o), † non es factor legis sed iudex (o). ¹² Unus est leg*islator* et iudex, qui potest † perdere et *liberare* (o). Tu autem quis es qui iudicas proximum ?	¹¹ †Nolite *retractare de* alterutro, frater (o). Qui *retractat de* fratre ET †iudicat fratrem suum (o), †*retractat* de lege et iudicat legem (o). Si autem †iudicas legem (o), † non es factor legis sed iudex (o). ¹² Unus est legUM *positor* et iudex qui potest †SALUARE et perdere (o). Tu autem quis es qui iudicas proximum.
V. ¹ Agite nunc diuites *plangite uos* ululantes *super* miserias UESTRAS quae *superuenirunt*. ² *diuitiis* uestris. PutruERUNT et †tini-	¹ Agite nunc diuites, plorate ululantes in miseriis quae ad uenient uobis. ² Diuitiae uestrae putr*aefactae sunt* et	¹ *Iam* nunc *locupletes* plorate ululantes in miseriis UESTRIS ad ueni*entibus*. ² Diuitiae uestrae putrIERUNT †*res* uestre

SPECULUM (m).	VULGATE (COD. AM.).	CORBEY MS. (ff).
AUERUNT uestes uestrae (o).	† uestimenta uestra a tineis comesta sunt (o).	tiniAUERUNT (o).
³ † Aurum et argentum uestrum (o) *quod reposuistis in nouissimis diebus* aeruginauit et aerugo eorum † in testimonium uobis erit (o) et *comedit* carnes uestras sicut ignis.	³ Aurum et argentum uestrum (o). eruginauit, et erugo eorum † in testimonium uobis erit (o) et manducabit carnes uestras sicut ignis.	³ † Aurum uestrum et argentum (o) eruginauit et erugo *ipsorum* † erit uobis in testimonium (o) et manducabit carnes uestras *tanquam* ignis.
⁵ *Et uos deliciati* estis super terram et lux*oriati* ESTIS : *creastis autem* corda uestra in die occisionis.	⁵ *Epulati* estis super terram et *in* lux*uriis enutristis* corda uestra in diem occisionis.	⁵ *Fruiti* estis super terram et *abusi* ESTIS. *Cibastis* corda uestra in die occisionis.

With this comparison before us, let us take each of the documents in turn and ask ourselves (1) whence it got the common matter which it shares with either or both the other documents, and (2) whence it got the matter which is peculiar to itself.

First as to m. I ought not to speak too positively, as I have not yet made a special study of m even in the Gospels, much less in the Epistles: but I believe that I shall not be far wrong in saying that m is a late African text, which has carried a step further the process that we find begun in e (Cod. Palatinus). In e an African base, identical probably with k, has been corrupted partly by internal development and partly by the admission of European readings. It is not likely that m has been corrupted directly from the Vulgate. The mixture probably took place higher up on the line of descent, through some ancestor of m crossing an ancestor of the Vulgate or some ancestor of the Vulgate crossing an ancestor of m. The two hypotheses do not exclude each other: both causes may have been at work at different times. The same kind of relation holds good between m and ff: there is an amount of scattered resemblance between the two MSS. which cannot be altogether the result of chance coincidence, and points to a definite mixture of the two texts at some stage or other of their previous history.

Let us examine the structure of m a little more in detail, taking the common elements first. The coincidences with the Vulgate are not very numerous, but some of them are important. These are all that I can at present stay to notice.

I. 27. 'Deum patrem:' there can be little doubt that this is the original Latin reading and that 'Dominum' in ff is a corruption.

— 'Immaculatum:'—also a well established reading in 1 Pet. i. 19; 2 Pet. iii. 14; and to be traced as far back as to Tertullian in 1 Tim. vi. 14; where, however, d Vulgate have 'sine macula,' the reading of ff here. The presence of a reading in Tertullian does not, I believe, necessarily prove that it is African; for I strongly suspect that besides his own direct translations from the Greek, he also became acquainted with the European text during his stay at Rome, and made use of it together with the African. But I wish to speak on all points relating to Tertullian as yet with great reserve. Cyprian is our true starting point in the history of the African Version.

II. 13. 'Judicium enim sine misericordia:' the reading of St. Augustine, as well as of Vulgate. The rendering is so natural for ἡ γὰρ κρίσις ἀνέλεος that it may conceivably have been original in both the African and European texts and not necessarily imply mixture. At the same time it may be an instance of European interpolation: the inverse relation is hardly so probable, but I doubt if anything can be affirmed with certainty.

II. 16. 'Ite in pace, et calefacimini et satiemini:' the reading of Vulgate is very near this, for the form 'caleficamini' of Am. (so Tischendorf, 'caleficiamini' appears to be found in some texts) is doubtful: 'calefaciens' is, I believe, the universal rendering of θερμαινόμενος in the four places where it occurs, except that in Mark xiv. 54, k has 'calfactans' (but 'calfacientem' in v. 67): e is not extant in any of the four passages: 'saturabuntur' is also the universal rendering of χορτασθήσεσθε in Matt. v. 6, including k Cypr.; e k both have 'saturare' in Matt. xv. 33, but e has 'satiati' in Matt.

xv. 37 ('saturati' m ; k not extant). The same MS. e has 'satiabuntur' in Luke vi. 21, so that we can see how the word crept into the African version, to the later stage of which it seems to belong. [It is however also found occasionally in single European texts, possibly from mixture, e. g. Luke ix. 17 a, xvi. 21 a, John vi. 26 b.]

II. 16. 'Necessaria corporis:' this is the only place where ἐπιτήδειος occurs in the New Testament : 'necessarius' is a word common to both the African and European Texts (e. g. Mark xi. 3).

III. 4. 'Impetus dirigentis voluerit :' the marked divergence of ff at this point goes to prove that there must be some real connexion between m and Vulgate : 'impetus' is another word that is common to both texts (cf. Matt. viii. 32 k, Mark v. 13 e); the use of the participle is also not un-African (cf. Matt. xiii. 3, where d e k have 'seminans' b ff q 'seminator,' a c f Am. 'qui seminat').

III. 5. 'incendit :' III. 6. 'inflammetur.' Both these words occur only in these passages: ἀνάπτειν is elsewhere rendered by 'accendo,' but it occurs only in two other places (Luke xv. 49. Acts xxviii). φλογιζομένη is a ἅπαξ λεγόμενον.

III. 7. 'serpentium :' this is the reading of d Vulgate Augustine in Acts x. 12, and of d e Vulgate in Romans i. 23.

III. 13. 'mansuetudine :' this is the Vulgate rendering of πραΰτης in nine out of the twelve places where it occurs ; Cyprian also has it in Gal. v. 23 (not Ephes. iv. 2).

IV. 1. 'Unde bella ?' 'unde rixae ?' With the insertion of 'et,' this is the reading of Jerome himself, though Vulgate has only 'bella' and ff only 'unde rixae.'

IV. 10. 'Humiliamini :' 'humiliari' and 'humiliare se' occur equally often in Vulgate (each six times) and were both found in Cyprian.

— 'Ante conspectum :' also a frequent rendering in Vulgate.

IV. 11. 'detrahere :' this too is a Vulgate word occurring besides frequently in Old Testament and in 1 Tim. iii. 11, 1 Pet. iii. 16. Cyprian renders καταλαλεῖν by 'retractare' (v. l. 'detractare').

V. 1. 'Agite:' the only other places where ἄγε is thus used adverbially is iv. 13 of this Epistle: the Vulgate there has 'ecce,' while ff has 'jam' as here.

— 'divites :' the usual Vulgate rendering.

V. 3. 'sicut :' very common in the European and Vulgate texts.

In all the above readings 'satiemini' alone is in any way specially characteristic of a text such as that of m; and that is merely an adaptation of a reading that otherwise belongs to the Vulgate stock: all the rest have more or less abundant analogies in the Vulgate. It is therefore on the whole more probable that the coincidences between m and Vulgate are caused by a pre-Vulgate element in m, and not by an m element in the Vulgate.

Let us now examine some of the more marked coincidences between m and ff.

I. 19, 20. 'iracundia:' though 'iracundia' occurs four times in the Vulgate New Testament, it is nowhere as a rendering of ὀργή: the only place in the Gospels where I have found it is in Mark iii. 5, where it is peculiar to a: it has very much the character of other peculiar renderings in that MS. It is also, I think, we may say certainly, the reading of Cyprian in Ephes. vi. 9 ('laxantes iracundiam' codd. W L M B, 'remittentes minas' cod. A, Hartel).

I. 26. 'fallens:' this word occurs only once in the Vulgate New Testament, and that in this Epistle as a rendering of παραλογιζόμενοι (I. 27); it is, however, a fairly well-established Africanism: Cyprian has it in four separate and widely removed quotations of Matt. xxiv. 4, 5 (two of these are given by Hartel as from Mark xiii. 6, and one is referred to both places, but they seem to be all really taken from St. Matthew). In the parallel passage, Mark xiii. 16, k has 'decipiat' and 'in errore promittent.' I have not, however, found 'fallo' elsewhere in Cyprian: 'decipio' seems to be the more usual African word.

I. 27. 'orfanos:' the universal Old-Latin (African and European) and Vulgate rendering in John xiv. 18, the only other place where the Greek word occurs in the New Testament.

I. 27. 'servare:' so τηρεῖν is rendered in Matt. xix. 17, a b e, etc., and repeatedly elsewhere; e has 'observavi' in Matt. xix. 20, where the rest have 'custodivi.'

II. 15. 'Defuerit:' 'indigeo' is sometimes avoided by the African text (e.g. Luke xii. 30 e, cf. b), but not always (e.g. Matt. vi. 32 k Cyprian rel.); 'deest' is, however, the common rendering in Matt. xix. 20, and elsewhere.

III. 1. 'accipie[tis]:' the common word in this connexion in both texts.

III. 2. 'fraenare:' the African text not seldom uses the simple verb, where other texts have the compound, but this relation is quite as often, or rather more often, inverted.

III. 3. 'totum:' 'totus' for 'omnis' or 'universus' is rather characteristic of the African text: k has it three times in St. Matthew, four times in St. Mark, but in three of these last instances along with a.

IV. 1. 'rixae:' the word μάχαι only occurs three times besides in the New Testament; in one of these places Cyprian has 'lites:' as Jerome himself has 'rixae' no stress can be laid on the deviation from the Vulgate here.

— 'voluntatibus' (for 'voluptatibus,' ff Jerome): similarly in Matt. xiii. 22, a has 'voluntates divitiarum,' e 'divitiarum voluntas,' while conversely in John iv. 34 d has 'voluptatem.'

IV. 12. 'salvare:' this word is frequently found in the African text, where the European MSS. have 'salvum facere,' but all our three documents have it above in ii. 14, so that no inference can be drawn from it.

V. 2. 'putruerunt et tiniaverunt:' of these two words 'tiniaverunt' is the more characteristic; it occurs in the Vulgate only in Baruch vi. 71, which belongs to the unrevised Old Latin.

Looking back over these expressions and taking also into account the minor points which have not been more particularly noticed, I think that they amount to proof that there is something more than an accidental connexion between the two texts m and ff, wide apart from each other as they may seem; but I am not so sure that we can affirm from which side the common element proceeds. It has on the whole a slight African tinge, and so far points to an African importation into the text of ff, but the total balance is not decided enough to allow us to speak confidently.

When we come to the peculiar points in m, their African character is clearer: and they are African, just of the kind that we should expect, not such as are found in the earliest stages of the version, but such as belong rather to its later stage. I must not stay to examine all these peculiar points, but will confine myself to indicating those the African origin of which is most apparent.

- I. 26. 'superstitiosum:' the only trace that I can find of this is in Col. ii. 18, Auctor *Quaest. ex Nov. Test.*, and Ambrosiaster, as given by Sabatier.
- I. 27. 'pura:' it is a rather remarkable coincidence that the only instance that I am aware of in which the word 'purus' occurs in the Gospels is in a single MS. (A) of Cyprian's *Testimonia*, where he is quoting Matt. v. 8; every other extant MS. and authority there, and so far as I know elsewhere in the Gospels, has 'mundus.' And this MS. of Cyprian, Cod. Sessorianus, is the very same that contains the text that Mai has edited of the *Speculum*: its text in Cyprian is I believe very similar to its text in the *Speculum*, degenerate African.
- — 'angustia:' so e alone in Matt. xiii. 21, where k has the older African reading 'pressura:' 'angustiis' is also a singular reading of d in Matt. xxiv. 9.
- II. 14. 16. 'prode est:' this form appears to be also characteristic of Cod. Sessorianus, from which Rönsch has collected four examples of it (*It. u. Vulg.* p. 468 f.); it is, however, found in other non-African MSS.
- II. 14. 'manere:' this is a word of which the African text at one of its stages appears to be rather fond: e introduces it against all other MSS. (including k) into Matt. xiii. 32, and k alone has it in Mark xiv. 34.
- II. 15. 'cibus:' a clear case cannot be made out for 'cibus' though k has it against the European MSS. in Matt. iii. 4; and Cyprian against most other authorities in 1 Cor. iii. 2; a b have it in Matt. xxiv. 45, where e has 'cibaria' and in John iv. 8, b has 'cibus,' e 'esca.'
- III. 1. 'multiloqui:' it is perhaps something more than a chance coincidence that k has 'multiloqui esse' in Matt. vi. 7, where the other texts have 'multum loqui.'
- III. 5. 'delinquimus:' 'delinquere,' 'delictum,' are predominantly African words; so the best MSS. of Cyprian in Eph. iv. 26, 1 John ii. 1, 2, and k in Matt. vi. 14, 15. In all these places the European texts have 'peccare,' 'peccatum.'

III. 6. 'geniturae,' 'genitura:' this word is distinctly African, and African of a very old type; it has disappeared from k, but Tertullian has it in Matt. i. 1: it does not occur in the Vulgate.

III. 7. 'avium:' so c d in Matt. xiii. 32, where all the others have 'volucres' or 'volatilia,' as here.

IV. 8. 'proximate,' 'proximavit:' so k in Mark xiii. 28; the word only occurs in the Vulgate New Testament in Heb. vii. 19.

V. 1. 'plangite:' African in Matt. v. 5, 'plangentes' k Cypr., 'qui lugent' or 'lugunt' a b d f, comp. John xvi. 20 'plangetis' de Cypr., 'lugebitis' a b.

— 'super,' 'superveniunt:' 'super' and its compounds are also frequent in the African text.

V. 3. 'quod reposuistis in novissimis diebus:' this seems to be a transposition from the end of the verse ('thesaurizastis iram in novissimis diebus' Vulgate).

— 'comedit:' African in Mark xii. 40 (a c k, 'devorant' rel.).

V. 5. 'deliciati estis:' this appears to be African; 'delicata est' is the true reading in Cyprian's quotation of 1 Tim. v. 6, where all the other texts have 'in deliciis est, agit, vivit;' the Greek is σπαταλῶσα, which is the word used here in St. James, and it occurs nowhere else in the New Testament.

It is possible that an enlargement of the data would modify some of the details in this evidence, but I do not think it likely that the general result would be altered. The text of m is no doubt neither early nor pure; it has suffered considerably both from degeneration and from mixture, but its original base is African, and as such it is separated from the two other texts by a wider chasm than that which separates them from each other.

The Vulgate and m are offshoots of two fundamentally different stocks. I cannot think that this is the case between the Vulgate and ff. Before passing to this question, however, it may be well to ascertain first a little more closely what is the character of the Vulgate text. This will turn mainly upon the character of the peculiar readings; for on those that are shared with m something has already been said, and on those that are shared with ff something will be said presently.

Of those in Ch. 1, 'ira,' 'seducens,' 'pupillos,' 'custodire,' are all wide-spread European renderings: for 'pupillos' see Mark xii. 40, where the word is interpolated in a b d i (not in e k). In ii. 13 Augustine is quoted by Sabatier as twice reading 'superexultat' (and Dombart's critical edition of the *De Civitate* gives the same reading) and twice 'superexaltat;' so that, whichever was the original form of the word, it was certainly in existence in this passage before the time of Jerome. 'Indigeat,' as we have seen, is common to all the texts: 'saturamini' is a regular European form: 'in semetipsa' has in it nothing unusual. In iii. 1 'plures' seems to be peculiar, but it is probably not due to Jerome himself: in Mark xii. 5, precisely the same change has taken place, a k reading 'multos,' b d (i? *ex silentio*) Vulg. 'plures.' In the same verse 'fieri' is found in Augustine (Sab.), who also has 'sumitis' (for λαμβάνετε), which is said to be the reading of the Memphitic version. Augustine again has 'in multis offendimus;' so has Leo; and an anonymous writer of about the same date has 'circumducere freno.' Lucifer as well as the Vulgate has a parallel for 'circumferimus' in Jude 12; the curious 'minentur' (= French 'mener') is not an uncommon Vulgate word (see Rönsch, *It. u. Vulg.* p. 236): 'modicus' is the reading not only of a b f, but of k, in Matt. vi. 30, though it is European and not African in Matt. viii. 26; the word is common enough. μεγάλα αὐχεῖ or μεγαλαυχεῖ is a ἅπαξ λεγόμενον in the Greek and is rendered by 'magna exaltat,' which is also peculiar in this sense; though the word occurs frequently both in the Vulgate and Old Latin (European and African at least of the e type) as the rendering of ὑψοῦν. I am not aware of any parallel for 'universitas,' which occurs only here in the Vulgate New Testament. 'Constituo' is a common Vulgate and European word; it occurs also in e: 'voluerum' is the more usual European word: 'ceterorum' (for 'cetorum') is as peculiar as the word ἐναλίων of which it is a translation. 'Inquietum,' the rendering of another peculiar word, ἀκατάστατον, occurs in Vulgate and Ambrosiaster as a rendering of ἄτακτος in 1 Thess. v. 14, and in Vulgate and Augustine as a rendering of ἀτακτεῖν in 2 Thess. iii. 7: 'ostendo' is the common European word for which in one place (Matt. viii. 4) k has 'demonstro,' but not elsewhere (Matt. iv. 7, Mark xiv. 15): there does not seem to be a hard and fast local division between the two words. 'Operatio' is a Vulgate word found also in Cyprian (2 Thess. ii. 10): 'lites' is found in all the authorities including Cyprian in 2 Tim. ii. 23: 'concupiscentia' is well established both in European and African texts of the Epistles: 'adpropinquo' is a common European word: 'detrahere' occurs in Vulgate and d of 1 Tim. iii. 11, and in Vulgate of 1 Pet. iii. 16, νομοθέτης and 'legislator' are both ἅπαξ λεγόμενα in the New Testament, though 'legislator' is found three times in the Vulgate Old Testament. The use of 'libero' for 'salvo' or 'salvum facio' is one about which I should like to know a little more: it occurs at least once as a singular reading in the best MSS. of Cyprian (Matt. xxiv. 22), and it occurs again in the Vulgate in 2 Tim. i. 9, where the European reading seems to be 'salvos fecit.' As to 'putrefactae sunt' there is no very decisive evidence: 'comeditur a tinea' occurs in Vulgate of Job xiii. 28, and 'tinea comedet' in Isa. l. 9. 'Epulor' is a regular European word: it occurs four times in the parable of the Prodigal Son where e has 'jucundor.' 'Enutrio' occurs in d Ambrosiaster, as well as in the Vulgate of 1 Tim. iv. 6; 'luxuria' is rather common in the Vulgate, and is a widespread reading in Gal. v. 19, where it goes back to the Latin version of Irenaeus, in Eph. v. 18 where it goes back to Tertullian, and in Tit. i. 6, where it is found in Lucifer.

What inferences are we to draw from all this as to the character of the Vulgate text in the Epistle? (1) Extremely little is due to Jerome himself. There is hardly a word that cannot be proved to have been in use before his time: in many cases where the evidence is slenderest as to the use of the word elsewhere the quotations in St. Augustine and Ambrosiaster prove that it was already found in this Epistle. The only expressions that may have been introduced by Jerome would seem to be 'minentur,' 'universitas,' 'cetorum,' and possibly 'inquietum,' 'a tineis comesta sunt.' (2) The main body of the Vulgate text has the same European, or perhaps Italic, base that it has in other parts of the New Testament. Perhaps it is with this that we are to connect the few possible Africanisms, such as 'salvare,' 'liberare,' just as occasional African readings are found in f (Cod. Brixianus), which appears to have been at the foundation of the Vulgate text in the Gospels. But (3) there may also be a small element, not necessarily African, which is peculiar and intrusive. The only word that appears to point distinctly to such an element is 'superexalto,' (for κατακαυχῶμαι, which is elsewhere rendered by 'glorior' in a way not very different from ff,) unless we are also to assign to this element some of the words just mentioned for which there is no direct pre-Vulgate evidence. To it too we may perhaps also attribute some of the peculiarities noted by Professor Wordsworth (p. 130) and Dr. Westcott.

And now, lastly, we come to the Corbey MS. (ff) itself. We will reserve a little longer the consideration of its fundamental relation to the Vulgate and ask ourselves first, what account is to be given of those features in it to which there is no parallel in either of the other documents.

- I. 26. 'infrenans:' the repetition of this compound in iii. 2, shows that it is really characteristic: as χαλιναγωγεῖν occurs only in these two places and neither passage appears to be quoted by any ancient writer, no light can be thrown upon it.
- I. 27. 'Dominum:' this is simply an error of transcription for 'Deum,' arising from a misunderstood abbreviation: in k 'Deum' is five times represented by 'dom.' (Matt. v. 8, vi. 24, xv. 31, Mark xii. 14, 32.) 'Deum' having been changed into 'Dominum,' 'patrem' would naturally be dropped, as the combination 'Dominum patrem' is, I believe, nowhere found.
- — 'sine macula:' it has been already observed (p. 245 above) that

this is the reading of d Vulgate in 1 Tim. vi. 14; it is therefore not far removed from the main line of Vulgate transmission.

II. 13. 'Juditium non miserebitur ei:' we are reminded of the way in which ἐλεηθήσονται is paraphrased in Matt. v. 7; a b c g h, representing in fact the main stock of the European version, all have 'ipsis miserebitur Deus:' and in Rom. xi. 32, the Latin Irenaeus has 'ut universis misereatur' (sc. Deus); Ambrose also has the dative 'omnibus,' otherwise the more usual reading is the genitive 'omnium.'

— 'super-gloriatur:' 'gloriari,' as we have seen, is a very widespread rendering of καυχᾶσθαι; especially European, but found even in Cyprian (e. g. Rom. v. 2, 3), though he never, I believe, uses 'gloria,' but always 'claritas.'

II. 16. 'Vadite:' common in all texts and sometimes (as in Luke xiii. 33 c, cf. l m r), a variant for 'ite.'

— 'calidi estote et satulli:' there is a partial but important parallel to this in Luke vi. 21, where a has 'saturi eritis,' the other European MSS. 'saturabuntur,' 'saturabimini,' and e 'satiabuntur.'

— 'alimentum:' it is remarkable that, not apparently any other text, but Vulgate Jerome (twice) have 'alimenta' in 1 Tim. vi. 8: the word ἐπιτήδεια, of which 'alimentum' is a rendering, does not occur elsewhere.

III. 2. 'erramus:' 'errare' is common to all the texts including k (Mark xii. 24, 27, in the latter verse with the construction 'multum erratis'); it occurs in the Vulgate rendering of i. 16, v. 19, as well as in ff.

— 'consummatus:' this also is a common word both in the Vulgate and in the European Latin generally: it occurs as an alternative for 'perficio' in the African text in Matt. xi. 1, Mark xiii. 4.

— 'potens est:' frequent in Vulgate as a rendering of δυνατός.

III. 3. 'convertimus:' very common in Vulgate, especially in the passive: in Matt. xxvi. 52, 'Converte gladium tuum in locum suum,' it appears to be almost, if not quite, the universal rendering, but no African authorities are extant other than Augustine.

IV. 4, 5. 'Parvulo,' 'parvulum:' this word is found in all the texts, but appears to be markedly characteristic of the revised European text and the Vulgate. cf. Matt. xiv. 21, xv. 38, xviii. 2. 3, 4. 5, xix. 13. 14. Mark x. 13, 14, 15, in all of which places it is found in f Vulgate, and not in any other leading MS.

IV. 4. 'voluntate eorum qui eas gubernant:' the form of phrase 'ille qui,' 'is qui,' for participle or substantive, appears to be characteristic of the African text: comp. in the chapters covered by k Matt. iv. 2, 'ille qui temptat' (rel. 'temptator'), v. 42, 'ab eo qui voluerit mutuari' (rel. 'volenti'), Matt. xiii. 18, 'ejus qui seminat' (rel. 'seminantis'), and no less than eight times in St. Mark (with one exception).

IV. 5. 'gloriantur:' as we have seen, common to all the texts, but characteristically European.

IV. 5. 'pusillum:' common to all the texts.

IV. 6. 'seculi:' rather more frequent in the African text.

— 'posita est:' the usual rendering of καθίστημι is 'constituo,' and the only instance that I have been able to find of 'pono' in this connexion is Matt. xxiv. 45, where Hilary has 'praeponit.' Comparing this instance with the peculiar use of 'exponentes' in i. 21, and 'legum positor' in iv. 12, it would seem that the Corbey text had a certain leaning to the use of 'pono.' It is not an uncommon phenomenon to find in a MS. a tendency to the use of certain words, often simple ones, in different combinations and as a rendering of different Greek.

— 'incenditur:' it is not easy to see why 'inflammat,' two lines above, should be changed to 'incenditur,' the Greek being the same, φλογίζεσθαι and φλογιζομένη; Vulgate and m both keep 'inflammo,' but as they also have 'incendit' in the verse before, the rendering in ff is not very far to seek; it may have been caused by the mental influence of the preceding word at a time when the Latin version was no longer accompanied by the Greek original.

III. 7. 'volatilium:' this word is found in both the African and the European texts, but is rather more common in the African (e.g. Matt. xiii. 4, 32).

— 'natantium:' occurs in Wisd. xix. 18, as a rendering of νηκτά: it will be remembered that the book of Wisdom was not revised by Jerome, so that its text belongs to the Old Latin.

— 'inconstans:' this is the rendering of ἀκατάστατος, not only in ff, but also in the Vulgate, in the only other place where it occurs, ch. i. 8 : the change would therefore appear to be in Vulgate and not in ff.

III. 13. 'disciplinosus :' as compared with the Vulgate 'disciplinatus' the only peculiarity here is the termination '-osus,' which is sufficiently common in ecclesiastical Latin (see Goelzer, *Latinité de St. Jérome*, p. 149): d has the curious form 'daemoniosus' in Luke xi. 14.

— 'demonstrat :' 'demonstro' is, as we have seen, a frequent alternative for 'ostendo.'

— 'clementiam :' this word occurs before in the Corbey text in ch. i. 21, it is only found once in the Vulgate New Testament (Acts xxiv. 4), as a rendering of ἐπιείκεια, neither have I succeeded in finding any trace of it in the other texts.

IV. 1. 'pugne :' compare 'pugnatis,' which is also peculiar, in v. 2 below : in Matt. xxiv. 6, 'pugnas' is peculiar to r (cod. Usserianus, at Dublin, lately published by Professor T. K. Abbot), and h (cod. Claromontanus), the main body of the European text having 'praelia' and the African 'bella :' the word only occurs three times in the Vulgate New Testament.

IV. 7. 'zabolo' (for 'diabolo') : this form is not at all uncommon, see Rönsch *It. u. V.* p. 457 : it occurs not only on African ground in MSS. of Cyprian and Lactantius, and in Commodian of Gaza (some additions may be made to the list in Rönsch, and k has 'ziabolus' in Matt. xiii. 39), but also in Hilary and Ambrose : nor is the form confined to this word, 'zacones' is also found for 'diacones,' 'zametrus' for 'diametrus,' 'zebus' for 'diebus,' and in the inscriptions collected by Schürer from the Jewish cemeteries at Rome ζὰ βίου occurs for διὰ βίου (Schürer, *Die Gemeinde-verfassung der Juden in Rom.* p. 23).

IV. 8. 'accedite,' 'accedit :' common in all the texts, but rather as a rendering of προσέρχεσθαι than of ἐγγίζειν, for which ff has in v. 8 the more usual 'adpropio.'

— 'Dominum :' see above on i. 27, a transcriptional substitution for 'Deum.'

IV. 10. 'Humiliate vos :' comp. v. 7.

IV. 11. 'retractare de,' 'retractat de :' the phrase occurs in a somewhat similar sense and with the same construction in Iren. *Adv. Haer.* v. ii. 1, and also apparently in Tertullian ; Cyprian has it as a rendering of καταλαλῶσιν in 1 Pet. ii. 12.

IV. 12. 'legum positor:' see above on iii. 6.

V. 1. Jam (ἄγε): ff is consistent with itself as it renders ἄγε by 'jam' in iv. 13, where Vulgate has 'Ecce:' these are the only two places where this use of ἄγε occurs in the New Testament.

— 'locupletes:' this is another instance in which ff is consistent with itself, as it has 'locuples' in i. 10, 11, ii. 5 (not ii. 6): the word is rare; it is however also found in Mark xv. 43, in n (Fragm. Sangall.), the peculiar element in the text of which is closely allied to that in a.

— 'tanquam:' peculiar to a in Mark ix. 3, 26, x. 15, xii. 25, and to a d in xii. 31: the common European word is 'sicut.'

V. 5. 'fruiti estis:' the nearest parallel appears to be 'fruitus fuero' in Rom. xv. 24 (Old Latin and Vulgate).

— 'abusi estis:' this rendering of ἐσπαταλήσατε appears to be quite peculiar.

— 'cibastis:' this occurs in an Arian fragment published by Mai (*Vat. Coll.* iii. p. 227) in a quotation of Matt. xxv. 35, where all the other texts, I believe without exception, have 'dedistis mihi manducare;' it appears however to be the universal reading in Rom. xii. 20, 'si esurierit inimicus tuus, ciba illum.'

This examination will, I think, have given us a sufficiently clear idea of the vocabulary of the Corbey MS. A large part of it is very similar in its character to that of the Vulgate. In many cases the word or phrase in ff might be substituted for that in the Vulgate without any real disturbance: in two at least ('inconstans,' and 'voluptatibus') the parallels quoted by Professor Wordsworth show that the text of ff is nearer than the Vulgate to that used by Jerome. And yet by the side of this Vulgate element two other distinct elements are also traceable: one African, which may be classed with the resemblances already noted between ff and m, and the other peculiar to ff. To this element I should be inclined to refer more especially 'infrenans' and 'infrenare,' 'calidi estote et satulli,' 'posita est' and 'legum positor,' the termination of 'disciplinosus,' 'clementiam,' 'pugne,' 'jam' (for ἄγε), 'locupletes,' 'abusi estis' and 'cibastis.' There is so much coherence about these readings and about others that occur in the Corbey text that I should be quite disposed to believe them due to a definite local recension, bearing very much the same sort of relation to the main text that the peculiar element of a in St. Mark and St. Luke bears to the main body of the European version: nor should I be surprised if it should be found ultimately—for at present we can only form guesses on the subject—to have had its origin in a not very distant region. The clearest indication that we possess, 'acquirit mortem,' in the quotation of Chromatius of Aquileia, and I suspect also, though of course in an inferior degree, 'cibastis' of the Arian fragment and 'locupletes' point in that direction.

I speak of a 'recension' of a version already existing and not of a new and distinct version, because there is much that prevents us from thinking that the hypothesis of such a distinct version is necessary. In the first place the amount of divergence between the Corbey MS. and the Vulgate does not seem enough to require it. The verses printed above from the text of ff in ch. i. contain in all sixty-three words; in these there are only six points that are peculiar, and only eleven in which ff differs from the Vulgate. Now, for the sake of comparison, we will take a MS. older in date than ff, of the eighth or ninth century instead of the tenth, and therefore with less time allowed for corruption and mixture, a MS. too of the Gospels where the language is simpler and less open to variation than an Epistle like this of St. James, but a MS. in other respects sufficiently resembling ff, the St. Gall fragment of an Irish lectionary designated p, and containing a considerable portion of St. John xi. If we take the first continuous section of this MS. we find in it sixty-nine words with thirteen variations from the Vulgate, which would represent a very similar ratio. Taking the passages given from chap. ii. I make in all ninety words with twenty-seven variations in ff; but there are seventy-four words ('At illa ... veni et vide') with twenty-eight variations in p. Yet there can be no doubt that p has the same common European base with the Vulgate. When we remember that the common ancestor of ff and the Vulgate was probably a long way removed from those texts as we have them, that in each case there has certainly been mixture and revision, and that the Vulgate certainly deviates from the original type in one direction if ff differs from it in another, when we remember this and all the other circumstances of the case, that the language of the Epistle is such as to invite change, and that MSS. descended from the same stock frequently do present marked variations; when all this is borne in mind the amount of difference between the two texts will not seem so very remarkable: it is certainly much greater in m, which I believe to have really had a separate origin. In chap. i. m has sixty words against sixty-three and twenty variations against eleven, or nearly double.

A second argument, which weighs in the same scale, is that the structure of the sentences and order of the words in ff and the Vulgate presents on the whole a decided preponderance of resemblance over differences. I have noted in all twenty-six variations of order. In one of these m agrees with ff against the Vulgate: in two more all three differ: of the remaining twenty-three, ff agrees with the Vulgate in fourteen, whereas m agrees with it only in eight, the ratio again being nearly double. This is a significant fact, and points, I think, to the fundamental identity of the two versions. This part of the subject, however, will need further investigation.

I shall be asked, perhaps, if the two versions are fundamentally the same, how it comes about that they also present such marked differences? What has been said above about the various strains of mixture and revision to which they have been subject, will, I hope, go far to account for this: but I should like, before I conclude, to quote a few words from an Essay by Lagarde, which seem to me to go to the root of the matter. They occur in the course of an important review of Hartel's Cyprian, with which I have only made acquaintance since this paper was begun (*Symmicta*, i. p. 68 f.). 'Herr Hartel,' he says, 'speaking of the scribe of the Verona MS. says on p. 17: this strange person has indulged in conjectures to such a degree that one might suppose oneself to have come upon a grammarian in the act of teaching boys by what devices to vary their expressions: for no probable cause can be imagined why he should have preferred *pacificis* to *pacatis*, *nefaria* to *nefanda*, *non factum* to *infectum*, *inquinatis* to *immundis*, *misissem* to *darem*, *fecistis* to *ministis*, *instruentes* to *insinuantes*, *tempus est* to *licet*, *violari* to *corrumpi*, *expugnandum* to *impugnandum*, *exerrare* to *oberrare*, *repellat* to *avertat*, *obrepserit* to *fefellerit*, *prohibitum* to *pulsum*, *ostende* to *demonstra*, *involvlam* to *vinclam*, and any number of the like.' 'The probable cause,' Lagarde replies to this, 'lay simply in this, that in the learned or popular speech of the district for which the MS. was intended the one word was not in use, and therefore had to be replaced by another.' The idea thus expressed has been floating before me for some time. I believe that the differences in the various forms of the Old Latin are largely differences of local usage. Something, no doubt, is due to simple caprice, and something has probably been also due at one stage, even before the time of Jerome, to learned revision. But the original versions, African and European, were not made, and the subsequent changes in them were not for the most part introduced, by practised scholars. They were essentially vernacular; and the scribes by whom they were copied were men of the people, who did not scruple to substitute forms and usages with which they were familiar for others that were strange to them. But when we think to what an extent dialects have survived in our own country, compact as it is, and easy as is the communication from one part to another, what must have been the diversities of usage in different parts of the Roman Empire? It is, I suspect, through these diversities, to an extent that we are as yet unable to define, that the Latin versions have assumed those varied forms in which they have come down to us.

But if this is so, surely a dazzling prospect lies open to the theologian. Besides his own proper subject, the study of the versions as versions, it is for him more than for anyone else to track out and delimitate these varieties of provincial speech. He possesses advantages which the classical philologist cannot hope for [1]. He has at his command a number of MSS. dating back to very early times; and, what is of especial importance, he has a large store of patristic quotations by comparison with which he can assign, more or less satisfactorily, the texts before him to certain fixed localities. And besides the versions of the Old and New Testaments he has a wealth of MSS. of writers such as Cyprian, which present the same kind of phenomena, and which will enable him to test and verify his conclusions.

No doubt, whoever undertakes this work, great circumspection will be needed. Every peculiar reading is not necessarily a characteristic reading of the text in which it is found. Nor would it at once follow that every reading that was characteristic of a MS. or writer was also characteristic of a particular locality. At every step a process of winnowing must take place, and the proportion of chaff to wheat will often be large.

An Essay like the present is of course the merest possible beginning to the working out of these problems. The inductions on which a great part of it rests are, I am well aware, much too narrow [2]. I should be sorry to seem to attach too great importance to them. But it is just because I am sensible how narrow and tentative this inquiry has been, and just because I feel that it is capable of almost indefinite expansion, that I am hopeful as to the method by which it has been conducted. It is a 'far cry' yet to the conclusions that I seem

---

[1] The work of Sittl, *Die lokalen Verschiedenheiten der lateinischen Sprache* (Erlangen, 1882), though useful, shows how soon classical philology comes to the end of its resources.

[2] What was said about k in the Gospels stands on a different footing from the views expressed respecting ff and the Vulgate in St. James. In the Gospels we are on far surer ground.

to see in the dim distance awaiting us. If the attempt is made to reach them by short cuts they will be apt to elude us altogether. We need to approach them by gradual, well considered, and systematic advances. The first step must be the comparing and collating of a number of different texts and the cataloguing of their peculiarities: each text must be isolated, and its individual character ascertained. Then, as fast as one is ascertained, it will supply us with the means of determining others, till we are able, as I hope we may ultimately be, to map out the whole ground and assign each text to its place with more or less accuracy.

Perhaps I am drawing too much on the imagination. Indeed I do not like to set down all the possibilities that present themselves to me. It is well to remember the caution, 'Let not him that girdeth on his harness boast himself as he that taketh it off.' And yet there is enough, I cannot but think, to encourage the worker in such a field, and to give him confidence that—whatever his own success or failure— there is at least a harvest to be secured, and that one generation, if not another, will secure it.

POSTSCRIPT.

More recent experience enables us to define rather more exactly one or two points in the above.

P. 238, l. 21. 'continuo' is shared by e with several European MSS. in St. Mark and St. Luke: 'protinus' is specially characteristic of a in those Gospels, while 'confestim' occurs four times, and 'statim' twice in European texts.

l. 22. 'comminor' alternates with 'increpo' in the European texts of St. Mark and St. Luke. The use of 'objurgo' in a is very marked.

l. 35. 'obsecro,' 'rogo:' there are interesting varieties here which it would take too much space to discuss, but which seem to have something of principle running through them.

P. 239, l. 5. 'similitudo' ceases to be peculiar to the African text in (St. Mark and) St. Luke. In St. Mark it occurs in iv. 2 b, vii. 17 a n, xiii. 28 a k; in St. Luke the usage is divided, b f Am. (with e) have almost consistently 'similitudo,' while a d have 'parabola.'

P. 246, l. 6 [satior]: add Mark vi. 42 a, vii. 27 a: the word is clearly characteristic of a, and belongs to that element which a has in common with e.

P. 250, l. 8. 'proximate,' 'proximavit:' add Luke xv. 25 d: the use of the other two words is again divided; 'adpropinquo' is read by a consistently (twelve places), by f almost consistently (eleven places), by e in six places (all but one of those in which it is extant), and by b and d in two each; 'adpropio' is read by d in nine places, by b in five (in several places b is not extant), by f in two, and by e in one.

l. 17. 'comedit:' add Luke xv. 30 a d e, Luke xx. 47 a d e.

THE END.

Clarendon Press, Oxford.

SELECT LIST OF STANDARD WORKS.

STANDARD LATIN WORKS . . . Page 1
STANDARD GREEK WORKS . . . „ 3
MISCELLANEOUS STANDARD WORKS . „ 7
STANDARD THEOLOGICAL WORKS . „ 8
NEW ENGLISH DICTIONARY . . „ 9

1. STANDARD LATIN WORKS.

Avianus. *The Fables.* Edited, with Prolegomena, Critical Apparatus, Commentary, &c., by Robinson Ellis, M.A., LL.D. 8vo. 8s. 6d.

Catulli Veronensis *Liber.* Iterum recognovit, Apparatum Criticum Prolegomena Appendices addidit, R. Ellis, A.M. 8vo. 16s.

Catullus, *a Commentary on.* By Robinson Ellis, M.A. *Second Edition.* 8vo. 18s.

Cicero. *De Oratore Libri Tres.* With Introduction and Notes. By A. S. Wilkins, Litt.D. 8vo. 18s.

Also, separately,
Book I. 7s. 6d. Book II. 5s.
Book III. 6s.

—— *Philippic Orations.* With Notes. By J. R. King, M.A. *Second Edition.* 8vo. 10s. 6d.

Cicero. *Select Letters.* With English Introductions, Notes, and Appendices. By Albert Watson, M.A. *Fourth Edition.* 8vo. 18s.

Horace. With a Commentary. By E. C. Wickham, M.A. *Two Vols.* 8vo.

Vol. I. The Odes, Carmen Seculare, and Epodes. *Second Edition.* 12s.

Vol. II. The Satires, Epistles, and De Arte Poetica. 12s.

Livy, *Book I.* With Introduction, Historical Examination, and Notes. By J. R. Seeley, M.A. *Second Edition.* 8vo. 6s.

Manilius. *Noctes Manilianae; sive Dissertationes in Astronomica Manilii. Accedunt Coniectura in Germanici Aratea.* Scripsit R. Ellis. Crown 8vo. 6s.

Oxford: Clarendon Press. London: Henry Frowde, Amen Corner, E.C.

Ovid. *P. Ovidii Nasonis Ibis.* Ex Novis Codicibus edidit, Scholia Vetera Commentarium cum Prolegomenis Appendice Indice addidit, R. Ellis, A.M. 8vo. 10s. 6d.

——— *P. Ovidi Nasonis Tristium Libri V.* Recensuit S. G. Owen, A.M. 8vo. 16s.

Persius. *The Satires.* With a Translation and Commentary. By John Conington, M.A. Edited by Henry Nettleship, M.A. Second Edition. 8vo. 7s. 6d.

Plautus. *Rudens.* Edited, with Critical and Explanatory Notes, by E. A. Sonnenschein, M.A. 8vo. 8s. 6d.

Quintilian. *M. Fabi Quintiliani Institutionis Oratoriae Liber Decimus.* A Revised Text, with Introductory Essays, Critical Notes, &c. By W. Peterson, M.A., LL.D. 8vo. 12s. 6d.

Scriptores Latini *rei Metricae.* Ed. T. Gaisford, S.T.P. 8vo. 5s.

Tacitus. *The Annals.* Edited, with Introduction and Notes, by H. Furneaux, M.A. 2 Vols. 8vo.

Vol. I, Books I–VI. 18s.

Vol. II, Books XI–XVI. 20s.

King and Cookson. *The Principles of Sound and Inflexion, as illustrated in the Greek and Latin Languages.* By J. E. King, M.A., and Christopher Cookson, M.A. 8vo. 18s.

——— *An Introduction to the Comparative Grammar of Greek and Latin.* Crown 8vo. 5s. 6d.

Lewis and Short. *A Latin Dictionary,* founded on Andrews' edition of Freund's Latin Dictionary, revised, enlarged, and in great part rewritten by Charlton T. Lewis, Ph.D., and Charles Short, LL.D. 4to. 1l. 5s.

Lewis. *A Latin Dictionary for Schools.* By Charlton T. Lewis, Ph.D. Small 4to. 18s.

Nettleship. *Lectures and Essays on Subjects connected with Latin Scholarship and Literature.* By Henry Nettleship, M.A. Crown 8vo. 7s. 6d.

——— *The Roman Satura.* 8vo. sewed, 1s.

Nettleship. *Ancient Lives of Vergil.* 8vo. sewed, 2s.

——— *Contributions to Latin Lexicography.* 8vo. 21s.

Papillon. *Manual of Comparative Philology.* By T. L. Papillon, M.A. Third Edition. Crown 8vo. 6s.

Pinder. *Selections from the less known Latin Poets.* By North Pinder, M.A. 8vo. 15s.

Sellar. *Roman Poets of the Augustan Age.* By W. Y. Sellar, M.A.; viz.

I. VIRGIL. New Edition. Crown 8vo. 9s.

II. HORACE and the ELEGIAC POETS. With a Memoir of the Author by ANDREW LANG, M.A., and a Portrait. 8vo. 14s.

——— *Roman Poets of the Republic.* Third Edition. Crown 8vo. 10s.

Wordsworth. *Fragments and Specimens of Early Latin.* With Introductions and Notes. By J. Wordsworth, D.D. 8vo. 18s.

2. STANDARD GREEK WORKS.

Allen. *Notes on Abbreviations in Greek Manuscripts.* By T. W. Allen. Royal 8vo. 5s.

Chandler. *A Practical Introduction to Greek Accentuation*, by H. W. Chandler, M.A. Second Edition. 10s. 6d.

Haigh. *The Attic Theatre.* A Description of the Stage and Theatre of the Athenians, and of the Dramatic Performances at Athens. By A. E. Haigh, M.A. 8vo. 12s. 6d.

Head. *Historia Numorum:* A Manual of Greek Numismatics. By Barclay V. Head. Royal 8vo. half-bound, 2l. 2s.

Hicks. *A Manual of Greek Historical Inscriptions.* By E. L. Hicks, M.A. 8vo. 10s. 6d.

King and Cookson. *The Principles of Sound and Inflexion, as illustrated in the Greek and Latin Languages.* By J. E. King, M.A., and Christopher Cookson, M.A. 8vo. 18s.

Liddell and Scott. *A Greek-English Lexicon*, by H. G. Liddell, D.D., and Robert Scott, D.D. Seventh Edition, Revised and Augmented throughout. 4to. 1l. 16s.

—— *An Intermediate Greek-English Lexicon*, founded upon the Seventh Edition of Liddell and Scott's Greek Lexicon. Small 4to. 12s. 6d.

Papillon. *Manual of Comparative Philology.* By T. L. Papillon, M.A. Third Edition. Crown 8vo. 6s.

Veitch. *Greek Verbs, Irregular and Defective.* By W. Veitch, LL.D. Fourth Edition. Crown 8vo. 10s. 6d.

Aeschinem et Isocratem, *Scholia Graeca in.* Edidit G. Dindorfius. 8vo. 4s.

Aeschines. See under **Oratores Attici**, and **Demosthenes**.

Aeschyli *quae supersunt in Codice Laurentiano quoad effici potuit et ad cognitionem necesse est visum typis descripta edidit* R. Merkel. Small folio. 1l. 1s.

Aeschylus : *Tragoediae et Fragmenta*, ex recensione Guil. Dindorfii. Second Edition. 8vo. 5s. 6d.

—— *Annotationes* Guil. Dindorfii. Partes II. 8vo. 10s.

Anecdota *Graeca Oxoniensia.* Edidit J. A. Cramer, S.T.P. Tomi IV. 8vo. 1l. 2s.

Anecdota *Graeca e Codd. mss. Bibliothecae Regiae Parisiensis.* Edidit J. A. Cramer, S.T.P. Tomi IV. 8vo. 1l. 2s.

Apsinis et Longini *Rhetorica.* E Codicibus mss. recensuit Joh. Bakius. 8vo. 3s.

Archimedis *quae supersunt omnia cum Eutocii commentariis* ex recensione J. Torelli, cum nova versione Latina. Fol. 1l. 5s.

Aristophanes. *A Complete Concordance to the Comedies and Fragments.* By H. Dunbar, M.D. 4to. 1l. 1s.

—— *J. Caravellae Index in Aristophanem.* 8vo. 3s.

Aristophanes. *Comœdiæ et Fragmenta*, ex recensione Guil. Dindorfii. Tomi II. 8vo. 11s.

—— *Annotationes* Guil. Dindorfii. Partes II. 8vo. 11s.

—— *Scholia Graeca* ex Codicibus aucta et emendata a Guil. Dindorfio. Partes III. 8vo. 1l.

Aristotle. Ex recensione Im. Bekkeri. Accedunt Indices Sylburgiani. Tomi XI. 8vo. 2l. 10s.

The volumes (except Vol. IX) may be had separately, price 5s. 6d. each.

—— *Ethica Nicomachea*. Recognovit brevique Adnotatione critica instruxit I. Bywater. 8vo. 6s.

—— *The Politics*, with Introductions, Notes, &c., by W. L. Newman, M.A. Vols. I and II. Medium 8vo. 28s.

—— *The Politics*, translated into English, with Introduction, Marginal Analysis, Notes, and Indices, by B. Jowett, M.A. Medium 8vo. 2 vols. 21s.

—— *Aristotelian Studies*. I. On the Structure of the Seventh Book of the Nicomachean Ethics. By J. C. Wilson, M.A. 8vo. Stiff covers. 5s.

—— *The English Manuscripts of the Nicomachean Ethics*, described in relation to Bekker's Manuscripts and other Sources. By J. A. Stewart, M.A. (Anecdota Oxon.) Small 4to. 3s. 6d.

—— *On the History of the process by which the Aristotelian Writings arrived at their present form.* By R. Shute, M.A. 8vo. 7s. 6d.

Aristotle. *Physics*, Book VII. Collation of various MSS.; with Introduction by R. Shute, M.A. (Anecdota Oxon.) Small 4to. 2s.

Choerobosci *Dictata in Theodosii Canones, necnon Epimerismi in Psalmos*. E Codicibus mss. edidit Thomas Gaisford, S.T.P. Tomi III. 8vo. 15s.

Demosthenes. Ex recensione G. Dindorfii. Tomi IX. 8vo. 2l. 6s.

Separately:—
Text, 1l. 1s. Annotations, 15s. Scholia, 10s.

Demosthenes and Aeschines. The Orations of Demosthenes and Aeschines on the Crown. With Introductory Essays and Notes. By G. A. Simcox, M.A., and W. H. Simcox, M.A. 8vo. 12s.

Euripides. *Tragoediae et Fragmenta*, ex recensione Guil. Dindorfii. Tomi II. 8vo. 10s.

—— *Annotationes* Guil. Dindorfii. Partes II. 8vo. 10s.

—— *Scholia Graeca*, ex Codicibus aucta et emendata a Guil. Dindorfio. Tomi IV. 8vo. 1l. 16s.

—— *Alcestis*, ex recensione G. Dindorfii. 8vo. 2s. 6d.

Harpocrationis Lexicon. Ex recensione G. Dindorfii. Tomi II. 8vo. 10s. 6d.

Hephaestionis *Enchiridion, Terentianus Maurus, Proclus, &c.* Edidit T. Gaisford, S.T.P. Tomi II. 10s.

Heracliti *Ephesii Reliquiae*. Recensuit I. Bywater, M.A. Appendicis loco additae sunt Diogenis

Laertii Vita Heracliti, Particulae Hippocratei De Diaeta Lib. I., Epistolae Heracliteae. 8vo. 6s.

Homer. *A Complete Concordance to the Odyssey and Hymns of Homer;* to which is added a Concordance to the Parallel Passages in the Iliad, Odyssey, and Hymns. By Henry Dunbar, M.D. 4to. 1l. 1s.

—— *Seberi Index in Homerum.* 8vo. 6s. 6d.

—— *A Grammar of the Homeric Dialect.* By D. B. Monro, M.A. 8vo. Second Edition. 14s.

—— *Ilias,* cum brevi Annotatione C. G. Heynii. Accedunt Scholia minora. Tomi II. 8vo. 15s.

—— *Ilias,* ex rec. Guil. Dindorfii. 8vo. 5s. 6d.

—— *Scholia Graeca in Iliadem.* Edited by W. Dindorf, after a new collation of the Venetian mss. by D. B. Monro, M.A. 4 vols. 8vo. 2l. 10s.

—— *Scholia Graeca in Iliadem Townleyana.* Recensuit Ernestus Maass. 2 vols. 8vo. 1l. 16s.

—— *Odyssea,* ex rec. G. Dindorfii. 8vo. 5s. 6d.

—— *Scholia Graeca in Odysseam.* Edidit Guil. Dindorfius. Tomi II. 8vo. 15s. 6d.

—— *Odyssey.* Books I–XII. Edited with English Notes, Appendices, &c. By W. W. Merry, D.D., and James Riddell, M.A. *Second Edition.* 8vo. 16s.

Oratores *Attici,* ex recensione Bekkeri:
 I. Antiphon, Andocides, et Lysias. 8vo. 7s.
 II. Isocrates. 8vo. 7s.
 III. Isaeus, Aeschines, Lycurgus, Dinarchus, &c. 8vo. 7s.

Paroemiographi Graeci, *quorum pars nunc primum ex Codd. mss. vulgatur.* Edidit T. Gaisford, S.T.P. 1836. 8vo. 5s. 6d.

Plato. *Apology,* with a revised Text and English Notes, and a Digest of Platonic Idioms, by James Riddell, M.A. 8vo. 8s. 6d.

—— *Philebus,* with a revised Text and English Notes, by Edward Poste, M.A. 8vo. 7s. 6d.

—— *Sophistes* and *Politicus,* with a revised Text and English Notes, by L. Campbell, M.A. 8vo. 18s.

—— *Theaetetus,* with a revised Text and English Notes, by L. Campbell, M.A. *Second Edition.* 8vo. 10s. 6d.

—— *The Dialogues,* translated into English, with Analyses and Introductions, by B. Jowett, M.A. 5 vols. medium 8vo. *Third Edition.* Cloth, 4l. 4s.; half-morocco, 5l.

—— *The Republic,* translated into English, with Analysis and Introduction, by B. Jowett, M.A. Medium 8vo. 12s. 6d.; half-roan, 14s.

—— *Index to Plato.* Compiled for Prof. Jowett's Translation of the Dialogues. By Evelyn Abbott, M.A. 8vo. Paper covers, 2s. 6d.

Plotinus. Edidit F. Creuzer. Tomi III. 4to. 1*l.* 8*s.*

Polybius. *Selections.* Edited by J. L. Strachan-Davidson, M.A. With Maps. Medium 8vo. buckram, 21*s.*

Sophocles. *The Plays and Fragments.* With English Notes and Introductions, by Lewis Campbell, M.A. 2 vols.

    Vol. I. Oedipus Tyrannus. Oedipus Coloneus. Antigone. 8vo. 16*s.*

    Vol. II. Ajax. Electra. Trachiniae. Philoctetes. Fragments. 8vo. 16*s.*

—— *Tragoediae et Fragmenta,* ex recensione et cum commentariis Guil. Dindorfii. *Third Edition.* 2 vols. Fcap. 8vo. 1*l.* 1*s.*
Each Play separately, limp, 2*s.* 6*d.*

—— *The Text alone,* with large margin, small 4to. 8*s.*

—— *The Text alone,* square 16mo. 3*s.* 6*d.*
Each Play separately, limp, 6*d.*

—— *Tragoediae et Fragmenta* cum Annotationibus Guil. Dindorfii. Tomi II. 8vo. 10*s.*

    The Text, Vol. I. 5*s.* 6*d.*
    The Notes, Vol. II. 4*s.* 6*d.*

Stobaei *Florilegium.* Ad mss. fidem emendavit et supplevit T. Gaisford, S.T.P. Tomi IV. 8vo. 1*l.*

—— *Eclogarum Physicarum et Ethicarum libri duo.* Accedit Hieroclis Commentarius in aurea carmina Pythagoreorum. Ad mss. Codd. recensuit T. Gaisford, S.T.P. Tomi II. 8vo. 11*s.*

Theodoreti *Graecarum Affectionum Curatio.* Ad Codices mss. recensuit T. Gaisford, S.T.P. 8vo. 7*s.* 6*d.*

Thucydides. Translated into English, with Introduction, Marginal Analysis, Notes, and Indices. By B. Jowett, M.A., Regius Professor of Greek. 2 vols. Medium 8vo. 1*l.* 12*s.*

Xenophon. Ex recensione et cum annotationibus L. Dindorfii.

    Historia Graeca. Second Edition. 8vo. 10*s.* 6*d.*

    Expeditio Cyri. Second Edition. 8vo. 10*s.* 6*d.*

    Institutio Cyri. 8vo. 10*s.* 6*d.*

    Memorabilia Socratis. 8vo. 7*s.* 6*d.*

    Opuscula Politica Equestria et Venatica cum Arriani Libello de Venatione. 8vo. 10*s.* 6*d.*

3. MISCELLANEOUS STANDARD WORKS.

Bentham. *An Introduction to the Principles of Morals and Legislation.* By Jeremy Bentham. Crown 8vo. 6s. 6d.

—— *A Fragment on Government.* By Jeremy Bentham. Edited, with an Introduction, by F. C. Montague, M.A. 8vo. 7s. 6d.

Casaubon (Isaac), 1559-1614. By Mark Pattison, late Rector of Lincoln College. Second Edition. 8vo. 16s.

Clinton's *Fasti Hellenici.* The Civil and Literary Chronology of Greece, from the LVIth to the CXXIIIrd Olympiad. Third Edition. 4to. 1l. 14s. 6d.

—— *Fasti Hellenici.* The Civil and Literary Chronology of Greece, from the CXXIVth Olympiad to the Death of Augustus. Second Edition. 4to. 1l. 12s.

—— *Fasti Romani.* The Civil and Literary Chronology of Rome and Constantinople, from the Death of Augustus to the Death of Heraclius. 2 vols. 4to. 2l. 2s.

Finlay. *A History of Greece from its Conquest by the Romans to the present time,* B.C. 146 to A.D. 1864. By George Finlay, LL.D. A new Edition, revised throughout, and in part re-written, with considerable additions, by the Author, and edited by H. F. Tozer, M.A. 7 vols. 8vo. 3l. 10s.

Gaii *Institutionum Juris Civilis Commentarii Quattuor;* or, Elements of Roman Law by Gaius. With a Translation and Commentary by Edward Poste, M.A. Third Edition. 8vo. 18s.

Gardthausen. *Catalogus Codicum Graecorum Sinaiticorum.* Scripsit V. Gardthausen Lipsiensis. With six pages of Facsimiles. 8vo. 25s.

Herculanensium Voluminum Partes II. 1824. 8vo. 10s.

Fragmenta Herculanensia. A Descriptive Catalogue of the Oxford copies of the Herculanean Rolls, together with the texts of several papyri, accompanied by facsimiles. Edited by Walter Scott, M.A., Fellow of Merton College, Oxford. Royal 8vo. 21s.

Hodgkin. *Italy and her Invaders.* With Plates and Maps. By Thomas Hodgkin, D.C.L. Vols. I-IV, A.D. 376-553. 8vo. 3l. 8s.

Justinian. *Imperatoris Iustiniani Institutionum Libri Quattuor;* with Introductions, Commentary, Excursus and Translation. By J. B. Moyle, D.C.L. Second Edition. 2 vols. 8vo. 22s.

Machiavelli. *Il Principe.* Edited by L. Arthur Burd. With an Introduction by Lord Acton. 8vo. 14s.

Pattison. *Essays by the late Mark Pattison,* sometime Rector of Lincoln College. Collected and Arranged by Henry Nettleship, M.A. 2 vols. 8vo. 24s.

Smith's *Wealth of Nations.* A new Edition, with Notes, by J. E. Thorold Rogers, M.A. 2 vols. 8vo. 21s.

Stokes. *The Anglo-Indian Codes.* By Whitley Stokes, LL.D.
Vol. I. Substantive Law. 8vo. 30s.
Vol. II. Adjective Law. 8vo. 35s.

4. STANDARD THEOLOGICAL WORKS.

Bigg. *The Christian Platonists of Alexandria;* being the Bampton Lectures for 1886. By Charles Bigg, D.D. 8vo. 10s. 6d.

Bright. *Chapters of Early English Church History.* By W. Bright, D.D. 8vo. 12s.

Clementis Alexandrini *Opera,* ex recensione Guil. Dindorfii. Tomi IV. 8vo. 3l.

Eusebii Pamphili *Evangelicae Praeparationis Libri XV.* Ad Codd. MSS. recensuit T. Gaisford, S.T.P. Tomi IV. 8vo. 1l. 10s.

—— *Evangelicae Demonstrationis Libri X.* Recensuit T. Gaisford, S.T.P. Tomi II. 8vo. 15s.

—— *contra Hieroclem et Marcellum Libri.* Recensuit T. Gaisford, S.T.P. 8vo. 7s.

Hatch. *Essays in Biblical Greek.* By Edwin Hatch, M.A., D.D. 8vo. 10s. 6d.

—— *A Concordance to the Greek Versions and Apocryphal Books of the Old Testament.* By the late Edwin Hatch, M.A., and H. A. Redpath, M.A. Part I. A–Βαριθ. 21s.

Nouum Testamentum Domino Nostri Iesu Christi Latine, secundum Editionem S. Hieronymi. Ad Codicum Manuscriptorum fidem recensuit Iohannes Wordsworth, S.T.P., Episcopus Sarisburiensis. In operis societatem adsumto Henrico Iuliano White, A.M.

    Fasc. I. *Euangelium secundum Mattheum.* 4to. 12s. 6d.

    Fasc. II. *Euangelium secundum Marcum.* 7s. 6d.

---

5. **A NEW ENGLISH DICTIONARY on Historical Principles,** founded mainly on the materials collected by the Philological Society. Vol. I (A and B). Imperial 4to, half-morocco, 2l. 12s. 6d.

    Part IV, Section 2, **C—CASS,** beginning Vol. II, price 5s.
    Part V, **CAST—CLIVY,** price 12s. 6d.
    Part VI, **CLO—CONSIGNER,** price 12s. 6d.
    Part VII. *In the Press.*

Edited by James A. H. Murray, LL.D.

    Vol. III, Part I (**E—EVERY**), edited by Henry Bradley, M.A., price 12s. 6d.

    Vol. III, Part II. *In the Press.*

Oxford
AT THE CLARENDON PRESS
LONDON: HENRY FROWDE
OXFORD UNIVERSITY PRESS WAREHOUSE, AMEN CORNER, E.C.

www.ingramcontent.com/pod-product-compliance
Lightning Source LLC
Chambersburg PA
CBHW031934230426
43672CB00010B/1923